A Practical Approach to Open Source Intelligence (OSINT) - Volume 1

This book delves into the fascinating world of Open-Source Intelligence (OSINT), empowering you to leverage the vast ocean of publicly available information to gain valuable insights and intelligence. The reader can explore the fundamentals of OSINT, including its history, ethical considerations, and key principles. They can learn how to protect your online privacy and enhance your web browsing security. They can master essential OSINT skills, such as navigating the underground internet, employing advanced search engine techniques, and extracting intelligence from various sources like email addresses and social media. This book helps the reader discover the power of Imagery Intelligence and learn how to analyze photographs and videos to uncover hidden details. It also shows how to track satellites and aircraft, and provides insights into global trade and security by investigating marine vessel, road, and railway movements. This book provides hands-on exercises, real-world examples, and practical guidance to help you uncover hidden truths, gain a competitive edge, and enhance your security. Whether you're a student, researcher, journalist, or simply curious about the power of information, this book will equip you with the knowledge and skills to harness the potential of OSINT and navigate the digital landscape with confidence.

Akashdeep Bhardwaj is a Professor at UPES, Dehradun, India. An eminent IT industry expert in Cybersecurity, Digital Forensics, and IT Operations areas, Dr. Akashdeep mentors graduate, master's, and doctoral students and leads several industry projects as the Head of Cybersecurity (Center of Excellence). Dr. Akashdeep is a Post-Doctoral candidate from Majmaah University, Saudi Arabia, and holds a PhD (doctoral) in Computer Science. Dr. Akashdeep has over 150 international publications (including SCI, Scopus, WoS papers, Copyrights, and Patents) and authored several books and chapters. He is certified in multiple technologies including Compliance Audits and Cybersecurity, and has industry certifications in Microsoft, Cisco, and VMware technologies.

A Practical Approach to Open Source Intelligence (OSINT) - Volume 1

Akashdeep Bhardwaj

CRC Press
Taylor & Francis Group
Boca Raton London New York

CRC Press is an imprint of the
Taylor & Francis Group, an **informa** business

Designed cover image: Shutterstock

First edition published 2026
by CRC Press
2385 NW Executive Center Drive, Suite 320, Boca Raton FL 33431

and by CRC Press
4 Park Square, Milton Park, Abingdon, Oxon, OX14 4RN

CRC Press is an imprint of Taylor & Francis Group, LLC

© 2026 Akashdeep Bhardwaj

ISBN: 978-1-032-80222-0 (hbk)
ISBN: 978-1-032-80596-2 (pbk)
ISBN: 978-1-003-49761-5 (ebk)

DOI: 10.1201/9781003497615

Typeset in Sabon
by codeMantra

Contents

Chapter 1

Open-source intelligence evolution and basics

1.1 INTRODUCTION

In the era of the internet and the digital revolution, information is more accessible than ever before. This democratization of information has given rise to a powerful and transformative field known as Open-Source Intelligence [1] or OSINT. OSINT is a multi-method approach to collect, analyze, and make decisions from publicly available data from a wide array of sources to extract valuable insights, make informed decisions, and mitigate risks in various domains, including national security, business intelligence (BI), and cybersecurity. In this chapter exploring OSINT, we will dive deep into its foundational concepts, principles, and methods, uncovering the extraordinary potential it offers in our interconnected world.

At its core, OSINT revolves around the collection, analysis, and interpretation of publicly accessible information. This information encompasses data from diverse sources, both online and offline, including:

- Public Records: Government documents, court records, and regulatory filings.
- Media and News Outlets: Newspapers, magazines, broadcast news, and online news articles.
- Social Media: User-generated content on platforms like Facebook, Twitter, Instagram, and YouTube.
- Websites and Forums: Data from blogs, forums, and websites, including academic publications and research papers.
- Commercial Data: Information from commercial databases, market research reports, and industry publications.

Effective OSINT relies on a set of fundamental principles that ensure the reliability, accuracy, and ethical use of information. These principles serve as the guiding framework for OSINT practitioners:

- Transparency: OSINT operates with transparency, ensuring that data sources are publicly available and legally obtained.

DOI: 10.1201/9781003497615-1

- Relevance: Information gathered should be relevant to the objectives of the analysis or investigation.
- Accuracy: OSINT practitioners prioritize accuracy in data collection and reporting, striving to eliminate misinformation.
- Legal and Ethical Compliance: Adherence to legal and ethical standards is paramount, safeguarding individual privacy and data rights.

This comprehensive exploration of OSINT serves as a foundational resource for those seeking to understand the principles, methods, and applications of OSINT in today's information-rich environment. It underscores the significance of OSINT as a discipline that continues to evolve and shape the way we navigate the complexities of the modern world. In an increasingly interconnected world characterized by the relentless flow of information, OSINT has emerged as a critical tool for understanding, analyzing, and mitigating risks across various domains. This chapter delves deep into the pivotal role OSINT plays in three key areas: national security, BI, and cybersecurity. It highlights the unparalleled importance of OSINT in each of these fields, demonstrating how this discipline has become a linchpin in navigating the complexities of the modern era. Examples of OSINT include:

- Financial Investigations: Unraveling a company's financial story by dissecting their official reports and deciphering news headlines.
- Digital Footprints: Delving into someone's past by following their online trails on social media, official records, and other digital directories.
- Political Pulse: Taking the temperature of a nation's political landscape by listening to local voices through news articles and social media buzz.
- Disease Detectives: Tracking the path of an illness by gathering data from healthcare websites and social media accounts, piecing together the puzzle.
- Political Watchdogs: Keeping tabs on a political organization's activities by scrutinizing their online presence and dissecting their messages.

1.2 INTELLIGENCE LIFECYCLE

As illustrated in Figure 1.1, the first phase starts with Planning & Direction, so imagine a client gave a contract to find details about a target, and then the 'who,' 'what,' 'when,' and 'were' aspects are gathered. The next phase is data collection where most of the time is spent. The third phase is processing the data to ensure that it is readable and legitimate. The next phase involves taking the data points and analyzing them for use, answering the 'how' and 'why,' which is typically production. The final phase is creating reports and sharing with the client, but the work is ongoing.

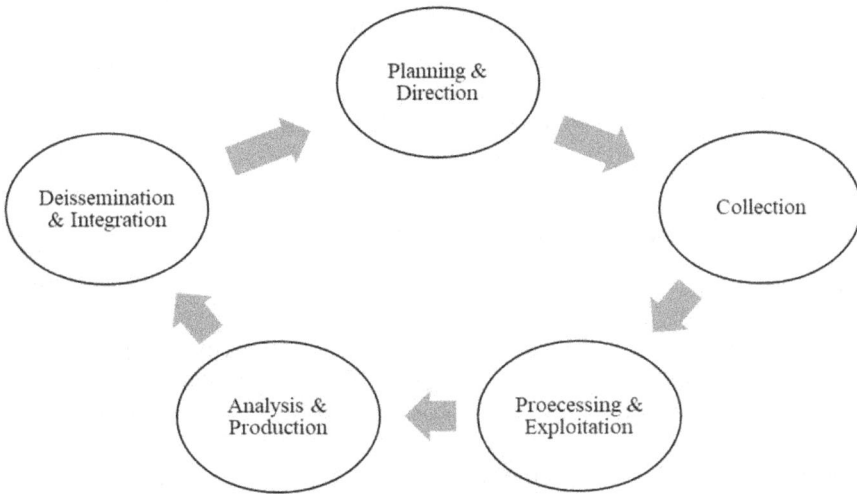

Figure 1.1 Intelligence lifecycle.

1.2.1 Stage 1: Planning and direction

The first stage in the OSINT lifecycle is planning and direction, where the foundation for the entire intelligence operation is laid. This involves defining the intelligence requirement, identifying the target, and developing a comprehensive collection plan. The initial step is to clearly articulate the specific information needed to address a question or problem. This involves understanding the context, identifying the decision-making process, and determining the desired outcomes. For instance, a government agency might need to gather information on a foreign leader's activities to assess potential threats, while a corporation may require data on market trends to inform its business strategies.

Once the intelligence requirement is defined, the target must be identified. This could be an individual, a group, an organization, or a geographic location. For example, a law enforcement agency might target a suspected terrorist organization, while a journalist may focus on a particular country's political situation. A comprehensive collection plan outlines the sources, methods, and tools to be used for data gathering. It should consider factors such as the target's digital footprint, the availability of public records, and the potential for human intelligence sources. For instance, a collection plan for a targeted individual might include social media monitoring, public records searches, and interviews with associates.

Example: A government agency tasked with monitoring a foreign terrorist organization might develop a collection plan that includes:

- Social Media Monitoring: Tracking the organization's online activities on platforms like Facebook, Twitter, and Telegram.

- Open-Source Forums: Monitoring online forums and discussion boards where the organization's members might communicate.
- Public Records Searches: Examining public records such as court documents, property records, and corporate filings.
- Human Intelligence: Cultivating relationships with individuals who may have information about the organization's activities.

1.2.2 Stage 2: Collection

The second stage of the OSINT lifecycle is collection, where the planned sources, methods, and tools are employed to gather relevant information. This stage involves a systematic and organized approach to acquiring data from various publicly available sources. One of the primary methods of data collection in OSINT is through online resources. This includes:

- Social Media: Platforms like Facebook, Twitter, Instagram, and LinkedIn can provide valuable insights into individuals, organizations, and events. By monitoring public profiles, groups, and discussions, analysts can gather information on interests, affiliations, and activities.
- News Articles: Online news outlets, both mainstream and niche, offer a wealth of information on current events, trends, and emerging issues. By analyzing news articles, analysts can identify key players, understand different perspectives, and track the evolution of events.
- Blogs and Forums: Blogs and forums can be valuable sources of information, especially for niche topics or communities. By monitoring these platforms, analysts can discover discussions, opinions, and insider knowledge that may not be readily available elsewhere.
- Public Records: Public records, such as court documents, property records, and corporate filings, can provide valuable information on individuals, organizations, and their activities. By accessing these records, analysts can uncover connections, identify patterns, and verify information obtained from other sources.

In addition to online resources, other collection methods may include:

- Human Intelligence: Cultivating relationships with individuals who may have information about the target or related topics. This can involve interviewing experts, contacting former associates, or conducting surveys.
- Physical Surveillance: Observing individuals or locations in person to gather information. This may involve following individuals, monitoring public spaces, or conducting reconnaissance missions.
- Technical Surveillance: Employing technological tools to gather information, such as intercepting communications or using geolocation techniques.

Example: A law enforcement agency investigating a suspected terrorist organization might employ the following collection methods:

- Social Media Monitoring: Tracking the organization's online activities on platforms like Facebook, Twitter, and Telegram.
- News Article Analysis: Examining news articles related to the organization's activities and identifying key players, locations, and events.
- Forum Monitoring: Monitoring online forums and discussion boards where the organization's members might communicate.
- Public Records Searches: Examining public records such as court documents, property records, and corporate filings.
- Human Intelligence: Cultivating relationships with individuals who may have information about the organization's activities.

1.2.3 Stage 3: Processing and exploitation

The third stage of the OSINT lifecycle is processing and exploitation, where the collected data is analyzed, evaluated, and integrated with other intelligence sources to extract meaningful insights. The first step in processing and exploitation is to analyze the collected data. This involves identifying patterns, trends, and anomalies within the information. Analysts may use various techniques, such as:

- Keyword Searching: Identifying relevant keywords or phrases within the data to locate specific information.
- Network Analysis: Mapping relationships between individuals, organizations, or entities to identify connections and patterns.
- Time Series Analysis: Examining data over time to identify trends, fluctuations, and anomalies.
- Data Visualization: Creating charts, graphs, and other visual representations of the data to facilitate understanding and analysis.

Once the data has been analyzed, it is important to evaluate its reliability. This involves assessing the credibility and accuracy of the sources. Analysts may consider factors such as:

- Source Reputation: The reputation and credibility of the source, including its track record, biases, and affiliations.
- Consistency: The consistency of the information with other sources and known facts.
- Context: The context in which the information was provided, including the time, place, and circumstances.
- Verification: The ability to verify the information through independent sources.

The collected OSINT data may be integrated with other intelligence sources to form a more comprehensive picture. This can include:

- Human Intelligence: Combining OSINT with information obtained from human sources, such as informants or agents.
- Signals Intelligence: Integrating OSINT with information obtained from electronic communications, such as intercepted phone calls or emails.
- Measurement and Signature Intelligence: Combining OSINT with information obtained from physical sensors, such as satellites or radars.

Example: A law enforcement agency investigating a suspected terrorist organization might analyze collected data to:

- Identify key individuals and their affiliations.
- Map the organization's network of contacts and connections.
- Track the organization's activities over time.
- Evaluate the reliability of the sources.
- Integrate the collected information with other intelligence sources, such as human intelligence or signals intelligence.

1.2.4 Stage 4: Analysis and production

The fourth stage of the OSINT lifecycle is analysis and production, where the processed and evaluated data is transformed into actionable intelligence products. The goal of analysis and production is to create concise, clear, and relevant intelligence products that can be easily understood and consumed by decision-makers. These products may include:

- Reports: Detailed reports that provide a comprehensive overview of the findings, including the methodology, data sources, and analysis.
- Briefings: Concise summaries of key findings that are designed for quick consumption by busy decision-makers.
- Alerts: Timely notifications of significant events or developments that may require immediate attention.
- Visualizations: Charts, graphs, and other visual representations of the data that can help to communicate complex information effectively.

Once the intelligence products have been created, they must be disseminated to relevant stakeholders in a timely and effective manner. This involves:

- Identifying the Target Audience: Determining who needs to receive the intelligence and tailoring the products accordingly.

- Selecting the Appropriate Channels: Choosing the best way to deliver the intelligence, such as email, secure messaging, or in-person briefings.
- Ensuring Confidentiality: Protecting the intelligence from unauthorized access or disclosure.

Example: A law enforcement agency investigating a suspected terrorist organization might produce the following intelligence products:

- Report: A detailed report outlining the organization's structure, leadership, and activities.
- Briefing: A concise summary of the organization's recent activities and potential threats.
- Alert: A notification of a planned attack or other significant event.
- Visualization: A map showing the organization's network of contacts and locations.

1.2.5 Stage 5: Dissemination

The fifth stage of the OSINT lifecycle is dissemination, where the intelligence products are delivered to relevant stakeholders and the significance of the findings is explained. The goal of dissemination is to ensure that the intelligence products are received by the intended audience in a timely and effective manner. This involves:

- Identifying the Target Audience: Determining who needs to receive the intelligence and tailoring the products accordingly.
- Selecting the Appropriate Channels: Choosing the best way to deliver the intelligence, such as email, secure messaging, or in-person briefings.
- Ensuring Confidentiality: Protecting the intelligence from unauthorized access or disclosure.

In addition to delivering the intelligence products, it is important to provide context to help stakeholders understand the significance of the findings. This may involve:

- Explaining the Implications: Discussing the potential consequences of the events or trends identified in the intelligence.
- Offering Recommendations: Suggesting actions that stakeholders can take to address the issues or opportunities identified in the intelligence.
- Providing Additional Information: Providing additional context or background information that may be relevant to understanding the intelligence.

Example: A law enforcement agency investigating a suspected terrorist organization might disseminate the following intelligence products:

- Delivering the Intelligence: Sending the intelligence products to relevant stakeholders, such as senior officials, field agents, and intelligence analysts.
- Providing Context: Explaining the potential threats posed by the organization, discussing the implications of the findings, and offering recommendations for action.

1.3 ROLE OF OSINT

The digital age has brought about unparalleled connectivity but has also exposed organizations to a myriad of cybersecurity threats. In an era where information flows ceaselessly through digital channels, the significance of OSINT looms larger than ever before. OSINT is a dynamic discipline that revolves around the collection, analysis, and interpretation of publicly available information from a myriad of sources. Its scope spans a vast and interconnected landscape, encompassing diverse fields, industries, and sectors. As we embark on a comprehensive exploration of OSINT, let us journey through the intricacies of this multifaceted discipline, unraveling its definition, principles, methods, and the expansive extent of its influence. OSINT has become a cornerstone of effective cybersecurity strategies:

- Threat Intelligence: OSINT provides valuable threat intelligence, helping organizations identify emerging threats and vulnerabilities in real time.
- Vulnerability Assessment: It assists in identifying weaknesses in systems and software that could be exploited by cybercriminals.
- Incident Response: OSINT plays a crucial role in incident response, helping organizations understand the scope and impact of security breaches.
- Phishing Detection: By monitoring the dark web and open sources, OSINT helps in the early detection of phishing campaigns and data breaches.

At its core, OSINT is the art and science of extracting valuable insights, knowledge, and actionable intelligence from openly available information. OSINT encompasses data from a multitude of sources, both online and offline, that are accessible to anyone. It represents a distinct branch of intelligence that contrasts with classified, sensitive, or proprietary information. OSINT derives its power from the fact that it is open, transparent, and, in most cases, legally obtainable by anyone with the tools and techniques to access it. The scope of OSINT is vast, reaching into various domains, sectors, and applications across the global landscape. This scope is characterized by its breadth and flexibility, allowing OSINT to adapt to evolving information ecosystems and emerging challenges. The multifaceted scope of OSINT and its diverse applications are described below.

Real-world examples:

- Dark Web Monitoring: Companies and security firms use OSINT to monitor the dark web for stolen data and cybercriminal discussions. This information helps them prepare against potential attacks.
- Threat Hunting: In the cybersecurity realm, OSINT is used for threat hunting, proactively seeking out signs of malicious activity before it can cause significant damage.

In a world where information is power, OSINT has risen to the forefront as a catalyst for informed decision-making and risk mitigation. Whether in the realm of national security, BI, or cybersecurity, the importance of OSINT cannot be overstated. In national security, OSINT is the guardian of a nation's interests, providing critical insights into threats and enabling governments to respond effectively. In BI, OSINT is the compass that guides companies through the competitive landscape, helping them adapt to changing market conditions and consumer preferences. In cybersecurity, OSINT is the early warning system, allowing organizations to defend against digital threats and protect their valuable assets. As OSINT continues to evolve, its importance will only grow, reshaping the way we perceive and navigate the information-rich world of the 21st century. The discipline's ethical use, adherence to principles, and integration with emerging technologies will determine its continued effectiveness and relevance in an ever-changing landscape. In embracing OSINT, we harness the power of open information to thrive, innovate, and safeguard our interests in a complex and interconnected global environment.

National security [2] is a paramount concern for every nation, and OSINT has revolutionized the way governments and intelligence agencies gather and analyze information to protect their interests. OSINT's importance in this realm cannot be overstated:

- Threat Assessment [3]: OSINT enables the continuous monitoring of global events, providing crucial insights into emerging threats and potential security risks.
- Counterterrorism [4]: It aids in tracking the activities of terrorist organizations and identifying their networks, helping governments take proactive measures to counteract them.
- Geopolitical Analysis [5]: OSINT informs governments about the evolving geopolitical landscape, helping them make informed foreign policy decisions.

- Disaster Response [6]: OSINT can be vital in disaster response efforts, helping governments assess the extent of damage and plan effective relief operations.
- Counterterrorism: OSINT aids in tracking the activities of terrorist organizations, identifying their networks, and preventing potential attacks.
- Crisis Response: During crises, OSINT helps governments gather real-time data, assess the extent of damage, and formulate effective response strategies.

Real-world examples:

- Monitoring Adversarial Nations [7]: Governments use OSINT to monitor the activities of adversarial nations. Analysis of satellite imagery and online discussions provides insights into military developments and intentions.
- Humanitarian Aid [8]: During natural disasters, OSINT is used to assess damage, locate survivors, and coordinate humanitarian aid efforts. For example, after the 2010 earthquake in Haiti, OSINT data played a crucial role in coordinating relief efforts.

In the corporate world, BI is the key to informed decision-making and maintaining a competitive edge. OSINT has emerged as a game-changer in the realm of BI, offering a treasure trove of data and insights. BI and Corporate Decision-Making: In the corporate world, information is power, and OSINT has become a linchpin in decision-making processes. Its applications in BI are profound:

- Market Research: OSINT enables businesses to collect data on market trends, consumer behavior, and competitor activities, empowering informed decision-making.
- Competitive Analysis: Through OSINT, companies keep a watchful eye on their competitors, monitoring product launches, pricing strategies, and customer feedback.
- Brand Reputation Management: OSINT helps protect and manage a brand's reputation by monitoring online sentiment, identifying potential public relation crises, and responding proactively.
- Risk Mitigation: OSINT allows organizations to identify potential risks and vulnerabilities, ranging from supply chain disruptions to cybersecurity threats.

Real-world examples:

- Competitor Analysis: Companies like Coca-Cola use OSINT to monitor competitor activity in real time. They track social media mentions, advertising campaigns, and pricing strategies to stay ahead.

- Supply Chain Resilience: OSINT helps organizations assess the vulnerabilities in their supply chains. For instance, during the COVID-19 pandemic, companies relied on OSINT to identify disruptions in their supply networks.

In the digital age, safeguarding sensitive information and digital assets is paramount for Cybersecurity and Information Security: OSINT forms an integral part of cybersecurity:

- Threat Intelligence: OSINT provides valuable threat intelligence, aiding organizations in identifying emerging threats and vulnerabilities in real time.
- Vulnerability Assessment: It assists in identifying weaknesses in systems and software that could be exploited by cybercriminals.
- Incident Response: OSINT is instrumental in incident response, helping organizations understand the scope and impact of security breaches.
- Phishing Detection: By monitoring the dark web and open sources, OSINT helps in the early detection of phishing campaigns and data breaches.

In the field of law enforcement and criminal investigations, OSINT serves as a critical tool in gathering evidence, tracking suspects, and solving cases:

- Digital Footprint Analysis: OSINT experts use online traces left by individuals to assist in criminal investigations, locating suspects and identifying connections.
- Social Media Investigations: Law enforcement agencies utilize OSINT to monitor social media platforms for criminal activities and threats.
- Missing Persons and Human Trafficking: OSINT aids in locating missing persons and combating human trafficking by tracking online activities and identifying potential victims.

In times of crisis and humanitarian emergencies, OSINT contributes significantly to disaster response efforts:

- Damage Assessment: OSINT is used to assess the extent of damage after natural disasters or conflict situations, guiding relief efforts.
- Resource Allocation: It helps humanitarian organizations identify areas in need of assistance and allocate resources effectively.
- Crisis Mapping: OSINT experts create real-time crisis maps using open-source data to visualize the impact of disasters and coordinate response efforts.

In the realms of academia and journalism, OSINT serves as a valuable resource for research, reporting, and investigation:

- Investigative Journalism: Journalists use OSINT to uncover stories, verify facts, and expose hidden information.
- Academic Studies: Researchers employ OSINT to gather data for various academic disciplines, including social sciences, political science, and geography.
- Fact-Checking: OSINT aids in fact-checking claims and statements made by individuals, governments, or organizations.

Beyond traditional BI, OSINT plays a pivotal role in competitive intelligence by offering insights into market dynamics and competitor strategies:

- Market Intelligence: OSINT assists in gathering data on emerging markets, market trends, and consumer preferences.
- Mergers and Acquisitions: Companies use OSINT to gather information about potential acquisition targets, assessing their financial health and market position.
- Product Development: By analyzing publicly available data, businesses can identify gaps in the market and develop products to meet consumer needs.

In the arena of diplomacy and foreign affairs, OSINT has become an indispensable tool for nations to navigate international relations:

- Foreign Policy Formulation: Governments employ OSINT to gather information on the policies and actions of foreign nations, aiding in diplomatic negotiations and decision-making.
- Monitoring International Agreements: OSINT ensures compliance with international agreements and treaties by monitoring activities and developments in partner countries.
- Predicting International Events: OSINT aids in predicting international events, such as elections and political developments, allowing nations to prepare for potential changes in the global landscape.

OSINT extends its reach to environmental monitoring and conservation efforts, contributing to the preservation of natural resources:

- Deforestation Tracking: OSINT is used to monitor deforestation activities and illegal logging in remote areas through satellite imagery and open data sources.
- Wildlife Conservation: Researchers employ OSINT to track and study the movements of endangered species, aiding conservation efforts.
- Climate Change Research: OSINT contributes to climate change research by providing data on environmental changes and weather patterns.

In urban planning and geospatial analysis, OSINT aids in understanding and managing urban environments:

* Urban Development: OSINT helps monitor urban growth, traffic patterns, and infrastructure development.
* Disaster Preparedness: It aids in disaster preparedness and response by providing data on vulnerable areas and population density.
* Land Use Planning: OSINT data informs land use planning and zoning decisions by providing insights into land ownership.

1.4 OPEN-SOURCE V/S CLASSIFIED INFORMATION

OSI [9] and Classified Information [10] represent two distinct categories of data, each with its own characteristics, accessibility, and implications. The differentiation between these two forms of information is vital, as it underpins the functioning of government, intelligence agencies, businesses, and individuals in an information-driven world. OSI encompasses data that is publicly available and accessible to anyone who seeks it. This information is not subject to strict controls or restrictions, and its sources can be diverse, including books, newspapers, magazines, websites, academic publications, social media, public records, and more. OSI is not inherently sensitive or confidential, and it is often disseminated through legitimate, authorized channels. One of the defining features of OSI is its transparency and accessibility. It is information that is readily available to the public or can be obtained through legal means. OSI is subject to the principles of transparency and openness, which means that its sources are not concealed, and individuals or organizations can access and utilize it without any legal constraints. In essence, OSI is the information that is in the public domain, making it valuable for research, analysis, and decision-making. Moreover, OSI carries no inherent classification or security markings. It does not require specialized security clearance or protective measures for its handling. This distinguishes OSI from classified information, which is subject to stringent security protocols and restrictions.

In stark contrast to OSI, Classified Information represents data that is deemed sensitive, confidential, or protected by national security interests. Classified Information is subject to strict control and access limitations, and its disclosure to unauthorized individuals can have severe legal and security consequences. This category of information is typically divided into different levels of classification, such as 'Confidential,' 'Secret,' and 'Top Secret,' depending on the degree of sensitivity and potential harm its release could cause. The hallmark of Classified Information is its restricted access. Only individuals with the requisite security clearances, a legitimate need-to-know, and compliance with security protocols are granted access to this information. Access is usually compartmentalized, meaning that individuals are only given access to the specific information necessary for their duties. Classified Information is protected by stringent security measures, both physical and digital, to prevent unauthorized disclosure or access. This includes secure storage, encryption, controlled access points, and strict handling procedures. Violations of these security measures can result in criminal charges, penalties, or severe repercussions for individuals involved. The classification of information is primarily based on the potential harm its disclosure could cause to national security, diplomatic relations, or individuals' safety. This assessment is conducted by government agencies and is subject to periodic review and declassification when the sensitivity of the information diminishes over time.

OSI and Classified Information are fundamentally distinct categories, differing in their accessibility, transparency, and security implications. OSI is publicly available and accessible, transparent, and subject to no inherent security classification. In contrast, Classified Information is highly restricted, protected by rigorous security measures, and subject to various levels of classification based on its sensitivity. The differentiation between these two types of information is crucial for individuals, organizations, and government agencies to operate effectively and securely in an information-rich world while safeguarding national security interests and protecting sensitive data.

1.5 OSINT PRINCIPLES

OSINT operates within a framework of key principles that guide its practice, uphold ethical standards, and ensure the responsible use of publicly available information. These principles serve as the foundation upon which OSINT practitioners build their methodologies and conduct their analyses. Three paramount principles in the realm of OSINT are transparency, legality, and relevance. In the following discussion, we will delve deep into these principles, exploring their significance, implications, and the role they play in shaping the practice of OSINT.

1.5.1 Transparency: unveiling the truth

Transparency is one of the foundational principles of OSINT, emphasizing the importance of clarity, openness, and honesty in the collection, analysis, and dissemination of information. Transparency is the cornerstone of ethical OSINT. It underscores the importance of clarity, openness, and honesty in the collection, analysis, and dissemination of information. Transparency not only fosters trust among stakeholders but also ensures accountability, enabling scrutiny and validation of OSINT findings. At its core, transparency in OSINT signifies the commitment to reveal the truth to the best of one's ability, ensuring that the information and the methodologies used are transparent, accessible, and verifiable. In OSINT, transparency starts with the selection of data sources. Practitioners should explicitly state the sources from which information is obtained, providing clear citations and references. Whether it's public records, social media, news articles, or academic papers, transparency dictates that the origins of data should be discernible, allowing others to independently verify the information.

Transparency extends to the methodologies employed in collecting and analyzing OSINT data. Researchers and analysts should be candid about the tools, techniques, and algorithms used. This openness enables peers and reviewers to assess the validity of the findings and potentially replicate the research, fostering a culture of trust and accountability. Transparent OSINT practitioners also acknowledge the limitations of their work. They recognize that publicly available information may be incomplete, inaccurate, or biased. Therefore, it is essential to disclose these limitations, providing context for the information and its potential shortcomings. Such transparency allows consumers of OSINT to make informed judgments.

1.5.2 Legality: operating within the boundaries of the law

Legality is an unequivocal pillar of OSINT, demanding that practitioners adhere to all applicable laws and regulations governing the collection and use of information. Legality is a fundamental ethical principle in OSINT, demanding adherence to all applicable laws and regulations governing the collection and use of information. While OSINT revolves around publicly accessible data, it is crucial to recognize that legal boundaries exist even within open sources. Legality not only safeguards against legal repercussions but also upholds the rights and dignity of individuals whose information is part of open-source data. While OSINT is rooted in the acquisition of publicly accessible data, it is crucial to recognize that legal boundaries exist even within the realm of open sources. OSINT professionals must respect privacy laws that protect individuals' personal information. Accessing or disseminating sensitive personal data without proper authorization or consent is a breach of privacy regulations and, in many jurisdictions, a punishable offense.

Another facet of legality in OSINT pertains to copyright and intellectual property rights. Practitioners should be diligent in ensuring they have the legal right to use and share information found in open sources. Unauthorized reproduction or distribution of copyrighted materials can lead to legal consequences. Beyond legal considerations, ethical data collection is intertwined with legality in OSINT. Respecting terms of service, terms of use, and community guidelines of online platforms is essential. Violating these rules can result in the suspension of accounts, loss of access to valuable sources, and even legal actions. They must respect privacy laws that protect individuals' personal information. Accessing or disseminating sensitive personal data without proper authorization or consent is a breach of privacy regulations and, in many jurisdictions, a punishable offense. OSINT practitioners need to ensure they have the legal right to use and share information found in open sources. Unauthorized reproduction or distribution of copyrighted materials can lead to legal consequences.

1.5.3 Relevance: focusing on what matters

The principle of relevance is a cornerstone of effective OSINT practice, emphasizing the importance of collecting, analyzing, and reporting information that is pertinent to the objectives at hand. In a world inundated with data, OSINT practitioners must discern what is significant and what is superfluous. Relevance begins with clearly defined objectives. OSINT efforts should have a specific purpose, whether it's national security threat assessment, competitive analysis for a business, or cybersecurity risk mitigation. These objectives guide the collection process, ensuring that only data germane to the mission is pursued. The digital age has ushered in a deluge of data, and it is easy to succumb to information overload. Relevance dictates that practitioners focus on the signal amidst the noise, filtering out extraneous information and concentrating on what directly contributes to the mission's success. Relevant OSINT is also timely. Information loses its relevance as it ages. Practitioners must prioritize current and up-to-date data to maintain the accuracy and efficacy of their analyses. This timeliness ensures that decisions and actions are based on the most recent and actionable information available.

The principles of transparency, legality, and relevance in OSINT are interconnected and often intersect in practice. Achieving a delicate balance between these principles is essential for ethical and effective OSINT operations. For instance, transparency reinforces legality by requiring practitioners to openly disclose their methods and sources while demonstrating compliance with laws and regulations. Likewise, relevance guides transparency by ensuring that disclosed information and methodologies align with the objectives, avoiding unnecessary or inappropriate disclosure. Legality, on the other hand, safeguards the ethical practice of OSINT by setting boundaries on data collection and use. It upholds the privacy rights of individuals and protects against the misuse of information. Relevance complements legality by ensuring that the data collected is not only legal but also essential for the intended purpose, minimizing the risk of inadvertently engaging in unlawful or unethical activities. Relevance intersects with transparency when practitioners clarify their objectives and methodology, ensuring that they are aligned with the mission's purpose. Practicing transparency in this manner not only fosters trust but also helps stakeholders understand the rationale behind data collection and analysis choices.

The principle of relevance is vital in ensuring that OSINT efforts are meaningful, focused, and aligned with their intended objectives. In an information-saturated world, practitioners must discern what is significant and what is superfluous. Relevance ensures that OSINT practitioners do not waste resources on irrelevant information and that their efforts remain aligned with their intended goals. Ethical OSINT practitioners:

- Define Clear Objectives: Relevance begins with well-defined objectives. OSINT efforts should have specific purposes, whether it's national security threat assessment, competitive analysis for a business, or cybersecurity risk mitigation. Clear objectives guide the collection process, ensuring that only data relevant to the mission is pursued.
- Avoid Information Overload: Ethical practitioners prioritize the signal amidst the noise, filtering out extraneous information and concentrating on what directly contributes to the mission's success. Information overload can lead to inefficiency, errors, and loss of focus.
- Embrace Timeliness and Currency: Relevant OSINT is also timely. Information loses its relevance as it ages. Ethical practitioners prioritize current and up-to-date data to maintain the accuracy and efficacy of their analyses.

These principles are not isolated silos but rather interwoven threads that guide responsible and effective OSINT practices. Operating within the boundaries of the law, maintaining transparency, and focusing on relevance collectively contribute to the ethical and valuable application of OSINT in a wide range of domains, from national security to BI to cybersecurity. Transparency, legality, and relevance stand as the ethical bedrock upon which the discipline of OSINT rests. They shape the conduct of OSINT practitioners, ensuring that the information they gather and analyze serves its intended purpose, respects legal boundaries, and maintains the highest standards of transparency. In an era characterized by the relentless flow of information, these principles guide practitioners in harnessing the power of open sources responsibly and ethically, preserving the integrity and efficacy of OSINT in a complex and interconnected world.

1.5.4 Ethical landscape of OSINT

In the digital age, where information flows abundantly and boundaries between public and private domains blur, the ethical considerations surrounding OSINT take center stage. OSINT, the art of collecting and analyzing publicly available information from various sources, presents practitioners with a complex ethical landscape. This comprehensive exploration delves into the multifaceted ethical aspects of OSINT, shedding light on the principles that guide ethical practice, the challenges faced, and the responsibilities that accompany the use of OSI. Ethics are the moral compass that steers the practice of OSINT, influencing every decision made by analysts, researchers, and organizations engaged in the collection and analysis of OSI. These ethical considerations are essential not only for ensuring responsible and lawful conduct but also for maintaining public trust and safeguarding individual rights. The ethical dimension of OSINT is characterized by a delicate balance between the pursuit of knowledge, respect for privacy, adherence to legal boundaries, and the preservation of transparency. In this exploration, we delve deep into the ethical considerations in OSINT, unpacking the principles that underpin them, the challenges they pose, and the responsibilities they demand. Ethical OSINT practices are anchored in a set of fundamental principles that guide the responsible and principled use of OSI. These principles are not just guidelines; they are the ethical underpinnings that shape the very essence of OSINT operations. Let's delve into these principles. Engage in Ethical Data Collection: Ethical data collection includes respecting terms of service, terms of use, and community guidelines of online platforms. Violating these rules can result in the suspension of accounts, loss of access to valuable sources, and even legal actions.

1.5.5 Pursuing truth and precision

Accuracy is an ethical imperative in OSINT, emphasizing the responsibility to strive for truth and precision in the collection and analysis of information. Accuracy is the linchpin of OSINT credibility. Ethical practitioners understand that their findings can influence decisions and actions, and, therefore, they strive for the highest level of accuracy in their work. Ethical practitioners are committed to:

- Verifying Information: They take the extra step to verify the accuracy of the data they collect, cross-referencing multiple sources and fact-checking information. This diligence minimizes the dissemination of false or misleading data.
- Avoiding Misinformation: Ethical OSINT practitioners refrain from knowingly disseminating false or unverified information. Spreading misinformation can have severe consequences, including damage to reputation and the potential to incite panic.
- Citing Sources Appropriately: In ethical OSINT, practitioners appropriately cite their sources, giving credit to the originators of information. This citation not only acknowledges the work of others but also allows for further verification and reference.

1.5.6 Upholding integrity & accountability

Integrity is the bedrock of ethical OSINT practice, encompassing honesty, credibility, and ethical conduct in all aspects of the profession. Integrity is not just an ethical principle but a moral commitment to conduct OSINT with honor, honesty, and ethical steadfastness. Ethical practitioners:

- Maintain Professional Integrity: They uphold the highest ethical standards, both within their organizations and in interactions with external stakeholders. Integrity is paramount in ensuring trustworthiness and reliability in the OSINT field.
- Avoid Bias and Prejudice: Ethical OSINT practitioners refrain from injecting personal bias or prejudice into their work. Their analyses should be objective, impartial, and free from undue influence.
- Protect Sources: Practitioners respect the confidentiality and anonymity of sources who provide sensitive or confidential information. They understand the importance of source protection in fostering trust and preserving open channels of information.
- Take Accountability: Taking Responsibility for Actions: Accountability is a fundamental ethical principle that entails taking responsibility for one's actions, decisions, and the consequences of OSINT activities.
- Acknowledge Mistakes: When errors or inaccuracies are identified, ethical OSINT practitioners promptly acknowledge and correct them. Accountability includes the willingness to admit mistakes and take corrective measures.

1.6 HISTORICAL EVOLUTION OF OSINT

OSINT is a crucial component of modern information gathering and analysis, playing a pivotal role in intelligence, security, and decision-making processes across various domains. OSINT, in essence, is the practice of collecting and analyzing publicly available information to gain insights, make informed decisions, and assess potential threats. While OSINT is now firmly embedded in contemporary intelligence practices, its historical roots stretch back through centuries of human civilization, evolving in response to changing technologies and geopolitical landscapes. This essay will explore the historical evolution of OSINT, tracing its development from ancient times to the digital age, and highlighting its significance in shaping the world of intelligence and security.

The foundations of OSINT can be traced back to antiquity, where information collection played a pivotal role in the strategies of empires, rulers, and military leaders. Ancient civilizations like the Egyptians, Greeks, and Romans practiced various forms of intelligence gathering, relying heavily on human sources, diplomacy, and espionage. The ancient Egyptians demonstrated an early understanding of the importance of information. Pharaohs utilized spies and diplomats to gather intelligence on neighboring kingdoms, trade routes, and potential threats. Hieroglyphics and papyrus scrolls contained valuable information about political affairs, trade, and military plans. In classical Greece, the concept of 'policing' emerged. The Athenians employed informants known as 'sycophants' to report on potential subversive activities. This early form of intelligence gathering was essential for maintaining social order and political stability. The Roman Empire employed a complex network of informers, messengers, and scouts. Roman legions relied on scouts to gather information about enemy forces and terrain. The practice of gathering and analyzing information contributed to the success of Roman military campaigns.

Early practices and techniques of OSINT have evolved significantly over time, reflecting the available technology, cultural norms, and geopolitical circumstances of their respective eras. The early practices and techniques of OSINT have come a long way, from relying on human sources and rudimentary codes to harnessing the power of the internet and digital technologies. Throughout history, the fundamental principles of collecting and analyzing publicly available information have remained constant, but the tools and methods have adapted and evolved to meet the changing needs of intelligence, security, and decision-making processes. Today, OSINT continues to play a critical role in various domains, from national security to BI and journalism, thanks to advances in technology and the increasing importance of open-source data. OSINT has a rich history that predates the digital age. Understanding its evolution provides insight into its present-day significance. OSINT's roots can be traced to the use of publicly available information in military intelligence, where open sources complemented classified data. OSINT in military intelligence can also be traced back to the earliest forms of intelligence gathering and reconnaissance. OSINT has a rich history within military operations, evolving in response to the changing nature of warfare, technology, and the need for information superiority. Ancient civilizations such as the Egyptians, Greeks, and Romans practiced various forms of intelligence gathering. Spies and informants were employed to collect information about enemy forces, strategic locations, and political developments. The use of scouts and reconnaissance missions allowed military commanders to gain insights into enemy positions and intentions, serving as a precursor to modern OSINT like:

- Human Sources: In ancient times, intelligence gathering heavily relied on human sources such as diplomats, spies, informants, and messengers. These individuals would infiltrate rival courts, gather information through conversations, and report back to their patrons.
- Interrogation: Interrogation techniques were used to extract information from captives or individuals under suspicion. Ancient civilizations, including the Roman Empire, employed skilled interrogators to elicit information.
- Signals and Codes: Early forms of signaling and codes were employed for communication. For example, the Greeks used the Scytale, a rod with a specific circumference, to encrypt and decrypt messages.

During the Middle Ages, the art of espionage and information gathering continued to evolve. Feudal lords, monarchs, and religious institutions sought to collect intelligence for various purposes, including securing power and wealth. The feudal system in medieval Europe relied on feudal lords to gather information about neighboring territories and potential threats. Spies and informants played a crucial role in these intelligence networks. The Catholic Church [11] had a vast network of informants, collecting information on heretics and potential threats to its authority. The Islamic world during the 8th to 13th centuries was a center of learning and innovation [12]. Scholars and travelers collected vast amounts of information about various cultures, technologies, and scientific advancements. This era saw the compilation of encyclopedic works that contained a wealth of open-source knowledge. During the Middle Ages, feudal lords and monarchs employed spies and informants to gather information about rival kingdoms and potential threats. Intelligence networks played a crucial role in maintaining power and security. Examples of Medieval Espionage include:

- Couriers and Messengers: In medieval Europe, couriers and messengers were vital for carrying sensitive information discreetly. They played a critical role in transmitting messages between monarchs, nobles, and military commanders.
- Cryptanalysis: While cryptographic techniques were often rudimentary, cryptanalysts sought to break codes and ciphers used by adversaries to protect their information. The ability to decrypt intercepted messages was a valuable OSINT skill.

The Renaissance [13] and Enlightenment periods marked a significant shift in the way information was collected and disseminated. The invention of the printing press by Johannes Gutenberg in the 15th century revolutionized the spread of knowledge, making information more accessible to the masses. European explorers, such as Christopher Columbus and Ferdinand Magellan, embarked on voyages of discovery, collecting information about newly encountered lands, peoples, and resources. Their explorations contributed to the expansion of knowledge and the emergence of global intelligence networks. Philosophers and thinkers like Voltaire and Montesquieu championed the principles of free speech and the dissemination of knowledge. Their writings laid the intellectual foundation for the open exchange of information that would later become integral to OSINT practices, which included:

- Diplomacy: The diplomatic corps of the Renaissance and Enlightenment periods served as key sources of information. Diplomats and ambassadors were often tasked with reporting on foreign courts, politics, and developments.
- Printed Materials: The invention of the printing press facilitated the dissemination of written information. Printed materials, including newspapers, pamphlets, and books, became valuable sources for OSINT analysts.

The 19th and 20th centuries witnessed the formalization and professionalization of intelligence agencies. Governments and military organizations began to develop structured intelligence services to gather information in a systematic and organized manner. World War I marked a significant shift in the formalization of military intelligence. Intelligence agencies, such as MI6 in the United Kingdom, played crucial roles in gathering and analyzing information about enemy forces and plans. During World War II, intelligence agencies like the American Office of Strategic Services (OSS) collected and analyzed OSI to support military operations, including information from newspapers, radio broadcasts, and captured documents. Both World Wars demonstrated the critical importance of intelligence gathering. Espionage and codebreaking became integral to military strategies. In World War I, intelligence agencies like MI6 and the American Black Chamber emerged. World War II saw the establishment of the OSS, a precursor to the Central Intelligence Agency. The Cold War era intensified intelligence operations as the United States and the Soviet Union engaged in espionage, counterintelligence, and propaganda warfare. The intelligence community expanded, encompassing agencies like the Central Intelligence Agency, FBI, and NSA. The Cold War era witnessed the development of technical OSINT capabilities, such as signal intelligence and imagery intelligence. These capabilities focused on intercepting and analyzing electronic communications and satellite imagery. Military intelligence agencies began to use advanced technology to enhance information collection and analysis. This included the use of satellites for reconnaissance and the interception of radio communications. Modernization of Intelligence involved:

- Espionage and Covert Operations: The development of modern intelligence agencies, such as MI6 and the OSS, led to more organized and systematic espionage efforts. Spies were trained in various skills, including codebreaking and covert operations.
- Aerial Photography: In the 20th century, the use of aerial photography became a groundbreaking OSINT technique. It allowed analysts to gather valuable information about enemy troop movements, military installations, and terrain.
- Signal Intelligence: The interception and analysis of electronic communications, such as radio signals and telegrams, became a critical OSINT technique during World War I and World War II.

OSINT has a rich and varied history that spans millennia, evolving in response to the changing needs of societies and the advancement of technology. From the ancient world to the digital age, the practice of gathering and analyzing publicly available information has been integral to intelligence, security, and decision-making processes. In today's interconnected world, OSINT plays a more vital role than ever before. The internet and digital technologies have exponentially expanded the sources of open-source data, making it an invaluable resource for governments, businesses, journalists, researchers, and humanitarian organizations. As the world continues to evolve, OSINT will undoubtedly adapt and remain at the forefront of information gathering and analysis, shaping the way.

1.7 MODERN OSINT

The digital revolution, which began in the mid-20th century and continues today, has transformed the landscape of intelligence gathering. The advent of the internet and digital technologies has ushered in a new era of OSINT. The internet, which emerged in the late 20th century, revolutionized information dissemination. It provided access to vast amounts of OSI, making OSINT more accessible and comprehensive. The rise of social media platforms like Facebook, Twitter, and Instagram transformed the way individuals and organizations share information. OSINT practitioners now leverage social media to monitor events, track trends, and assess public sentiment. The development of advanced data analytics tools and automation has enabled OSINT analysts to process and analyze vast amounts of data quickly. Machine learning and natural language processing techniques have become integral to OSINT practices. The digital age has brought about new threats, including cyberattacks and online disinformation campaigns. OSINT plays a critical role in monitoring and countering these threats by collecting and analyzing digital evidence.

In the 21st century, OSINT has become an indispensable tool for governments, law enforcement agencies, private sector organizations, and researchers. Its applications extend to a wide range of fields, including national security, BI, and journalism. Governments around the world rely on OSINT to monitor terrorist activities, assess geopolitical risks, and gather information about potential threats to national security. OSINT has played a crucial role in identifying and tracking terrorist networks. Private sector organizations use OSINT to gain insights into market trends, competitors, and consumer sentiment. It helps businesses make informed decisions, develop marketing strategies, and protect intellectual property. Journalists and investigative reporters use OSINT techniques to uncover hidden information, verify sources, and report on issues of public interest. OSINT has been instrumental in exposing corruption, human rights abuses, and government misconduct. OSINT is valuable in academic research, particularly in fields like political science, geography, and social sciences. Humanitarian organizations also utilize OSINT to assess and respond to crises, such as natural disasters and conflicts. With the advent of the internet and digital technologies, OSINT underwent a significant transformation. Military intelligence agencies began to incorporate online sources of information into their analysis, such as monitoring websites, social media platforms, and forums. Geospatial Intelligence became a critical component of OSINT, allowing military intelligence to analyze geographic data, satellite imagery, and geolocation information to assess threats and targets. Cybersecurity and cyber intelligence became essential aspects of military OSINT, focusing on monitoring and countering cyber threats and attacks. Digital Age and the internet techniques included:

- Online Searches: The internet revolutionized OSINT by providing access to vast amounts of OSI. Early practitioners learned to use search engines and databases to retrieve information from websites, forums, and social media platforms.
- Social Media Monitoring: OSINT analysts began monitoring social media platforms to track events, public sentiment, and individuals of interest. This practice has since become an integral part of OSINT, especially in tracking emerging trends and threats.
- Data Mining and Analysis: With the rise of big data, OSINT practitioners adopted data mining and analysis tools to process and make sense of the enormous amounts of open-source data available online.
- Geospatial Intelligence: Geospatial Intelligence techniques, including satellite imagery analysis and geolocation, have become prominent in modern OSINT, enabling analysts to assess physical locations and activities.

The digital age has ushered in an era of unprecedented access to information, transforming the practice of OSINT in profound ways. Social media platforms, online communities, and digital communication channels have become invaluable sources of open-source data, reshaping the landscape of intelligence gathering, analysis, and decision-making across various domains. This essay explores the multifaceted role of social media and online communities in OSINT, highlighting their significance, challenges, and ethical considerations. The digital revolution, marked by the proliferation of the internet and digital technologies, has democratized access to information. It has given individuals, organizations, and governments the ability to share and access vast amounts of data instantaneously.

The digital age has expanded the scope and impact of OSINT, making it a critical tool for intelligence agencies, law enforcement, businesses, journalists, researchers, and even the public. Social media and online communities play a central role in this evolution. Social media platforms such as Facebook, Twitter, Instagram, LinkedIn, and TikTok have billions of active users worldwide. These platforms are rich sources of user-generated content, including text, images, videos, and location data. Social media provides real-time updates on events, crises, and developments. OSINT practitioners can monitor breaking news, natural disasters, protests, and geopolitical events as they unfold. Many social media platforms allow users to tag their locations when posting. This geospatial information can be harnessed to track events, assess the spread of information, and analyze trends. Profiles on social media platforms often contain personal information, interests, affiliations, and connections. This data can be used to build profiles, understand behavior, and identify potential threats.

1.8 OSINT DATA SOURCES

OSINT draws information from various publicly accessible sources, offering a wealth of data for analysis. Some of the key OSINT sources and the challenges associated with these data sources are listed below.

- Websites: These are rich repositories of information. Data from official sites, forums, blogs, and news articles can be crucial for understanding trends, events, and perspectives. Government websites for official documents, news websites for real-time updates, and forums for discussions on specific topics. Personal blogs and websites offer unique perspectives, opinions, and firsthand experiences. Independent bloggers sharing insights on technology, travel, or personal experiences. APIs (Application Programming Interfaces) access data from online platforms, which provide a structured way to interact with and retrieve information. Financial analysts use APIs provided by stock exchanges to collect real-time stock market data for analysis. Twitter API allows developers to retrieve tweets for social media analysis. Challenges in this data source include the dynamic content of websites which makes it challenging to capture and analyze information consistently along with access restrictions imposed by web portals that often require authentication or have content hidden behind paywalls, limiting accessibility. This leads to limitations such as accuracy concerns as data on websites may not always be accurate, and outdated content can mislead analysts and websites may not provide a comprehensive view of a topic or event.
- Social Media Platforms: These are a treasure trove of user-generated content, providing insights into opinions, trends, and activities. Twitter for example provides real-time updates and opinions, Facebook for personal and group information, LinkedIn for professional profiles, and Instagram for visual content. The sheer volume and speed of content on social media platforms make it difficult to process and analyze in real time, and the privacy settings on social media profiles often limit the visibility of certain information. Fake Accounts and Misinformation also affect the reliability of data.
- Public Records: Government records, court documents, and other official databases contain information related to individuals, organizations, and events. Birth and death records, property ownership records, court proceedings, business registrations, and licensing databases are some of the examples. However, public records are often

scattered across different databases, requiring significant effort to consolidate. Errors or outdated information may exist in public records, leading to inaccuracies. Certain details in public records may be redacted due to privacy concerns or legal restrictions and the availability of public records can vary by jurisdiction and may not cover all aspects of an individual's or organization's activities. Government reports may use technical or bureaucratic language that requires interpretation. Such reports may have a lag in data collection and publication, making them less timely. Governments may selectively report information, leading to a biased representation of certain issues, and some data may be classified or unavailable to the public.

- News Outlets and Agencies: Report on various news related events and issues, offering a timely and comprehensive view of current affairs. CNN, BBC, Al Jazeera, NDTV, ANI, and local news outlets report on global, national, and regional events. Political analysts examine news articles to understand public opinion on a particular political event. Media monitoring tools like Meltwater or Google News can aid in this analysis. But news sources can exhibit bias or sensationalism, influencing the perception of events. Some events may not be covered by mainstream media, limiting the scope of information. Breaking news often lacks verified information, leading to reliance on unconfirmed reports. News reports at times only provide a surface-level understanding without delving into the intricacies of a situation. Journalists search court records to gather information about a legal case. Public records can include birth and death certificates, property records, and business registrations.

- Academic Publications: Research manuscripts and scholarly articles contribute to in-depth knowledge in various fields. Journals (like IEEE, Elsevier, Taylor & Francis, MDPI), conference proceedings, and university repositories contain studies on topics ranging from science and technology to social sciences. However, academic papers often use specialized terminology that may be challenging for non-experts. Publications are often behind paywalls, restricting access to certain audiences. Researchers may publish positive results more frequently, potentially skewing the overall picture of a subject. The time it takes for research to be conducted, reviewed, and published can result in outdated information.

- Online Forums and Communities: These offer discussions and insights into specific interests, hobbies, or professions. Reddit has specialized forums (e.g., Stack Exchange) and online groups related to specific industries or hobbies. Limitations are when users in online forums utilize aliases, making it challenging to verify their identity. Some forums have troll or disinformation campaigns that impact the reliability of information. Information on forums can be highly specialized and not representative of broader perspectives. Also, the credibility of information on forums varies, requiring careful validation. Personal websites and blogs may contain subjective opinions rather than objective facts. Information on personal websites lacks external validation and often personal websites offer a limited perspective, especially if they focus on niche topics. Also, authors' views on personal websites can evolve over time, making historical analysis challenging.

- Dark web: While not openly accessible, contains hidden websites and forums, often associated with illicit activities. Tor network websites and forums dealing with illegal goods, hacking services, or other confidential information. Law enforcement agencies conduct dark web monitoring to track illegal trade or activities. Tools like Tor and specialized search engines like Grams can be used for such monitoring. But accessing and navigating the dark web involves legal and ethical challenges. Dark web content is often encrypted, making it harder to track and analyze. Information from the dark web may come from unreliable or untrustworthy sources and engaging with dark web sources raises legal and ethical dilemmas.
- Satellite Imagery: This provides visual data for mapping, monitoring, and analyzing physical locations. Google Earth, satellite imagery services like Maxar, and government satellite programs providing high-resolution images and extensive satellite imagery datasets. Environmental researchers may use satellite imagery to monitor deforestation or track changes in ice cover. Security analysts may perform geospatial analysis to identify high-crime areas in a city using crime incident data and geographical maps. However, satellite imagery may not always provide the level of detail required for certain analyses and cloud cover can obstruct satellite views, limiting the availability of clear images. Thus, satellite imagery may not offer real-time data, impacting the timeliness of analysis and acquiring high-resolution satellite imagery can be expensive.

The combination of these sources allows OSINT analysts to gather a comprehensive and diverse range of information for analysis, providing valuable insights in fields such as security, BI, and research. But understanding the challenges and limitations is essential for responsible and effective OSINT practices. Analysts need to employ a combination of sources, triangulate information, and exercise critical thinking to mitigate these challenges and enhance the reliability of their intelligence assessments. OSINT relies on a variety of data collection methods to gather information from publicly available sources. Some of the key data collection techniques include web scraping, data mining, and the roles of Human Intelligence and Social Media Intelligence (SOCMINT).

- Web scraping involves extracting data from websites by using automated tools or scripts to navigate web pages and collect relevant information. Cybersecurity analysts use web scraping to monitor online forums for discussions related to potential security threats. Tools like BeautifulSoup in Python or Scrapy are commonly employed for web scraping.
- Data mining discovers patterns and extracts valuable knowledge from large datasets. It involves the use of statistical, mathematical, and machine learning techniques. Business analysts use data mining to analyze customer purchase patterns from e-commerce websites. This can help identify trends, preferences, and potential areas for business improvement. Data mining tools include Weka, RapidMiner, and the scikit-learn library in Python.
- Human Intelligence involves gathering information through direct human interaction, relying on human sources to provide insights or intelligence. Military intelligence interviews residents to gather information about potential threats in a specific region. The gathered intelligence may include observations, opinions, or insider knowledge.
- SOCMINT focuses on collecting and analyzing information from social media platforms. It involves monitoring user-generated content to gain insights into public sentiment, trends, and events. Marketing teams use SOCMINT to analyze social media posts and comments to understand customer opinions about a product launch. Tools like Hootsuite, Brandwatch, and Mention are used for social media monitoring.
- OSINT frameworks are comprehensive tools that integrate multiple data collection methods and sources into a unified platform. Maltego is an OSINT framework that allows analysts to visualize relationships between entities by aggregating information from various sources. It can incorporate data from social media, public records, and more.

It's important to note that while these methods are valuable, ethical considerations, legal boundaries, and the responsible use of collected information are crucial aspects of OSINT practices. Additionally, combining multiple techniques and sources often provides a more comprehensive and accurate intelligence picture.

1.9 CRITICAL THINKING AND OSINT PROCESS

The landscape of OSINT is dynamic, with new tools, sources, and challenges emerging regularly. Critical thinking fosters a mindset of continuous learning, encouraging analysts to stay informed, adapt to changes, and refine their analytical skills. Critical thinking is of paramount importance in OSINT analysis, as it forms the foundation for effective and reliable decision-making. OSINT involves collecting information from diverse sources and evaluating it to draw meaningful insights. Critical thinking allows analysts to assess the credibility, reliability, and motive of information sources. Understanding the context and intent behind the data helps in gauging its trustworthiness. OSINT involves collecting data from multiple sources. Critical thinking helps analysts cross-reference and triangulate information, identifying patterns and inconsistencies to form a more accurate and comprehensive understanding. Critical thinking enables analysts to interpret information within its broader context. This involves considering cultural, political, or historical factors that may impact the meaning and significance of the data.

Analysts need to recognize and account for biases in the information they encounter. Critical thinking helps identify subjective viewpoints, political leanings, or cultural influences that may affect the objectivity of the data. OSINT analysts must verify the accuracy of the information they collect. Critical thinking skills guide the process of fact-checking, ensuring that data is reliable and supported by multiple trustworthy sources. In the era of fake news and disinformation, critical thinking is essential for identifying misleading or manipulated content. Analysts need to question the authenticity of data and recognize signs of misinformation. Critical thinking also allows analysts to adapt to evolving situations. As new information emerges, they can reassess their conclusions, adjust hypotheses, and refine their understanding of the subject matter. Ethical dilemmas may arise during OSINT analysis, especially concerning privacy and the responsible use of information. Critical thinking guides analysts to make ethical decisions and navigate potential ethical challenges.

OSINT often involves drawing inferences and making deductions from incomplete or indirect information. Critical thinking skills aid in making logical and well-reasoned conclusions based on available evidence. Critical thinking is integral to problem-solving in OSINT. Analysts must navigate through a multitude of data, identify relevant information, and solve complex puzzles to gain a comprehensive understanding of a situation. Clear and effective communication of findings is crucial in OSINT. Critical thinking enables analysts to articulate their assessments and conclusions in a manner that is understandable to decision-makers or stakeholders. Thus, critical thinking acts as the cornerstone of sound OSINT analysis. It empowers analysts to navigate the complexities of information gathering, evaluation, and interpretation, ensuring that the intelligence derived is reliable, unbiased, and valuable for decision-makers across various domains.

The process of collecting, evaluating, and verifying OSINT data is a crucial aspect of ensuring the reliability and accuracy of the information gathered. Throughout the entire process, OSINT practitioners should adhere to ethical guidelines, respect privacy, and operate within legal boundaries. Continuous learning and improvement are essential to enhance the effectiveness of

Step 1: Define Objectives and Scope	Step 2. Identify Sources and Methods	Step 3: Collect Data	Step 4: Evaluate Source Credibility	Step 5: Cross-Check Information
Step 10: Use Geolocation and Context	Step 9: Check for Red Flags	Step 8: Corroborate Details	Step 7: Verify Timeliness	Step 6: Assess Bias and Objectivity
Step 11: Apply Digital Forensics	Step 12: Engage with Subject Matter Experts	Step 13: Maintain a Chain of Custody	Step 14: Document and Record Findings	Step 15: Report and Communicate Results
				Step 16: Adapt and Iterate

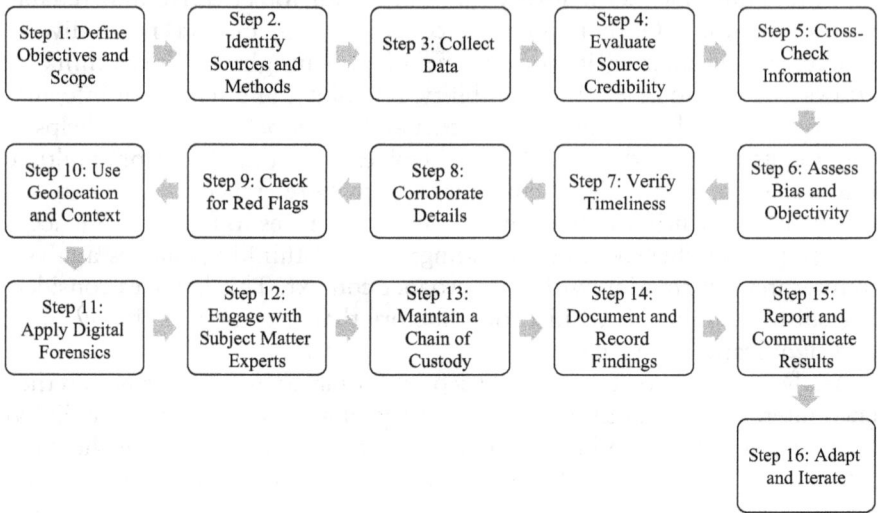

Figure 1.2 OSINT process.

OSINT efforts and contribute to responsible intelligence analysis. Figure 1.2 illustrates the steps involved in this process, which are listed below.

Step 1: Define Objectives and Scope
- Clearly define the objectives of the OSINT operation.
- Determine the scope, including the specific topics, entities, or events of interest.

Step 2: Identify Sources and Methods
- Identify relevant data sources based on the objectives and scope.
- Choose appropriate data collection methods, such as web scraping, data mining, social media monitoring, or human intelligence.

Step 3: Collect Data
- Utilize selected methods to collect data from various sources.
- Ensure compliance with legal and ethical guidelines during the data collection process.

Step 4: Evaluate Source Credibility
- Assess the credibility of each information source.
- Consider the reputation, reliability, and motive of the source.
- Evaluate the context in which the information was presented.

Step 5: Cross-Check Information
- Cross-reference data from multiple sources to verify consistency.
- Identify patterns or discrepancies in information obtained from different sources.

Step 6: Assess Bias and Objectivity
- Evaluate the potential bias of information sources.
- Consider the political, cultural, or personal perspectives that might influence the presentation of data.

Step 7: Verify Timeliness
- Ensure that the collected data is current and relevant to the objectives.
- Consider the timestamp of information, especially in fast-changing situations.

Step 8: Corroborate Details
- Verify key details and facts through additional sources.
- Seek confirmation from independent and reliable sources to enhance accuracy.

Step 9: Check for Red Flags
- Be vigilant for red flags, such as inconsistent information, sensationalism, or indications of manipulation.
- Scrutinize the context and language used in sources for signs of misinformation.

Step 10: Use Geolocation and Context
- Utilize geolocation data to confirm the origin or location of information.
- Consider the context in which the information was shared to understand its true meaning.

Step 11: Apply Digital Forensics
- Employ digital forensics techniques to verify the authenticity of digital content.
- Evaluate metadata, image forensics, and other digital traces for signs of manipulation.

Step 12: Engage with Subject Matter Experts
- Consult subject matter experts to validate technical or specialized information.
- Experts can provide insights into the accuracy and relevance of data within their domain.

Step 13: Maintain a Chain of Custody
- Document the source of each piece of information and maintain a clear chain of custody.
- Establish a record of the steps taken in the data collection and verification process.

Step 14: Document and Record Findings
- Document all findings, including the sources, methods, and verification steps.
- Maintain a record of the confidence level associated with each piece of information.

Step 15: Report and Communicate Results
- Present the verified and evaluated OSINT findings in a clear and organized manner.
- Clearly communicate the limitations and uncertainties associated with the information.

Step 16: Adapt and Iterate
- Be adaptable and open to revising findings based on new information or changing circumstances.
- Iterate the process as needed to incorporate additional data or refine conclusions.

1.10 CONCLUSION

OSINT stands as a crucial linchpin in the contemporary information landscape, wielding its influence across diverse domains such as national security and BI. As explored in this chapter, the evolution of OSINT from its roots in military intelligence to its present-day multifaceted applications reflects its adaptability and significance. Delving into the basics of OSINT, we have dissected its definition, ethical considerations, and core principles, shedding light on its role in decision-making and interest protection across industries. The exploration of various sources and methods, from web scraping and data mining to the indispensable Human Intelligence, has unveiled the intricacies and challenges inherent in OSINT practices.

The author anticipates that the next stage of information collection and analysis will be shaped by the confluence of social media creating an increasingly linked OSINT environment. As the information era develops, OSINT continues to be vital and dynamic. By navigating its progress and understanding its nuances, practitioners will be able to utilize its power ethically and efficiently, guaranteeing its continuing relevance in a technological context that is always changing. Exciting developments are anticipated in the future, and the combination of cutting-edge technology will be essential to opening new possibilities in the field of OSINT. Social media and online communities have redefined the practice of OSINT, offering a wealth of open-source data for various domains and applications. The role of OSINT in national security, law enforcement, business, journalism, research, and humanitarian efforts is now more prominent than ever. However, with this prominence comes a responsibility to navigate ethical considerations, privacy concerns, and data security challenges. As technology continues to shape OSINT practices, it is crucial to strike a balance between harnessing the power of social media and online communities for intelligence and ensuring ethical and responsible engagement with these digital spaces. Ultimately, OSINT's continued development will be pivotal in addressing the complex challenges of our interconnected world.

REFERENCES

1. R. Gill, "What Is OSINT (Open-Source Intelligence?) | SANS Institute," Feb. 23, 2023. https://www.sans.org/blog/what-is-open-source-intelligence/
2. "Open-Source Intelligence Has Arrived," https://www.orfonline.org/research/open-source-intelligence-has-arrived (accessed Jan. 29, 2024).
3. "OSINT Risk Assessment | OSINT Tools | OSINT Techniques," https://www.neotas.com/osint-risk-assessment/ (accessed Jan. 29, 2024).
4. "How We Work | Tech against Terrorism," https://techagainstterrorism.org/how-we-work (accessed Jan. 29, 2024).
5. SpecialEurasia, "The Importance of Open Source Intelligence in Geopolitics," Apr. 17, 2023. https://www.specialeurasia.com/2023/04/17/open-source-intelligence-osint/
6. "Unleashing the Power of Open Source Intelligence (OSINT): A Comprehensive Guide," https://www.linkedin.com/pulse/unleashing-power-open-source-intelligence-osint-comprehensive/ (accessed Jan. 29, 2024).
7. "Assessed Cyber Structure and Alignments of North Korea in 2023," https://cloud.google.com/blog/topics/threat-intelligence/north-korea-cyber-structure-alignment-2023/ (accessed April 11, 2025).
8. "Open Source Intelligence – OSINT Framework, Techniques, Tool". https://www.neotas.com/open-source-intelligence-osint/ (accessed Jan. 29, 2024).
9. A. de Borchgrave, T. M. Sanderson, and N. J. M. Iii, "Open Source Information," Mar. 2006 [Online]. Available: https://www.csis.org/analysis/open-source-information (accessed Jan. 29, 2024).
10. Wikipedia Contributors, "Classified Information," Jul. 17, 2019. https://en.wikipedia.org/wiki/Classified_information
11. Britannica, "Roman Catholicism – The Church of the Early Middle Ages | Britannica," 2019. Available: https://www.britannica.com/topic/Roman-Catholicism/The-church-of-the-early-Middle-Ages
12. Boundless, "The Islamic Golden Age | World Civilization," 2008. https://courses.lumenlearning.com/suny-hccc-worldcivilization/chapter/the-islamic-golden-age/
13. Britannica, "Renaissance," Oct. 17, 2018. Available: https://www.britannica.com/event/Renaissance

## Chapter 2

Online privacy and secure browsing techniques

2.1 INTRODUCTION

In the networked world of the internet, where data is shared effortlessly, it is more important than ever to protect one's online identity. I was inspired to start with this topic after delivering an OSINT course. A few participants had brought computers so they could try the methods I was presenting in the workshop. During a break, I saw many students using laptops from patrol cars to browse Facebook; private investigators accessing suspects' blogs on legacy Windows OS; and security experts visiting hacker websites with no proper security controls like script blockers. Although I was aware of virus and malware attacks, all I would do if I sensed something went wrong was reinstall Windows OS. Thinking in this way was reactive, but as I acquired and analyzed data online, I now know that it is essential to proactively mitigate online privacy and protect browsing risks.

Entering the world of OSINT requires a strong defense against the many risks to online privacy. This is because the gateway to efficient data collection and analysis is required. This introduction deconstructs the complex world of digital security, preparing the reader for an investigation into online privacy and safe surfing practices. The widespread availability of digital connection has permanently changed how we communicate, work, and use information. But as technology has advanced, several risks have emerged, endangering the confidentiality of personal information. The digital realm is full of potential perils, ranging from the subtle tracking systems used by marketers to the more sinister activities of thieves seeking illegal access. Think about the widespread use of third-party cookies, which covertly monitor our internet behavior and create intricate profiles for customized ads. In this context, it becomes essential for anyone trying to securely navigate the digital world to comprehend the subtleties of online risks.

Following prominent data breaches and privacy scandals, the need for internet privacy has been increasingly apparent to the public. Examples such as the Cambridge Analytica incident [1], in which user information from a well-known social media platform was utilized for political ends, highlight how sensitive personal data is in the digital sphere. In a society

DOI: 10.1201/9781003497615-2

where private information is frequently viewed as a commodity, the right to privacy is recognized as inalienable. This chapter explains how these occurrences highlight the necessity of taking preventative action to protect our digital identities against targeted and opportunistic threats. To put it simply, this introduction acts as a compass for people who are new to the digital frontier to arm themselves with the information and resources necessary to protect their digital identities. This chapter establishes the framework for an in-depth investigation of online privacy and secure browsing, providing the foundation for accountable and durable digital behaviors. The argument that a secure computing environment serves as the cornerstone for ethical and responsible OSINT techniques is reaffirmed in this chapter's conclusion, enabling people to navigate the digital terrain with resilience against possible dangers with confidence.

2.2 UNDERSTANDING THE THREAT LANDSCAPE

Before fortifying our digital fortresses, it is crucial to comprehend the varied threats that lurk in the digital shadows. There are significant risks from malicious actors, which can range from state-sponsored organizations pursuing espionage to hackers looking for financial gain. The increase in phishing attacks, in which people are tricked into disclosing private information by means of misleading emails, is a relevant example. People should effectively customize their defenses by being aware of the strategies these dangers use.

2.2.1 Rise of surveillance capitalism

The digital era has made personal data a desirable commodity, contributing to the phenomenon sometimes referred to as 'surveillance capitalism.' Businesses gather enormous amounts of data to improve their goods, target ads, and affect customer behavior. Examples from the real world are the extensive profiles that tech companies create from consumers' online activity. The consequences of surveillance capitalism are examined in this section, along with ways that people might lessen its negative effects on their privacy.

Surveillance capitalism [2], a term coined by academic Shoshana Zuboff [3], refers to the commodification of personal data for economic gain. In this paradigm, large corporations amass vast amounts of user information, employing sophisticated algorithms to analyze and monetize individuals' online behaviors. The pervasive collection of data has profound implications for online privacy, as it extends beyond targeted advertising to influence various aspects of society. The key characteristics are:

- Data Extraction: Surveillance capitalism relies on the extraction of extensive data from users' online activities. This includes not only explicit data shared on platforms, but also implicit data derived from user behaviors and interactions.

- Behavior Prediction: Advanced algorithms analyze collected data to predict user behavior. By understanding individuals' preferences, habits, and sentiments, companies can tailor products, services, and advertisements with unprecedented precision.
- Monetization of Predictions: The predictions generated from user data become valuable commodities. Companies monetize this information by selling targeted advertising, influencing consumer choices, and even shaping political narratives.
- Influence on Decision-Making: Surveillance capitalism has the power to influence decision-making on a massive scale. By manipulating the flow of information and tailoring content to individual preferences, it can shape opinions, beliefs, and political inclinations.

Certain nation states leverage surveillance capitalism for various purposes, both domestically and internationally. While motivations may differ, these states recognize the power that vast data collection has in influencing and controlling populations. Authoritarian regimes often exploit surveillance capitalism to maintain social control. By monitoring citizens' online activities, these states can identify dissent, suppress opposition, and shape public discourse in ways that align with their political agendas. For instance, China's social credit system integrates surveillance data to monitor and control citizens' behavior, affecting everything from travel privileges to financial transactions.

Nation states engaged in cyber espionage utilize surveillance capitalism techniques to gather intelligence on foreign governments, organizations, and individuals. By infiltrating social media platforms, collecting metadata, and exploiting vulnerabilities, these states can conduct sophisticated information warfare campaigns. Some nation states also leverage surveillance capitalism to influence democratic processes in other countries. This can involve spreading disinformation, conducting targeted social media campaigns, and exploiting divisive issues to sow discord and undermine trust in self-governing institutions. The 2016 U.S. presidential election is a notable example [4] of online digital interference. Nation states often collaborate with or co-opt tech companies to create extensive digital profiles of individuals. These profiles can be used for intelligence purposes, monitoring activists, and even implementing social engineering tactics to influence key figures. While surveillance capitalism poses significant challenges to online privacy, concerted efforts on legislative, technological, and societal fronts can contribute to mitigating its impact and fostering a more privacy-respecting digital environment.

2.2.2 Encryption and anonymization

Technologies like SSL/TLS protocols [5] are examples of security communication, which acts as a barrier against intercepting or eavesdropping to strengthen digital web browsing. Anonymization methods such using Virtual Private Networks (VPNs) and Tor provide the ability to hide their IP addresses and surf the internet anonymously by protecting sensitive information, ensuring the confidentiality of communications, and shielding individuals from unwarranted surveillance. A professional working remotely and utilizing a VPN to encrypt their connection and shield private work-related conversations from prying eyes is a real-world example.

To stop unwanted access, SSL/TLS encryption transforms data into a code. It protects communication secrecy, making it difficult for bad actors to intercept and decode private information. Encryption is used by secure communication channels, such HTTPS (Hypertext Transfer Protocol Secure), to safeguard data while it is being transmitted. Only the intended receiver will be able to decode the encrypted communication, thanks to end-to-end encryption. Encrypted communication between the user's browser and the website server is ensured while using HTTPS-enabled websites. HTTPS guards against illegal access to data during transmission, man-in-the-middle attacks, and eavesdropping. It is essential for protecting private data, including e-commerce and login passwords. End-to-end encryption is used by messaging apps like Signal and WhatsApp to shield communication information from other parties, including service providers. Data storage has been secured by encryption; it is not just for communication routes. Even in the event that physical hardware is hacked, data-at-rest encryption prevents unwanted access to data stored on servers or devices. Encryption serves as a powerful defense against mass surveillance by both state and non-state actors. By encrypting data, individuals can maintain a level of privacy and prevent indiscriminate data collection.

Anonymization involves concealing the identity of individuals in datasets. It enables users to interact with online platforms without revealing their true identities. Internet traffic is anonymized by use of a network of servers run by volunteer organizations, such as anonymous browsers like Tor. Anonymization protects user privacy by dissociating online activities from personal identities. This is particularly important in situations where individuals may face retribution for expressing dissent or unpopular opinions. Anonymization is integral to secure browsing. It prevents websites, advertisers, or governments from tracking users' online behavior and building comprehensive profiles.

While the tension between privacy advocates and law enforcement persists, it is crucial to strike a balance that upholds individual privacy rights while addressing legitimate security concerns. Encouraging an open dialogue and international collaboration on encryption standards and privacy practices is essential for navigating this complex landscape. The challenge lies in finding solutions that preserve individual freedoms without compromising overall security.

2.3 PRIVACY-FOCUSED TECHNIQUES

Privacy-focused techniques are essential for individuals seeking to protect their online privacy, especially in a landscape where tracking and monitoring have become ubiquitous. These techniques aim to minimize the collection of personal data, enhance anonymity, and secure online activities. This section presents a variety of privacy-focused techniques and resources against online privacy tracking and user browsing.

2.3.1 Virtual private networks or VPNs

By encrypting data transmission and hiding the user's IP address, VPNs provide secure tunnels between a user's device and a server, which also helps protect against surveillance by Internet Service Providers (ISPs) and other entities, making it challenging for websites to track users based on their IP addresses. Additionally, they enhance security on public Wi-Fi networks.

2.3.1.1 NordVPN

NordVPN [6] is a service designed to provide users with enhanced online privacy, security, and anonymity, which operates a vast network of 5,200 servers located in 59 countries around the world. When a user connects to NordVPN as illustrated in Figure 2.1, their internet traffic is encrypted. NordVPN uses robust encryption protocols, such as OpenVPN, IKEv2/IPsec, and NordLynx (a proprietary protocol based on WireGuard), to secure the data transmitted between the user's device and the VPN server.

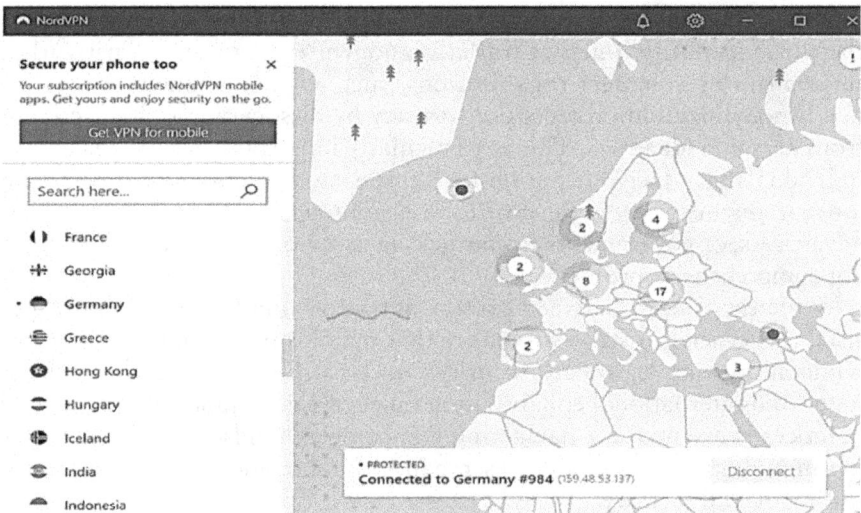

Figure 2.1 NordVPN.

NordVPN requires user authentication to establish a secure connection. Users typically log in using their account credentials (username and password). This authentication process helps ensure that only authorized users can connect to the VPN. After authentication, NordVPN establishes a secure tunnel between the user's device and the chosen VPN server. This tunnel is encrypted, preventing third parties, including hackers, ISPs, or government authorities, from intercepting or monitoring the user's online activities.

When connected to NordVPN, the user's internet traffic appears to originate from the VPN server's location. This helps mask the user's real IP address, providing a level of anonymity and privacy. Websites and online services only see the IP address of the VPN server, not the user's actual IP address. NordVPN allows users to connect to servers in different countries, enabling them to access content that may be geo-restricted or blocked in their region. By choosing a server in a specific location, users can appear as if they are browsing from that region. NordVPN offers a feature called Double VPN or Multi-hop, which routes the user's internet traffic through two VPN servers for an additional layer of security and anonymity. NordVPN has a strict no-logs policy, meaning the service does not record or store any information about users' online activities, connection timestamps, or IP addresses.

This commitment to privacy is designed to ensure that user data remains private and secure. NordVPN includes a kill switch feature that automatically disconnects the user from the internet if the VPN connection drops unexpectedly. This prevents the user's real IP address and online activities from being exposed. NordVPN provides users with options to customize their VPN experience. This includes features like CyberSec (blocking malicious websites and ads), split tunneling (allowing specific apps or websites to bypass the VPN), and more.

Link: https://nordvpn.com

2.3.1.2 ExpressVPN extensions

ExpressVPN [7] provides a browser extension primarily for Google Chrome and Mozilla Firefox. It's important to note that while browser extensions are available, ExpressVPN primarily operates as a standalone VPN application at the system level. This browser extension works by establishing a secure encrypted tunnel between the user's browser and one of ExpressVPN's servers, as shown in Figure 2.2. The extension uses strong encryption protocols such as OpenVPN with TLS/SSL to secure the data transmitted between the user's browser and the VPN server. ExpressVPN includes features to protect against WebRTC leaks, a potential vulnerability that could reveal a user's real IP address even when using a VPN. The extension ensures that WebRTC requests are routed through the VPN tunnel.

Figure 2.2 ExpressVPN.

While the ExpressVPN application operates at the system level and directs all internet traffic through the VPN, the browser extension specifically routes only the browser's traffic through the VPN connection. This allows users to have more granular control over which parts of their online activities are protected by the VPN. This extension allows users to select a server location, effectively spoofing their geographic location. This helps users access content that may be geo-restricted in their actual location. Users can configure the extension to automatically connect to the VPN when they open their browser. This ensures that their browser traffic is consistently protected. The extension handles Domain Name System requests made by the browser, preventing potential Domain Name System leaks that could reveal the user's true location. The extension connects to one of ExpressVPN's servers located in various countries around the world. The extensive server network allows users to choose from a wide range of locations for better privacy, security, and content access.

Link: https://www.expressvpn.com

2.3.2 The Onion Router (Tor) browser

Tor [8] networks route internet traffic through a series of volunteer-operated servers, making user activities difficult to trace. Tor or The Onion Router is a privacy-focused browser that allows users to access the internet with a higher degree of anonymity. Tor provides anonymous browsing by encrypting and bouncing internet traffic through multiple servers, as illustrated in Figure 2.3. This prevents websites and online services from easily tracking user locations and activities. Each node in the network peels off a layer of encryption, hence the term 'onion,' before passing the traffic to the next node. This process helps obfuscate the source of the data. The Tor network consists of thousands of volunteer-operated servers running the Tor software. These nodes contribute to the anonymity and privacy of users by routing their traffic through a series of randomly selected nodes.

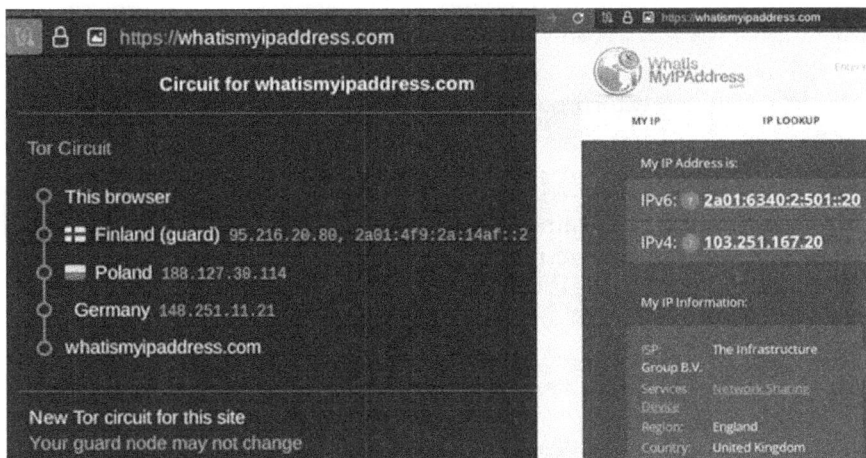

Figure 2.3 Tor browser routing.

The user's connection to the Tor network starts with an entry node, which is the first node to receive the encrypted data. The entry node only knows the IP address of the user, and it can't see the original content of the data. After passing through the entry node, the data is routed through several middle nodes. Each middle node only decrypts a layer of encryption, making it impossible for any single node to know both the source and destination of the data. The final node in the Tor network is the exit node. This node decrypts the last layer of encryption and sends the data to its intended destination on the internet. Importantly, the exit node does not know the original source of the data. Tor uses encryption throughout the entire process to protect the confidentiality of the data. The connections between nodes are encrypted using the Tor protocol, preventing eavesdroppers from deciphering the transmitted information. Tor browser is a modified version of Mozilla Firefox that is configured to work seamlessly with the Tor network. The browser is designed to prevent websites from tracking users and collecting identifying information. Tor browser is configured to reject most cookies, which are small pieces of data stored on the user's computer by websites. This helps prevent tracking based on cookie information.

Tor browser includes the HTTPS Everywhere extension, which ensures that connections to websites are encrypted whenever possible. This helps protect users from various types of attacks and surveillance. The browser includes the NoScript extension, which disables JavaScript, Java, Flash, and other potentially exploitable content by default. Users can choose to enable scripts on trusted sites, reducing the risk of malicious code execution. By routing traffic through a series of nodes and using a different IP address at each stage, Tor provides a high level of anonymity for users. However, it's essential to note that Tor is not completely immune to all forms of surveillance, and users need to be aware of potential risks. Tor browser may display warning messages to users when attempting to access websites with mixed content or other potential security risks, promoting user awareness.

Link: https://www.torproject.org

2.3.3 Privacy-focused search engines

Privacy-focused search engines prioritize user privacy by not storing search histories or tracking user activities. These search engines provide users with a private search experience, free from personalized tracking and targeted advertising commonly associated with major search engines.

2.3.3.1 DuckDuckGo

This is a privacy-focused search engine, as presented in Figure 2.4, which provides the users with a more private and secure online browsing experience. This search engine does not track users or store their personal information. Unlike other search engines like Google, this does not create, track, or log user profiles based on search history, IP addresses, or other identifying information, which allows users to search the internet anonymously. DuckDuckGo [9] uses encrypted SSL encrypted connections (HTTPS) by default, which helps protect user data during transmission. This prevents third parties from intercepting and eavesdropping on the communication between the user and the search engine.

DuckDuckGo provides the same search results for all users, regardless of their past search history or preferences. This approach helps avoid

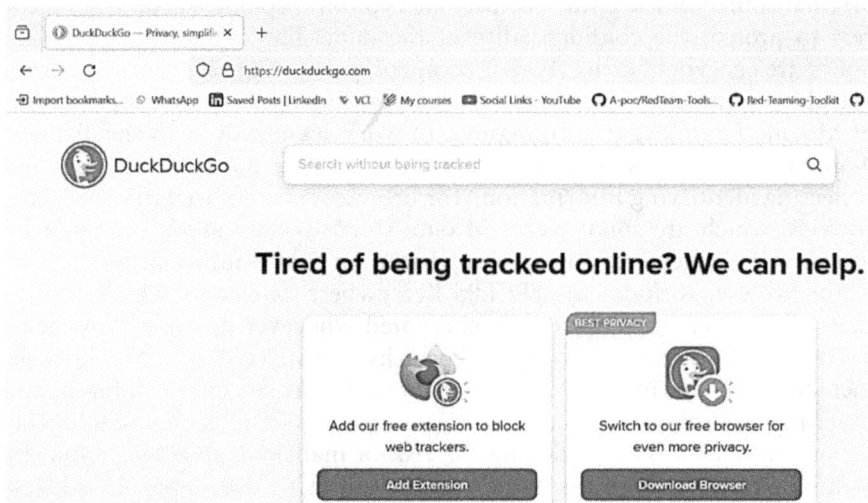

Figure 2.4 DuckDuckGo.

filter bubbles, where users are only exposed to information that aligns with their existing beliefs and interests. DuckDuckGo also offers browser extensions for popular web browsers (like Chrome, Firefox, and Safari) that enhance privacy. These extensions can block trackers, force encrypted connections where possible, and provide a privacy rating for visited websites. DuckDuckGo uses a combination of its web crawler and sources like Bing and Yahoo to deliver search results. This helps provide a comprehensive search experience without compromising user privacy. DuckDuckGo's search engine includes various built-in features designed to enhance privacy, such as the ability to force encrypted connections, block trackers, and provide instant answers without the need to click on search results.

Link: https://duckduckgo.com

2.3.3.2 Startpage

Privacy browser extensions are plugins that users can add to their web browsers to enhance online privacy and security. Extensions like Startpage [10] provide additional features and settings to protect users from various online threats and tracking practices. This helps block third-party trackers, advertisements, and force secure connections when available. These extensions enhance user privacy by preventing websites from collecting information through tracking scripts and by securing connections to websites through encryption. When you visit a webpage, parts of the page may come from domains and servers other than the one you asked to visit. This is an essential feature of hypertext. On the modern web portals, embedded images and code often use cookies and other methods to track users, often to display advertisements and track browsing habits. The domains that do this are called 'third-party trackers.'

Startpage is a privacy-focused proxy between the user and the search engine, as illustrated in Figure 2.5. When a user submits a search query, Startpage fetches the search results from Google (by default) on behalf of the user. This process helps to shield the user's IP address from being directly exposed to the search engine.

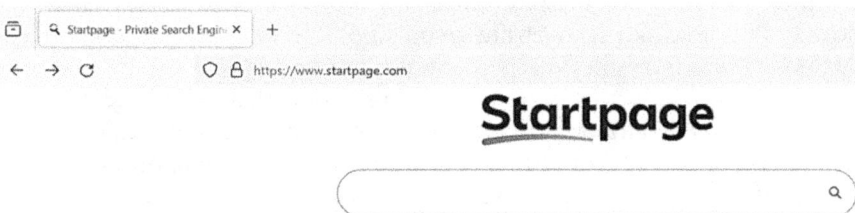

Figure 2.5 Startpage.

Startpage does not use tracking cookies to follow users across different websites. This prevents third parties from creating a comprehensive profile of a user's online activities. Startpage generates anonymous identifiers for each user session, and these identifiers are not linked to any personally identifiable information. This helps maintain user privacy during search sessions.

Link: https://www.startpage.com

2.3.3.3 Privacy settings

Regularly reviewing and adjusting privacy settings on devices, operating systems, and applications is essential. Many devices and platforms offer privacy settings that allow users to control what information is shared. Adjusting these settings helps limit data collection and sharing. Comprehensive privacy suites like Brave and Epic Privacy Browser bundle various privacy-enhancing features into a single package. These may include ad-blocking, tracker-blocking, fingerprinting protection, and other tools designed to protect user privacy.

2.3.3.4 Private browsing

This is known as Incognito mode in Chrome and Private Window in Firefox; private browsing is a feature that allows users to browse the internet with increased privacy by preventing the storage of certain information locally. In Private Window mode, Firefox doesn't save the browsing history. This means that the list of visited websites, searches, and download history is not stored. Firefox won't save any form data or search suggestions. This is particularly useful for preventing the browser from remembering search queries and other input. Cookies are not stored after closing the Private Window. This prevents websites from remembering the user's login status and other preferences between sessions. Temporary files and cached content are not saved during a Private Window session. This ensures that pages are not cached on the user's device. In this mode, Firefox doesn't store site-specific data, such as cached images, offline data, and other content, after the Private Window is closed.

Chrome Incognito mode performs similarly, as the browser does not save the browsing history. Pages visited, searches made, and other activities are not recorded. Chrome doesn't store cookies after the session is closed. This means that websites won't be able to track the user across sessions. Temporary files, cached content, and other site-specific data are not stored locally. Each Incognito session starts with a clean slate. Chrome doesn't save form data or search suggestions in Incognito mode. This helps prevent the browser from remembering user inputs. Temporary files are not saved during an Incognito session, ensuring that pages are not cached locally. Files downloaded during an Incognito session won't be listed in the download history.

2.3.4 Privacy extensions

Web browser privacy extensions are add-ons or plugins that users can install in their web browsers to enhance privacy and security while browsing the internet. These extensions typically provide additional features and tools that help users control their online privacy, block tracking elements, and secure their browsing experience.

2.3.4.1 uBlock Origin

The uBlock Origin [11] browser extension uses filter lists to identify and block content such as banner ads, pop-ups, tracking scripts, and other elements that can compromise user privacy or affect page loading speed. These lists contain rules that define which content to block based on patterns found in URLs. Users can customize these lists or add additional ones based on their preferences. uBlock Origin provides an element picker tool that allows users to select specific elements on a webpage and choose whether to block or unblock them. This feature gives users granular control over the content they want to see. uBlock Origin supports dynamic filtering, allowing users to control how web pages can connect to external domains. This feature helps prevent tracking scripts and third-party content from loading unless explicitly allowed by the user. In addition to blocking ads, uBlock Origin can block other types of resources such as scripts, frames, and images. This can enhance privacy and improve page loading times. uBlock Origin is designed to be efficient and lightweight. It aims to use minimal system resources while still providing robust ad-blocking capabilities. This contributes to faster page loading times and a smoother browsing experience.

Link: https://chromewebstore.google.com/detail/ublock-origin/cjpalhdln bpafiamejdnhcphjbkeiagm

2.3.4.2 Privacy Badger

The Privacy Badger [12] extension differs from traditional ad-blocking extensions in two ways: First, while most other blocking extensions prioritize blocking ads, Privacy Badger is purely a tracker blocker. The extension doesn't block ads unless they happen to be tracking you; in fact, one of our goals is to incentivize advertisers to adopt better privacy practices. Second, most other blockers rely on a human-curated list of domains or URLs to block. Privacy Badger is an algorithmic tracker blocker, which defines what tracking looks like, and then Privacy Badger, as illustrated in Figure 2.6, blocks or restricts domains that it observes tracking in the wild. What is and isn't considered a tracker is entirely based on how a specific domain acts, not on human judgment. When you view a webpage, that page will often be made up of content from many different sources. For example, a

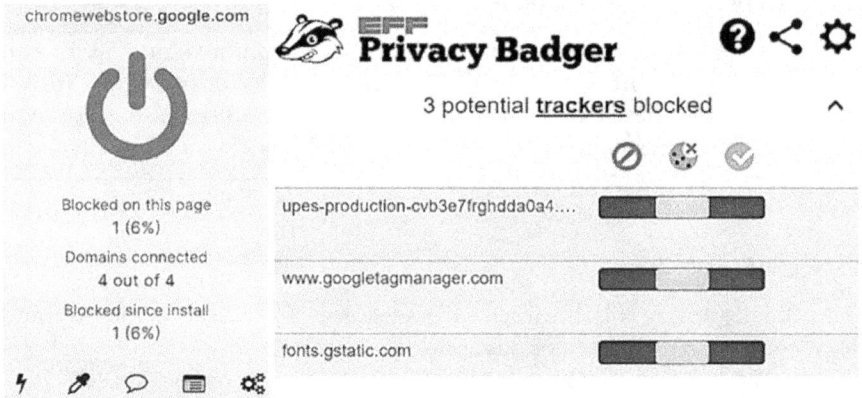

Figure 2.6 uBlock origin and Privacy Badger Chrome extensions.

news webpage might load the actual article from the news company, ads from an ad company, and the comments section from a different company that's been contracted out to provide that service. Privacy Badger keeps track of all of this. If as you browse the web, the same source seems to be tracking your browser across different websites, then Privacy Badger springs into action, telling your browser not to load any more content from that source. And when your browser stops loading content from a source, that source can no longer track you.

Privacy Badger keeps note of the 'third-party' domains that embed images, scripts, and advertising in the pages you visit. Privacy Badger looks for tracking techniques like uniquely identifying cookies, local storage 'super-cookies,' and canvas fingerprinting. If it observes a single third-party host tracking you on three separate sites, Privacy Badger will automatically disallow content from that third-party tracker. Privacy Badger analyzes the cookies from each site; unique cookies that contain tracking IDs are disallowed, while 'low entropy' cookies that perform other functions are allowed. For instance, a cookie like LANG=fr that encodes the user's language preference, or a cookie that preserves a very small amount of information about ads the user has been shown, would be allowed provided that individual or small groups of users' reading habits could not be collected with them.

Link: https://chromewebstore.google.com/detail/privacy-badger/pkehgijc mpdhfbdbbnkijodmdjhbjlgp

2.3.4.3 HTTPS Everywhere

Major web browsers like Firefox and Chrome offer native support for an HTTPS-only mode. HTTPS-only mode [13] forces all connections to websites to use a secure encrypted connection called HTTPS. Most websites already support HTTPS:// some support both HTTP and HTTPS.

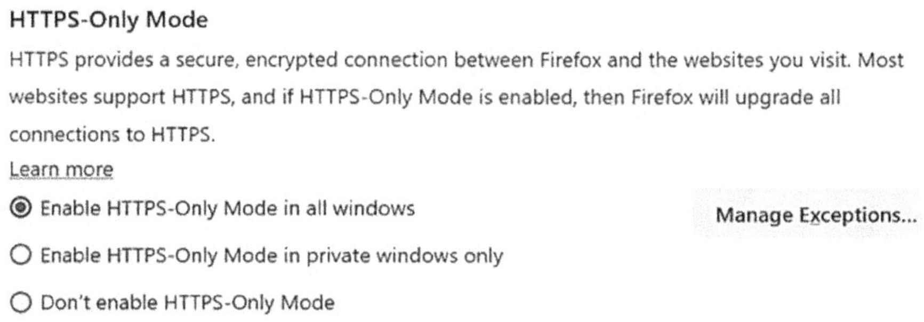

HTTPS-Only Mode

HTTPS provides a secure, encrypted connection between Firefox and the websites you visit. Most websites support HTTPS, and if HTTPS-Only Mode is enabled, then Firefox will upgrade all connections to HTTPS.

Learn more

◉ Enable HTTPS-Only Mode in all windows   Manage Exceptions...

○ Enable HTTPS-Only Mode in private windows only

○ Don't enable HTTPS-Only Mode

Figure 2.7 Firefox HTTPS-only mode.

Enabling this mode guarantees that all your connections to websites are upgraded to use HTTPS and hence secure.

For Firefox: HTTPS-only for mobiles is currently only available in Firefox Developer mode, which advanced users can enable in **about:config**. By clicking Settings → Privacy & Security → Scroll to Bottom → Enable HTTPS-only mode, as shown in Figure 2.7.

For Google Chrome: HTTPS-only is available for both desktop and mobile in Chrome 94. Click on Settings → Privacy and Security → Security → Scroll to bottom → Toggle 'Always use secure connections,' as illustrated in Figure 2.8. This feature is also under the flag **chrome:// flags/#https-only-mode-setting**.

2.3.4.4 SquareX

The current generation of endpoint security products operate using a Probabilistic Security Model. They strive to classify a file, website, or digital resource as malicious or safe and block access to anything detected as malicious. Besides being plagued by both false positives and negatives, blocking access can significantly impact user productivity. This leads to users at times disabling security products as a workaround to getting work done. Moreover, since every product uses different detection algorithms, the same file or website marked as safe by one product might be flagged as malicious by another. This inconsistency leads to confusion and panic.

SquareX [14] is the world's first product built from the ground up using a Deterministic Security Model applied to all attack vectors. Unlike existing

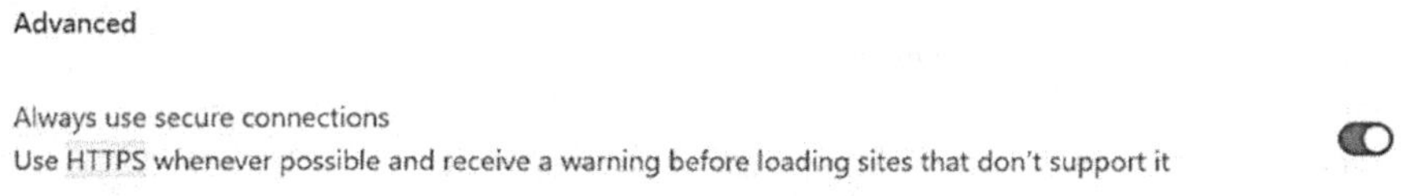

Advanced

Always use secure connections
Use HTTPS whenever possible and receive a warning before loading sites that don't support it

Figure 2.8 Google chrome HTTPS-only mode.

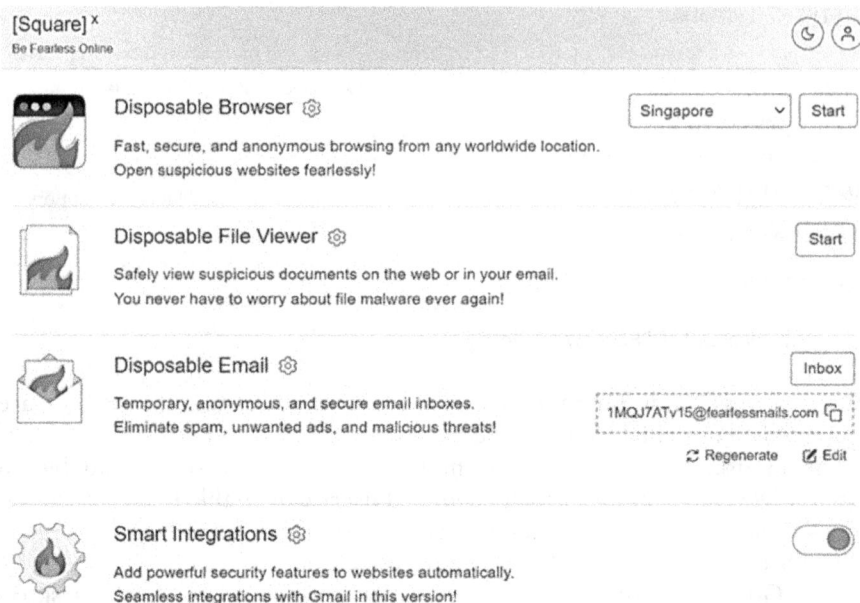

[Square] ˣ
Be Fearless Online

Disposable Browser ⚙

Fast, secure, and anonymous browsing from any worldwide location.
Open suspicious websites fearlessly!

Singapore ⌄   Start

Disposable File Viewer ⚙

Safely view suspicious documents on the web or in your email.
You never have to worry about file malware ever again!

Start

Disposable Email ⚙

Temporary, anonymous, and secure email inboxes.
Eliminate spam, unwanted ads, and malicious threats!

Inbox

1MQJ7ATv15@fearlessmails.com

↻ Regenerate   ✎ Edit

Smart Integrations ⚙

Add powerful security features to websites automatically.
Seamless integrations with Gmail in this version!

Figure 2.9 SquareX integrated solution.

products, SquareX never blocks access to files or websites; it allows users to open any suspicious file or website (including those with real malware) with absolutely zero chance of getting hacked. With SquareX as illustrated in Figure 2.9, users don't have to worry about whether a file or website is safe or malicious. Opening it with SquareX guarantees safety. SquareX achieves this by having the user's browser work in tandem with its cloud service. Files or websites are opened in disposable cloud environments, but they are integrated seamlessly into the user's browser, ensuring no change in workflow. The disposable cloud environments create watertight sandboxes, so even if the file or website contains malware or exploits, it can neither attack the user nor SquareX's infrastructure. After the user has finished with the file or website, they can dispose of the environment with a single click, which destroys all session data, including the files, viewing history, and any changes made.

2.3.4.5 Ghostery

Ghostery [15] is a browser extension designed to enhance online privacy and security by blocking trackers and other elements that collect user data. Ghostery operates by identifying and blocking trackers, which are scripts, pixels, and other elements embedded on websites to collect user data. These trackers are often used for advertising, analytics, and other purposes.

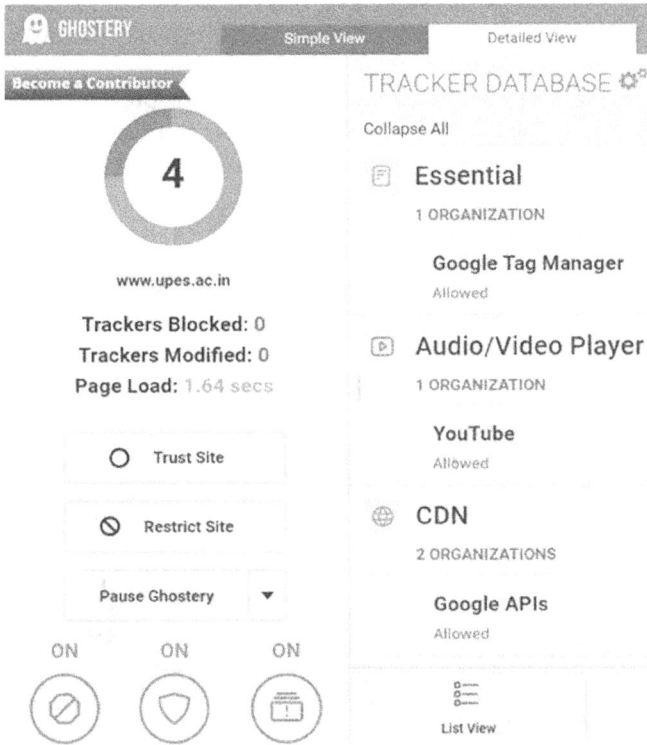

Figure 2.10 Ghostery plugin.

Ghostery, as presented in Figure 2.10, maintains a database of known trackers and employs heuristics to identify potential trackers based on their behavior.

This database includes information about the types of trackers, their purposes, and the companies behind them. When a user visits a website, Ghostery compares the elements on the page against its database to identify and categorize trackers. Once trackers are identified, Ghostery prevents them from loading and executing on the user's browser. This blocking action helps protect user privacy by limiting the amount of data collected about the user's online behavior. Ghostery provides users with a user interface that allows them to view and control the trackers on each website they visit. Users can see detailed information about the trackers detected, choose to block or unblock specific trackers, and adjust their privacy settings according to their preferences.

Users have the option to whitelist certain websites or trackers if they choose to support specific content or services. Additionally, Ghostery offers customizable settings, allowing users to adjust the level of tracking protection based on their privacy requirements. Ghostery offers an optional feature called GhostRank, which allows users to contribute anonymous data about the trackers they encounter. This data is aggregated and used to improve Ghostery's tracker database, helping the extension stay up to date with new tracking technologies. By blocking unnecessary trackers, Ghostery can improve page loading times as it prevents the loading of additional scripts and elements. This can contribute to a faster and more efficient browsing experience. Ghostery is available as an extension for various web browsers, including Chrome, Firefox, Edge, and others. Users can install the extension on their preferred browser to enjoy consistent privacy protection across different platforms.

2.3.5 Cookie managers

Cookies are small pieces of data stored by websites on a user's browser to track user behavior. By managing cookies, users can limit the information available for tracking and reduce the chances of being targeted by personalized advertising. Cookie Management is done by adjusting browser settings to limit or block cookies and periodically clearing cookies and browser history. Cookie managers [16] such as Cookie AutoDelete and EditThisCookie, as presented in Figure 2.11, allow users to control and delete cookies stored by websites. Cookies can be used for tracking, and these extensions give users more granular control over their cookie preferences.

Users can install cookie manager extensions from their respective browser's extension store (e.g., Chrome Web Store, Firefox Add-ons). Once installed, the extension integrates with the browser and becomes part of its functionality. After installation, the cookie manager detects and displays information about the cookies stored by websites. Users can access this information through the extension's interface, typically accessible via the browser's toolbar. Users can choose to whitelist certain websites or specific cookies from deletion. This is useful for preserving login sessions and maintaining preferences on trusted sites. Cookie managers allow users to set

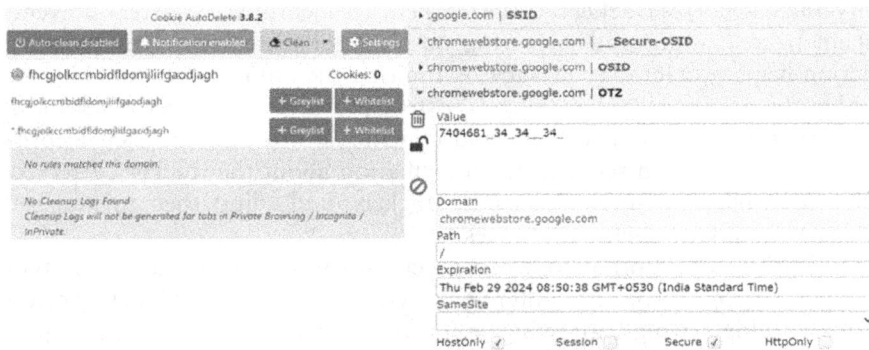

Figure 2.11 Cookie managers.

policies for cookie deletion. For example, users can configure the extension to automatically delete cookies when the browser is closed or after a certain period of inactivity on a particular website.

Cookie managers, like EditThisCookie, provide more advanced features, allowing users to edit, add, or delete specific cookies manually. This level of control is particularly useful for users who want to fine-tune their cookie settings. Certain cookie managers enable users to export or import their cookie settings. This feature allows users to transfer their preferences across different browsers or devices. Users can set permissions for cookies, deciding which cookies are allowed, blocked, or deleted based on criteria such as the cookie's origin, type, or purpose. Cookie managers prioritize user privacy and security by giving users control over their digital footprint. They help prevent tracking by third-party cookies and minimize the risk of security vulnerabilities associated with cookies.

2.3.6 Password managers

While primarily known for security, password managers like LastPass, 1Password, and Bitwarden contribute significantly to privacy by securely storing and generating strong, unique passwords for different websites. This helps users avoid password reuse and enhances account security.

- LastPass: LastPass [17] securely stores passwords, usernames, and other sensitive information in a vault protected by strong encryption. The master password is used to unlock this vault. LastPass can generate complex and unique passwords for each online account, reducing the risk associated with using weak or repetitive passwords. LastPass streamlines the login process by auto-filling credentials for websites. It helps users log in with a single click, minimizing the chances of password-related vulnerabilities. LastPass allows users to store secure notes and personal information in addition to passwords. This feature is useful for storing sensitive details like credit card information and secure notes. LastPass supports two-factor authentication, adding an extra layer of security beyond the master password. Users can enable 2FA methods like authenticator apps or hardware tokens. LastPass allows users to securely share login credentials without revealing the actual passwords. This is useful for collaboration or sharing accounts with trusted individuals.
- 1Password: 1Password [18] uses end-to-end encryption, ensuring that only the user has access to their stored data. Even the service provider cannot access or decrypt the user's passwords and sensitive information. 1Password includes a Travel Mode feature that allows users to remove sensitive information from their devices when traveling and restore it later. This adds an extra layer of privacy protection. 1Password's Watchtower features monitor and alert users about

security vulnerabilities, such as compromised passwords and websites with security issues. 1Password keeps a history of changes made to items in the vault. Users can review and restore previous versions of stored information. 1Password supports biometric authentication methods like fingerprint and face recognition, adding an additional layer of security for accessing the vault.

- Bitwarden: Bitwarden [19] is an open-source password manager, allowing users to review its source code for transparency and security assurance. Bitwarden offers a self-hosted option, enabling users to host their Bitwarden server for added control over their data. Bitwarden employs zero-knowledge encryption, meaning that only the user knows the master password, and the service provider cannot access or decrypt user data. This also supports synchronization across various devices, ensuring that users have access to their passwords and secure notes on different platforms, and supports two-factor authentication, providing an extra layer of security for accessing the vault. Bitwarden includes a built-in password generator to create strong, randomized passwords for increased security.

2.3.7 Script blockers

Script blockers such as NoScript and ScriptSafe [20] give users control over the execution of JavaScript, Java, Flash, and other scripting languages on websites by providing a mechanism to selectively enable or disable scripts on a per-site basis. When you install a script blocker, it usually starts by globally blocking the execution of scripts on all websites by default. This means that no scripts, including JavaScript, Java, Flash, etc., are allowed to run unless explicitly permitted. Users can create a whitelist of trusted websites where scripts are allowed to run without restrictions. This allows users to define a set of websites that they consider safe and trustworthy, ensuring a smooth browsing experience on those sites. Script blockers provide a user interface that allows users to manage permissions on a per-site basis. When you visit a website for the first time, all scripts are blocked. The user can then choose to enable scripts selectively for that specific site. Users often have the option to grant temporary or permanent permissions for scripts. Temporary permissions may last only for the current browsing session, while permanent permissions persist across multiple visits to the same site.

Script blockers offer granular control over different types of scripts. For example, users may have the ability to allow or block JavaScript, Java, Flash, and other scripting languages independently. Some script blockers come with additional features such as the ability to block other web elements like iframes, plugins, or certain types of content that can be used for tracking or security vulnerabilities. Script blockers often provide visual indicators on the browser interface to show whether scripts are allowed or blocked on a particular page. This helps users quickly identify the security status of the website they are visiting. Users can update their script blocker's rules regularly to stay protected against new threats. Additionally, these tools often allow users to customize settings based on their preferences and needs. By offering these features, script blockers empower users to take control of their online security and privacy. Users can decide which websites are allowed to run scripts, reducing the risk of malicious activities, such as cross-site scripting (XSS) attacks, and preventing unwanted tracking by third-party scripts. However, users should be aware that blocking scripts on certain websites may affect the functionality of those sites, and they need to make informed decisions about which sites to trust.

2.3.8 Privacy shields

Privacy Possum and Privacy-Oriented Origin Policy (Privacy-OOP) are browser extensions designed to enhance user privacy by blocking or disguising tracking mechanisms employed by websites. Each extension operates differently, so let's explore the general principles behind these types of privacy-focused extensions:

- Privacy Possum: This aims to protect against fingerprinting, a technique used by websites to identify and track users based on unique characteristics of their browsers and devices. It achieves this by providing false or random values for certain elements that can be used for fingerprinting. The extension [21] blocks third-party tracking elements, such as cookies and scripts, that are commonly used by websites and advertisers to monitor user behavior across different sites. This interferes with attempts to store or access data in the browser's local storage and Document Object Model to prevent tracking. The extension may have an aggressive mode that increases its effectiveness in blocking various tracking elements, but this could potentially affect the functionality of some websites.
- Privacy-Oriented Origin Policy (Privacy-OOP): This enhances the Same-Origin Policy [22] in browsers, which is a security feature that restricts web pages from making requests to a different domain than the one that served the original page. Privacy-OOP strengthens Same-Origin Policy to limit cross-site tracking. The extension works to reduce the likelihood of websites inadvertently leaking identifiable information across different origins. This helps prevent tracking across websites. Privacy-OOP may disguise certain identifiers that websites use to track users across different origins, making it more challenging for trackers to correlate user activities. The goal is often to enhance user privacy without significantly breaking the functionality of websites. By focusing on origin-based policies, the extension aims to mitigate tracking risks.

These privacy-focused techniques collectively empower individuals to take control of their online privacy, reducing the footprint of personal data available to websites, advertisers, and potentially malicious actors. While these measures enhance privacy, users should remain vigilant and stay informed about emerging privacy threats and evolving best practices.

2.4 CONCLUSION

I believe that executing much of the content in this chapter is vital before proceeding through the rest of this book. The methods discussed here help protect you, your computers, and your internet connection. The browsers and extensions make online research easier and more efficient. The casual searcher may have no need for virtual machines or VPNs. However, the global security team that monitors threats from violent people cannot afford to go without these.

REFERENCES

1. The Guardian, "The Cambridge Analytica Files | The Guardian," 2018. https://www.theguardian.com/news/series/cambridge-analytica-files
2. R. Kulik, "Surveillance Capitalism | Definition, History, & Facts | Britannica," Dec. 14, 2023. https://www.britannica.com/topic/surveillance-capitalism
3. "Harvard STS Program Science and Democracy Lecture Series»" News & Events Shoshana Zuboff, 2024. https://sts.hks.harvard.edu/events/lectures/shoshana-zuboff/ (accessed Oct. 14, 2024).
4. Victoria University, "Library Guides: Evaluating Information: Fake News in the 2016 US Elections," 2016. https://libraryguides.vu.edu.au/evaluating_information_guide/fakenews2016
5. SSL Support Team, "What is SSL/TLS: An In-Depth Guide," Nov. 24, 2023. https://www.ssl.com/article/what-is-ssl-tls-an-in-depth-guide/
6. Nord VPN, "What Is A VPN? Virtual Private Network Explained | NordVPN," Oct. 21, 2015. https://nordvpn.com/what-is-a-vpn/
7. Express VPN, "High-Speed, Secure & Anonymous VPN Service | ExpressVPN," 2016. https://www.expressvpn.com/
8. "The Tor Project | Privacy & Freedom Online," https://www.torproject.org/download/
9. DuckDuckGo, "DuckDuckGo — Privacy, Simplified," 2019. https://duckduckgo.com/
10. "Startpage.com – The World's Most Private Search Engine," 2019. https://www.startpage.com/
11. "uBlock Origin – Free, Open-Source Ad Content Blocker," https://ublockorigin.com/.
12. "Privacy Badger," May 2014. https://addons.mozilla.org/en-US/firefox/addon/privacy-badger17/ (accessed Oct. 14, 2024).

13. "HTTPS Everywhere Chrome Extension Overview," 2024. https://daily.dev/blog/https-everywhere-chrome-extension-overview (accessed Oct. 14, 2024).

14. Square X, "SquareX for Beginners – SquareX Labs," Nov. 07, 2023. https://labs.sqrx.com/squarex-for-beginners-ae8fac17ea68 (accessed Oct. 14, 2024).

15. "Ghostery – Privacy Ad Blocker," Nov. 15, 2008. https://addons.mozilla.org/en-US/firefox/addon/ghostery/ (accessed Oct. 14, 2024).

16. "Cookie Manager," Mar. 29, 2017. https://addons.mozilla.org/en-US/firefox/addon/a-cookie-manager/ (accessed Oct. 14, 2024).

17. "Free Password Manager App | LastPass," https://www.lastpass.com/password-manager.

18. "Demos | 1Password," 2024. https://1password.com/demos (accessed Oct. 14, 2024).

19. "Bitwarden Resources | Bitwarden," 2024. https://bitwarden.com/resources/ (accessed Oct. 15, 2024).

20. "NoScript – JavaScript/Java/Flash Blocker for a SAFER FIREFOX EXperience! – what is it? – InformAction," 2014. https://noscript.net/

21. Cowlicks, "Cowlicks/Privacypossum," Jul. 18, 2019. https://github.com/cowlicks/privacypossum

22. "Privacy-Oriented Origin Policy for Firefox – gHacks Tech News," https://www.ghacks.net/2019/01/19/privacy-oriented-origin-policy-for-firefox/

Chapter 3

Building OSINT skills and workflow process

3.1 INTRODUCTION

In the digital age, the landscape of intelligence gathering has undergone a profound transformation. The proliferation of publicly accessible information, coupled with advancements in technology, has given rise to a new paradigm: OSINT stands for OSINT. Information gathered and analyzed from publicly accessible sources, including the internet, social media, news media, and public documents, is referred to as OSINT. This intelligence can be used for a wide range of purposes, from national security to corporate investigations to personal research. The concept of OSINT is not entirely new. For centuries, individuals and organizations have relied on publicly available information to make informed decisions. However, the advent of the internet has dramatically expanded the scope and accessibility of such information. Today, an unprecedented amount of data is available online, providing a treasure trove for those who know how to find and utilize it effectively.

The ability to effectively gather and analyze OSINT has become a valuable skill in today's information-driven world. It requires a combination of technical expertise, critical thinking, and a deep understanding of human behavior. OSINT practitioners must be able to navigate the vast digital landscape, identify relevant sources, and extract meaningful insights from raw data. This introduction will explore the key concepts, techniques, and applications of OSINT. We will discuss the various skillsets and the ethical considerations that must be considered. Readers will have a firm grasp of the non-technical abilities needed to become an effective OSINT practitioner by the end of this chapter.

3.2 PSYCHOLOGY

Having a solid understanding of psychology [1] can be highly beneficial in several ways. One of the most important ways is to identify and understand the motivations, behaviors, and decision-making processes of individuals and groups that are the focus of an investigation. For example, in a case

DOI: 10.1201/9781003497615-3

where an individual or group is suspected of involvement in illegal or unethical activities, a psychological understanding can help an investigator to identify key personality traits or patterns of behavior that may indicate a greater likelihood of involvement in such activities. This could include a tendency toward impulsivity, a lack of empathy, or a need for power and control.

Another important aspect of psychology in OSINT investigations is the ability to effectively communicate and interact with individuals and groups that may be providing information or assistance during an investigation. Understanding and relating to people on a psychological level can help build trust and rapport, which can lead to more valuable and accurate information being provided. An example of this is in the case of an OSINT investigation into a suspected fraud ring. An investigator with a strong understanding of psychology may better identify key individuals within the group and understand how they are likely to interact and communicate with one another. This information can then be used to develop more effective communication strategies and tactics for interacting with these individuals and gathering information.

Another example is in the case of an investigation into a group or individual who is suspected of radicalization or terrorist activity. An investigator with a deep understanding of psychology may be able to identify key personality traits, behaviors, and decision-making processes that are associated with radicalization and use this information to develop a more effective strategy for detecting and preventing such activities. Thus, a solid understanding of psychology can be a valuable tool for OSINT investigators in various contexts. It can help to identify potential suspects and understand their motivations and behaviors, as well as help to build trust and rapport with individuals and groups that may be providing information or assistance during an investigation.

3.3 COMMUNICATIONS & PEOPLE SKILLS

Effective communication and people skills [2] are essential to gather and disseminate information successfully. To effectively conduct investigations, it is vital to be able to clearly articulate your findings and recommendations to clients, colleagues, and other stakeholders. One key aspect of effective communication in OSINT investigations is the ability to convey complex technical information clearly and concisely. This is particularly important when working with clients needing a more technical background. For example, an OSINT investigator may need to explain the details of a phishing attack to a non-technical executive in a way they can easily understand. Another important aspect of effective communication in OSINT investigations is building and maintaining relationships with a wide range of people. This includes colleagues, clients, and other stakeholders, as well as individuals who may have information relevant to the investigation. Building trust and rapport with these individuals can help facilitate the collection of information and can also be critical in situations where sensitive information is required.

One example of the importance of effective communication and people skills in OSINT investigations can be seen in the case of a company experiencing a high employee turnover rate. An OSINT investigator was brought in to determine the cause of the problem. Through interviews with current and former employees, the investigator discovered that the root cause of the turnover was poor communication and management practices within the company. By clearly communicating these findings to the company's leadership, the investigator was able to help the company make significant changes to its management practices, resulting in a substantial reduction in employee turnover.

Another example of the importance of effective communication and people skills in OSINT investigations can be seen in the case of a company experiencing a high cyberattack rate. An OSINT investigator was brought in to determine the source of the attacks. Through a combination of technical analysis and interviews with current and former employees, the investigator discovered that the attacks were launched by a disgruntled ex-employee who had access to sensitive information. By clearly communicating this information to the company's management, the investigator was able to help the company take steps to prevent future attacks and protect its sensitive information.

Effective communication and people skills are essential for the success of OSINT investigations. These skills are critical for clearly communicating technical information, building and maintaining relationships with key individuals, and facilitating the collection and dissemination of information. Through the examples and case studies provided above, the importance of communication and people skills must be considered in OSINT investigations.

3.4 NUMERICAL ANALYSIS

For the investigator, numerical analysis skills [3] are essential to effectively analyze and interpret the vast amount of data collected during an investigation. This data can come in many forms, including numerical data, such as financial records or statistics, or non-numerical data, such as text or images. One key example of the importance of numeracy skills in OSINT investigations is the analysis of financial records. To uncover hidden assets or illicit financial transactions, an OSINT investigator must be able to understand and analyze financial data, including balance sheets, income statements, and transaction records. This requires a strong understanding of mathematical concepts such as ratios, percentages, and statistical analysis.

Another example of the importance of numerical analysis in OSINT investigations is the use of data visualization tools. These tools, such as graphs and charts, can help investigators quickly identify patterns and trends in large datasets. However, to effectively use these tools, investigators must have a strong understanding of the underlying numerical data and be able to interpret the visualizations correctly. In one case study, an OSINT investigator uncovered a money laundering scheme by analyzing a company's financial records. Using ratio analysis, the investigator was able to identify unusual patterns in the company's transactions, leading to the discovery of large amounts of money being transferred to offshore accounts. This information was crucial in building a case against the individuals involved in the scheme. In another case, an OSINT investigator could track down a fraudster using data visualization techniques. By creating a graph of the fraudster's financial transactions over time, the investigator was able to identify a pattern of increasing spending and cash withdrawals, which led to the discovery of the fraudster's whereabouts.

Thus, numeracy skills are a crucial aspect of OSINT investigations, as they allow investigators to analyze and interpret the vast amount of collected data effectively. Without these skills, uncovering hidden assets, illicit financial transactions, and other criminal activities would be much more challenging.

3.5 RESEARCH

Being a good researcher or having good research skills [4] is crucial to effectively gather and analyze information from a wide variety of sources. These sources might range from government papers and news stories to social media and internet discussion forums.

One key aspect of research in OSINT investigations is the ability to verify the credibility and reliability of sources. This is particularly important when dealing with information found on the internet, as anyone can publish anything online. Therefore, it's essential to be able to critically evaluate the source of information, as well as its content, to determine its credibility. Another critical aspect of research in OSINT investigations is the ability to analyze and make connections between different pieces of information. This can involve using tools such as link analysis and social network analysis to uncover hidden relationships and patterns in the data. For example, in a suspected fraudster case, an OSINT investigator might start by researching the individual's social media profiles and online presence. By analyzing the information found on these profiles, the investigator may uncover connections to other individuals or organizations involved in the alleged fraud. Additionally, by searching for news articles and government documents related to the case, the investigator may be able to uncover additional information that helps to build a more complete picture of the situation.

Another example is in a case involving a suspected terrorist organization, an OSINT investigator might start by researching the group's history, ideology, and tactics. By analyzing the information found through this research, the investigator may uncover the group's key leaders, members, and financial supporters. Additionally, by searching for news articles and government documents related to the group, the investigator may be able to uncover additional information that helps to build a more complete picture of the group. Research skills are essential in OSINT investigations as they allow investigators to gather and analyze information from various sources effectively, verify the credibility and reliability of sources, and make connections between different pieces of information. This, in turn, enables them to build a more accurate picture of the situation at hand.

3.6 ETHICS

As an OSINT investigator, one of the most critical aspects of our work is maintaining a solid ethical foundation [5]. This is because the information we gather and use can have real-world consequences for individuals and organizations, and it is our responsibility to ensure that we are collecting and using the information legally and responsibly.

One example of the importance of ethics in OSINT investigations can be seen in the case of doxxing, where an individual's personal information is publicly released without their consent. This can have severe consequences for the individual, including harassment, stalking, and even physical harm. As OSINT investigators, it is our responsibility to ensure that we are not contributing to this type of behavior and that we are only gathering and sharing information that is legally obtained and used for a legitimate purpose. Another example of the importance of ethics in OSINT investigations is in privacy. As investigators, we often have access to sensitive information about individuals and organizations and must ensure that this information is not misused. This involves not disclosing information to unauthorized parties or using it for private benefit.

In addition to these instances, OSINT investigators must remain current on the laws and rules pertaining to the collection and exchange of information. This includes data privacy legislation, such the California Consumer Privacy Act in the US and the General Data Protection Regulation in the EU. Ethics plays a vital role in OSINT investigations. It is our responsibility as investigators to ensure that the information we gather and use is obtained and used legally and responsibly. We are not contributing to harmful behaviors like doxxing or violating individuals' privacy. By maintaining a solid ethical foundation and staying current on current laws and regulations, we can ensure that our investigations positively impact the individuals and organizations we serve.

3.7 LEGAL SKILLS AND KNOWLEDGE

A strong understanding of legal principles and regulations [6] is crucial in ensuring that the information collected during an investigation is admissible in court and that all investigation methods are ethical and lawful. One of the key areas where legal knowledge is essential is understanding and adhering to privacy laws. Strict laws are in place to safeguard people's right to privacy in many different nations. As an OSINT investigator, it's crucial to understand these laws and to ensure that any information collected is obtained legally and without violating an individual's privacy rights.

Another area where legal knowledge is critical is in understanding and following copyright laws. OSINT investigators often need to access and use a wide range of information from various sources, including online content, images, and videos. Understanding copyright laws and ensuring that any information used is obtained legally and that proper credit is given to the original source is essential. In addition, legal knowledge is critical in understanding the laws and regulations surrounding the use of various OSINT tools and techniques. For example, there are laws in place that regulate the use of social media scraping tools and the use of data obtained through these tools. It's essential to understand these laws and to ensure that any tools or techniques used are legal and ethical.

One example of where legal knowledge played a critical role in an OSINT investigation is the case of United States v. Aaron Swartz. Swartz, an internet activist and computer programmer, was accused of 13 federal offenses for downloading millions of scholarly papers from the digital library JSTOR using MIT's computer network. He was also charged with computer fraud, wire fraud, and other crimes. Swartz's defense team argued that the government's charges were too severe and that the Computer Fraud and Abuse Act was not intended to be used this way. They also argued that the government's use of the Computer Fraud and Abuse Act to prosecute Swartz violated his First Amendment rights. In the end, Swartz committed suicide before the trial could conclude. Still, the case highlights the importance of understanding the legal implications of OSINT investigations and the need to use ethical and lawful methods.

Legal knowledge is critical as it helps ensure that the information collected is admissible in court, investigation methods are ethical and lawful, and the rights of individuals are protected.

3.8 PROBLEM-SOLVING

We must gather and analyze information from publicly available sources to help organizations make informed decisions. One of the most critical skills I possess is problem-solving [7], as it enables me to effectively navigate the vast and often overwhelming amount of information available online. To understand why problem-solving is so essential in OSINT investigations, it's vital first to understand the nature of the work. Investigating OSINT frequently entails sorting through vast volumes of data from a variety of sources, such as government websites, news stories, forums, and social media. This data can be unstructured, inconsistent, and of varying quality, making it challenging to piece together a coherent picture of the situation.

Problem-solving skills help me overcome these challenges by breaking down complex problems into smaller, manageable pieces. For example, when investigating a potential security breach at a company, I might start by identifying the key players involved and the timeline of events. From there, I can begin to piece together the various pieces of information available to me, such as social media posts, email exchanges, and news articles, to build a complete picture of what happened. Another critical aspect of problem-solving in OSINT investigations is the ability to think creatively. Often, the information I need may be limited, and I must develop new and innovative ways to find it. For example, I may use social media scraping tools to gather information on a specific individual or organization or text analytics to identify patterns and trends in large datasets. In addition to problem-solving, critical thinking, and creativity, it's also essential to have a strong understanding of the legal and ethical considerations of OSINT investigations.

For example, as an OSINT investigator, I must ensure that any information I gather is obtained legally and ethically and that the people I am investigating are not subjected to any unwarranted intrusion into their privacy. Hence, problem-solving skills are essential for success in OSINT investigations, as they allow investigators to effectively navigate the vast and complex landscape of publicly available information. OSINT investigators can find important information and assist businesses in making better judgments if they have the necessary abilities and attitude.

> Case Study 1: A financial services company wanted to investigate a potential fraud case. The company noticed that a large amount of money had been transferred from one of their customers' accounts to an unknown one. The OSINT investigator was able to use problem-solving skills to track the money trail by analyzing transaction records, social media, and other publicly available information. This investigation led to the identification of a criminal organization and the recovery of the stolen money.
>
> Case Study 2: A large retail company wanted to investigate a data breach. The company noticed that a large amount of customer data had been stolen and was being sold on the dark web. The OSINT investigator used problem-solving skills to track down the source of the breach by analyzing network logs, social media, and other publicly available information. This investigation led to the identification and arrest of the individual responsible for the breach.

3.9 TECHNICAL SKILLS

Numerous technologies, including behavioral science, machine learning, and predictive analysis, have improved OSINT's ability to comprehend the patterns and behavior of data subjects. In terms of the information found on news, social media, and gray literature, intelligence technology operates in many phases, according to the RAND model of OSINT. These steps are:

   i. Collection
  ii. Acquisition
 iii. Retention
 iv. Processing
   v. Translation
 vi. Aggregation
 vii. Exploitation
viii. Authentication
 ix. Credibility Evaluation
   x. Contextualization
 xi. Production
 xii. Classification
xiii. Dissemination

These actions make the intelligence more trustworthy and genuine. It takes more time and effort for data scientists to gather and handle such complex processes if machine learning or artificial intelligence is used. Because OSINT conducts extensive research and includes in-depth analysis, there are several obstacles to overcome when putting OSINT into practice.

3.10 PATIENCE

As an OSINT investigator, one of the most essential skills to have is Patience [8]. Collecting and analyzing information can be time-consuming and requires excellent attention to detail. One example of patience in action is the investigation of a phishing scam. A phisher may set up a fake website that looks like a legitimate company's website and sends emails to potential victims, asking them to enter their personal information. An OSINT investigator may start by identifying the IP address of the phisher's website and then use that information to track down the registration information for the domain name. They may also use various tools to track the email headers of phishing emails to see if they can identify the source of the emails. These initial steps may yield little information and can take several hours or even days to complete. But an investigator with patience will continue to dig deeper, using more advanced techniques such as using virtual machines to interact with the phisher's website or using social media to identify the phisher's identity.

Another example is when an investigator tries to track down a suspect who has committed an online crime such as hacking or identity theft. In this case, the investigator may gather information about the suspect's online activities, such as their email addresses, social media accounts, and IP addresses. This information can then be used to track down other accounts and websites associated with the suspect. Tracking a suspect can be time-consuming, as the suspect may have taken steps to hide their identity. But an investigator with patience will continue to gather information, cross-reference it, and eventually build a comprehensive profile of the suspect. This profile can be used to identify the suspect's real-world identity and potentially bring them to justice.

One example of where patience is crucial in OSINT investigations is in the process of verifying information. In today's digital age, it's easy for anyone to create a website or social media profile, and it can take time to determine the authenticity of the information being presented. It's essential to take the time to thoroughly investigate the source of information, looking for any inconsistencies or red flags that may indicate that the data needs to be more legitimate. Another example is when researching a particular individual or organization. It's essential to take the time to gather as much information as possible, even if it seems insignificant at first. This information can be used to build a complete picture of the subject and can often lead to discovering additional information that may have yet to be found.

Patience is an essential quality for OSINT investigators. It allows for a thorough and methodical approach to gathering information, leading to a more complete understanding of the subject. Being patient allows the investigator to dig deeper, verify information, and find the key pieces of evidence that can make all the difference in an investigation.

3.11 OSINT WORKFLOW PROCESS

Whether we tackle computer, digital, or cyber forensics with one or a thousand data sources is irrelevant. What those data sources are is irrelevant. OSINT has a fundamental, built-in workflow mechanism that may be described as follows:

- Identification: This relates to the collection of intelligence. Details about the data we require. Data sources are mapped to information. What information is needed? Where can I get it? How can I get it? Which order? Are pre-acquisition or pre-seizure activities necessary? The Identification phase should anticipate and attempt to address the difficulties that may arise during the analysis and presentation stages. An acquisition plan should be the final step in the identification process.
- Acquisition: The acquisition plan developed during the Identification phase is being carried out during this phase. Getting forensic copies of all digital data that will be needed for the analysis phase is the aim of the acquisition phase. Both snapshot and live datasets are included in this digital data as needed. Live data is obtained in a notarized fashion, and all sources of snapshot data are confiscated or forensically photographed. The complete fulfillment of the acquisition plan should

mark the end of the acquisition phase. Every digital piece of information required for analysis should be easily accessible.

- Analysis: At this stage, collected data turns into digital proof. The main steps in data analysis include aggregation, correlation, filtering, transformation, and the creation of meta-data. The way in which the examiner interacts with data will determine if the resulting findings are forensically sound and as such can be accepted as digital evidence. The analysis phase should conclude with a set of digital evidence enough to cover the needs defined in the Identification phase.
- Presentation: This last step is writing a final report that presents the digital evidence gathered and, if necessary, provides support for a liturgical procedure. All pertinent activities completed during the Identification, Acquisition, and Analysis stages must be represented in this report, which must be a written record that is self-contained and self-explanatory. Digital evidence should be provided with all the information required for an impartial examiner to replicate and verify it. Optionally, a report can include other sets of information as a copy of the evidence or specific subsets of the data analyzed.

It is the responsibility to preserve evidence, whether you are gathering it or examining it. The benefit of digital evidence over DNA evidence, for example, is that you can make a million digital copies, and if the hashes match, the evidence is deemed identical. The most used hash in digital forensics is still the MD5 hash. This is because even if there was a collision (two different plaintexts turning into the same ciphertext), the plaintext still needs to be verified. A hash is a fixed-length value. No matter how much data you put in, you still get a fixed length of data in your hash. With that said, even a smaller hash like MD5 is difficult to get a collision with. For example, MD5 uses hex and is 32 characters long. That means there are 16^{32} possibilities in the hash. That is a lot of possibilities. It should be remarked that though the process is generally straightforward, you might have to back up some steps occasionally.

- You can discover throughout the acquisition that you need to reconsider your acquisition plan in order to incorporate more data sources.
- References to unsourced data sources may be discovered during analysis.
- You could be asked questions during the presentation that call for more research in order to produce adequate responses.

3.12 CONCLUSION

We need to integrate the soft and technical skills discussed in this chapter. When the OSINT investigator combines soft skills with technology, tools & techniques, like Psychology, Global Politics, Law Enforcement Agencies of a country, National Security, cyber security, Privacy Laws, Data Protection Laws, Intellectual Property Laws, Intelligence, and Criminology, the overall accuracy and effectiveness of an OSINT research becomes top notch. OSINT needs a collection of all these skills molded to excel in a career of OSINT investigation.

REFERENCES

1. G. Owl, "OSINT & Psychology: Profiling and Behavioral Analysis through Open Source Intelligence," Medium, May 07, 2024. https://goldenowl.medium.com/osint-psychology-profiling-and-behavioral-analysis-through-open-source-intelligence-a888b3920b2f (accessed Oct. 15, 2024).
2. "OSINT Techniques – Elevating Open Source Data Gathering and Analysis | Neotas – Enhanced Due Diligence," https://www.neotas.com/osint-techniques/
3. "SEC587: Advanced Open-Source Intelligence (OSINT) Gathering and Analysis | SANS Institute," https://www.sans.org/cyber-security-courses/advanced-open-source-intelligence-gathering-analysis/
4. "OSINT: Advanced Search Skills–i-intelligence," Apr. 24, 2023. https://i-intelligence.eu/courses/osint-advanced-search-skills
5. S. Bolen, "The Ethical Considerations of OSINT: Privacy vs. Information Gathering," Medium, Jan. 04, 2024. https://medium.com/@scottbolen/the-ethical-considerations-of-osint-privacy-vs-information-gathering-63b5b2f76c55
6. "Open-Source Intelligence (OSINT) & Its Legal and Ethical Aspects – EITHOS – European Identity Theft Observatory System," Jul. 25, 2024. https://eithos.eu/open-source-intelligence-osint-its-legal-and-ethical-aspects/
7. K. Tongs, "How to Solve the Top 3 Challenges of Open-Source Intelligence," Silobreaker, Jun. 09, 2023. https://www.silobreaker.com/blog/solutions-to-common-osint-challenges-using-open-source-intelligence/
8. "Patience – OSINT Team," 2019. https://osintteam.blog/tagged/patience (accessed Oct. 15, 2024).

Chapter 4

Search underground internet

4.1 INTRODUCING THE DARK WEB

In general, the internet may be separated into three layers: the dark web [1], the Deep Web [2], and the Surface Web [3]. Before delving into the technical aspects of the dark web, it's essential to differentiate it from various web levels. The internet is divided into three sections: the Surface Web, which is open to the public, the Deep Web, which is hidden and needs special access, and the dark web, which is a subset of the Deep Web that places a higher priority on privacy and anonymity.

The most well-known aspect of the internet is the Surface Web. It is made up of webpages that search engines like Google, Bing, and Yahoo index. Anyone with a web browser and an internet connection may readily view these websites. Examples of Surface Web content include news articles, social media platforms, e-commerce websites, and blogs. The term 'Deep Web' refers to any online information that search engines do not index. This covers dynamic content, password-protected regions, and private databases. A subclass of the Deep Web called the dark web was created expressly to offer secrecy and anonymity. Much of the material on the Deep Web, sometimes referred to as the Invisible Web, is not indexed by search engines. This includes websites that are password-protected, dynamic content, and private databases. While the Deep Web is not inherently malicious, it can be difficult to access without specific credentials or knowledge. Academic databases, internal company networks, medical records, and online banking portals are a few examples of Deep Web material.

A subsection of the Deep Web called the 'dark web' was created expressly to offer secrecy and anonymity. It is accessible through specialized networks like Tor (The Onion Router), which use encryption to mask users' identities and locations. Although the dark web is frequently linked to illicit activities like drug trafficking, the selling of weapons, and hacking, it may also be utilized for good causes like activism and whistleblowing. Dark web websites typically have onion domain names, which are not accessible through traditional browsers. The Onion Router (Tor) network is the foundation of the dark web. Tor is a decentralized network that encrypts and

DOI: 10.1201/9781003497615-4

routes communication across a number of relays, making it challenging to identify the original source. This layered encryption, often referred to as 'onion routing,' ensures a high degree of anonymity for users.

A portion of the internet that is not indexed by conventional search engines is known as the 'dark web.' Only certain software or settings, such as the Tor browser, which offers an encryption layer that makes it difficult for anybody to track a user's identity or behavior, may access it. The dark web is often associated with illegal activities, such as drug sales, hacking, and terrorism, but it is also used for legitimate purposes, such as whistle-blowing and freedom of speech. Accessing the dark web is not as simple as typing in a URL or clicking on a link. It requires the use of specialized software or configurations, such as the Tor browser, which can be downloaded for free. The Tor network uses a series of encrypted relays to bounce a user's connection around the world, making it difficult for anyone to trace their location or activity. However, it is important to note that the use of Tor or other dark web tools can potentially be illegal in some jurisdictions, and users should take care to use them responsibly and lawfully. Dark web sites are often referred to as 'hidden services' because they are not indexed by search engines. These sites are accessed through unique.onion addresses. The Hidden Service Directory, a decentralized database, lists known hidden services and allows users to discover them.

4.2 ETHICAL CONSIDERATIONS

Dark web raises significant ethical questions regarding its use. It is linked to illicit operations, including drug and human trafficking and the selling of stolen data, but it may also serve as a platform for lawful endeavors like advocacy and whistleblowing. As technology continues to evolve, the dark web is likely to become increasingly complex and challenging to navigate. Understanding its technical intricacies is crucial for researchers, law enforcement, and individuals who wish to engage with this hidden corner of the internet. Dark web employs various encryption protocols to protect user data and communications. In order to ensure that data is delivered securely, HTTPS is frequently used to encrypt connections between clients and servers. Secure email and communications also use end-to-end encryption methods like PGP (Pretty Good Privacy).

Despite its focus on anonymity and privacy, the dark web is not entirely immune to vulnerabilities. Law enforcement agencies have developed techniques to track and identify users on the dark web, albeit with varying degrees of success. Furthermore, it may be challenging to handle problems like fraud, scams, and unlawful activity due to the decentralized structure of the dark web. Using the dark web comes with several privacy and security risks. Users may be vulnerable to viruses, hacking, identity theft, and other forms of criminality since the dark web is frequently linked to illicit activity. Furthermore, individuals may be apprehended and charged for engaging in unlawful activity, and law enforcement organizations worldwide are attempting to apprehend criminals operating on the dark web. When you access the dark web make sure you access it in a controlled environment where you don't know which website you are accessing, I mean what harm can they do to your system?

4.3 LAW ENFORCEMENT AND THE DARK WEB

Law enforcement organizations worldwide are attempting to stop illicit activity on the dark web in spite of the difficulties it presents. This includes the development of specialized tools and techniques for tracking down criminals, as well as international collaborations and partnerships. Some notable examples of successful law enforcement actions against dark web marketplaces include the takedown of Silk Road in 2013 and the more recent seizure of the Wall Street Market in 2019.

The use of the dark web raises several ethical considerations, including the balance between privacy and security, freedom of speech, and the potential for illegal activities. While the dark web can be used for legitimate purposes, such as whistleblowing and the protection of human rights, it is important for users to be mindful of the potential for illegal activity and to use the platform responsibly.

Pros:

- Anonymity: High levels of anonymity and privacy are offered by the dark web, which may be particularly beneficial for people who live in nations with repressive regimes or for whistle-blowers who wish to cover delicate subjects without worrying about reprisals.
- Access to Restricted Information: The dark web can be a valuable source of information that is not easily accessible on the regular internet. For example, it may contain research studies or data that are not available to the public due to legal or ethical concerns.
- Online Activism: The dark web can be a platform for political activism and advocacy, particularly for individuals living in countries where freedom of speech and expression are restricted.
- Privacy and Security: The dark web provides a layer of encryption and security that can protect users from hacking, identity theft, and other types of cybercrime.

Cons:

- Illegal Activity: The dark web is well known for harboring illicit operations, including people and drug trafficking, among other criminal activities. Users may be vulnerable to identity theft, hacking, malware, and other forms of online criminality.

- Law Enforcement: Users may be apprehended and charged for engaging in illicit activities, and law enforcement organizations worldwide are attempting to apprehend criminals operating on the dark web.
- Unregulated Marketplace: Dark web markets are unregulated, meaning that there is no oversight to ensure that sellers are providing safe or quality products. This can lead to users receiving counterfeit or dangerous items.
- Cyber-Attacks: The dark web can be a breeding ground for cyber-attacks and hacking, as criminals use it to exchange hacking tools and techniques.

4.4 DARK WEB SITES

Many dark web marketplaces and services rely on peer-to-peer (P2P) networks to facilitate transactions. These networks enable direct communication between users, bypassing centralized intermediaries. Cryptocurrencies [4], such as Bitcoin, are commonly used for payments on the dark web due to their decentralized nature and privacy features. The dark web's illicit products and services bazaar is one of its most well-known features. These marketplaces operate similarly to traditional online marketplaces, with sellers offering items such as drugs, weapons, counterfeit goods, and stolen data. These marketplaces can only be accessed through the dark web, and payment is often made using cryptocurrencies such as Bitcoin, which can be difficult to trace. There are a variety of sites on the dark web that cater to different interests and needs. For example, some sites may offer forums for discussion, while others may provide access to illegal goods and services. The following are a few examples of dark web sites:

4.4.1 The Hidden Wiki

The Hidden Wiki [5] is a decentralized directory of websites on the dark web, accessible only through the Tor network. Users can find hidden services—websites that are not indexed by conventional search engines—by using it as a central location. The Hidden Wiki is known for its anonymity and privacy features, making it a popular destination for those seeking to access content that is not readily available on the Surface Web as illustrated in Figure 4.1.

Hidden Wiki relies heavily on the Tor network to provide anonymity and privacy for its users. Tor is a decentralized network that encrypts and routes communication across a number of relays, making it challenging to identify the original source. This layered encryption ensures that user identities and browsing history remain hidden. This portal functions as a directory of hidden services, which are websites on the dark web that are accessed through unique.onion addresses. These addresses are not accessible through traditional browsers, requiring users to use Tor browser or other specialized dark

OnionLinks × The Hidden Wiki × +

C paavlaytlfsqyvkg3yqj7hflfg5jw2jdg2fgkza5ruf6lplwseeqtvyd.onion

The Hidden Wiki

The Hidden Wiki

Main Page

Welcome to The Hidden Wiki
New hidden wiki url http://paavlaytlfsqyvkg3yqj7hflfg5jw2jdg2fgkza5ruf6lplwseeqtvyd.onion 🔗 Add it to bookmarks and spread it!!!!

Short v2 .onion links are insecure and will stop working in october 2021, bookmark us for the latest v3 .onion links.

Editor's picks

Pick a random page from the article index and replace one of these slots with it.

1. Mixaba – Bitcoin mixer
2. OnionLinks – .Onion link directory.
3. Bitpharma – Biggest european .onion drug store
4. DarkWebHackers – Dark Web Hackers For Hire.
5. Cardshop – USA CVV KNOWN BALANCE & Worldwide CC & CVV .

Introduction Points

- OnionLinks 🔗 – .Onion link directory.
- The Hidden Wiki 🔗 – New Hidden Wiki
- Another Hidden Wiki 🔗 Another hidden wiki like link collection.
- The Dark Web Pug 🔗 Pug's Ultimate Dark Web Guide .

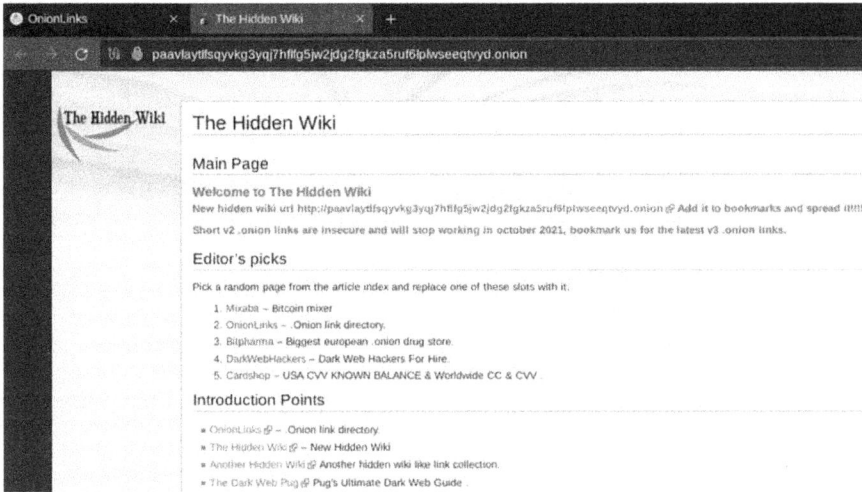

Figure 4.1   The Hidden Wiki.

Financial Services

Currencies, banks, money markets, clearing houses, exchangers:

- AceMarket 🔗 - Premium Paypal, Ebay and bank accounts.
- Cardshop 🔗 - USA CVV KNOWN BALANCE & Worldwide CC & CVV .
- Dark Mixer 🔗 - Anonymous bitcoin mixer
- Mixabit 🔗 - Bitcoin mixer
- VirginBitcoins 🔗 - Buy freshly mined clean bitcoins .
- ccPal 🔗 - PayPals, Ebays, CCs and more
- Webuybitcoins 🔗 - Sell your Bitcoins for Cash, Paypal, WU etc
- HQER 🔗 - High Quality Euro bill counterfeits
- Counterfeit USD 🔗 - High Quality USD counterfeits
- EasyCoin 🔗 - Bitcoin Wallet and Mixer
- Onionwallet 🔗 - Anonymous and secure bitcoin wallet and mixer

Drugs

- DCdutchconnectionUK 🔗 - The dutch connection for the UK
- DrChronic 🔗 - Weed straight from the source
- TomAndJerry 🔗 - Cocaine, Heroin, MDMA and LSD from NL
- 420prime 🔗 - Cannabis in dispensary quality from the UK
- Bitpharma 🔗 - Biggest european .onion drug store
- EuCanna 🔗 - First Class Cannabis
- Smokeables 🔗 - Finest organic cannabis from the USA
- CannabisUK 🔗 - UK wholesale cannabis supplier
- Brainmagic 🔗 - Best Darkweb psychedelics
- NLGrowers 🔗 – Coffee Shop grade Cannabis from the netherlands
- Peoples Drug Store 🔗 - The Darkwebs best Drug supplier!
- DeDope 🔗 - German Weed Store

Figure 4.2   Hidden Wiki pages.

web browsers. This is a decentralized platform, meaning it is not controlled by a single entity. This decentralized nature makes it resilient to censorship and attacks. If one server hosting the Hidden Wiki goes offline, others can continue to provide access to the directory as shown in Figure 4.2.

Hidden Wiki prioritizes anonymity and privacy for its users. It does not collect or store personal information, and it uses encryption to protect user communications. This makes it a popular choice for those who value their online privacy. The portal is constantly updated with new listings of hidden services. Users are guaranteed to have access to the most recent information on the dark web due to its dynamic nature. Hidden Wiki is organized into categories to help users find the hidden services they are looking for. These categories include topics such as markets, forums, news, and services. Hidden Wiki is available in multiple languages, making it accessible to users from around the world. Hidden Wiki is accessible through any device with an internet connection and a Tor browser. This makes it a versatile platform that can be used on computers, smartphones, and tablets.

Despite its many advantages, the Hidden Wiki also faces challenges and limitations. These include:

- Censorship: While the decentralized nature of the Hidden Wiki makes it difficult to censor, governments and law enforcement agencies have attempted to shut it down or block access to it.
- Unreliability: The Hidden Wiki can be unreliable at times, with servers going offline or listings becoming outdated.
- Illegal Activities: The Hidden Wiki is frequently linked to illicit operations, including hacking, weapon sales, and drug trafficking. Law enforcement authorities are now paying closer attention as a result of this.
- Limited Functionality: Figure 4.3 presents Hidden Wiki as the primarily a directory of hidden services, and it does not provide any additional features or functionality.

4.4.2 Silk Road

Under the alias 'Dread Pirate Roberts,' Ross Ulbricht founded the dark web marketplace Silk Road [6] in 2011, and it soon became known as a center for illegal activity. It became one of the largest online marketplaces for

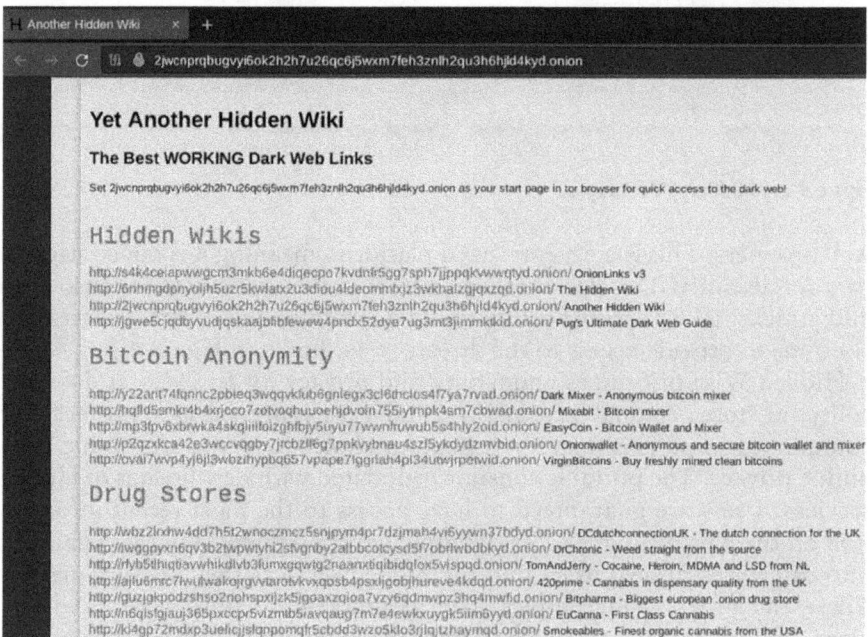

Figure 4.3 Another Hidden Wiki.

illegal drugs and other illicit goods and services, with a reported revenue of over $1.2 billion before it was shut down by law enforcement in 2013. Silk Road operated using Bitcoin as its primary currency, which made transactions difficult to trace and provided an additional layer of anonymity. The platform leveraged the Tor network's anonymity features to protect the identities of both buyers and sellers. Transactions were conducted using Bitcoin, a cryptocurrency that further enhanced privacy. Among the many goods and services provided by Silk Road were illicit narcotics, fake passports, and hacking tools.

To access Silk Road, users had to navigate the dark web using the Tor browser and find the marketplace's specific URL. Once inside, they could browse listings, place orders, and communicate with sellers anonymously. The site employed a reputation system where buyers could leave reviews of sellers, fostering trust within the community. However, Silk Road's illicit activities did not go unnoticed. Law enforcement agencies, particularly the FBI, began investigating the platform. In 2013, the FBI shut down Silk Road, arrested Ulbricht, and seized a significant amount of Bitcoin. The closure of Silk Road marked a turning point in the battle against online crime, demonstrating the potential for law enforcement to infiltrate and disrupt dark web marketplaces.

Despite the demise of the original Silk Road, similar platforms have emerged in its wake, continuing to offer a haven for illegal activities on the dark web, illustrated in Figures 4.4–4.6. The difficulties of controlling the

Figure 4.4   Dark web hackers.

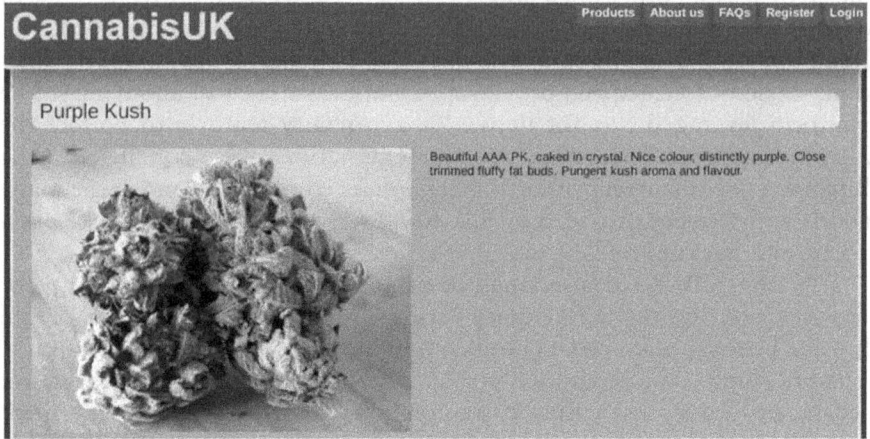

Figure 4.5 Cannabis UK.

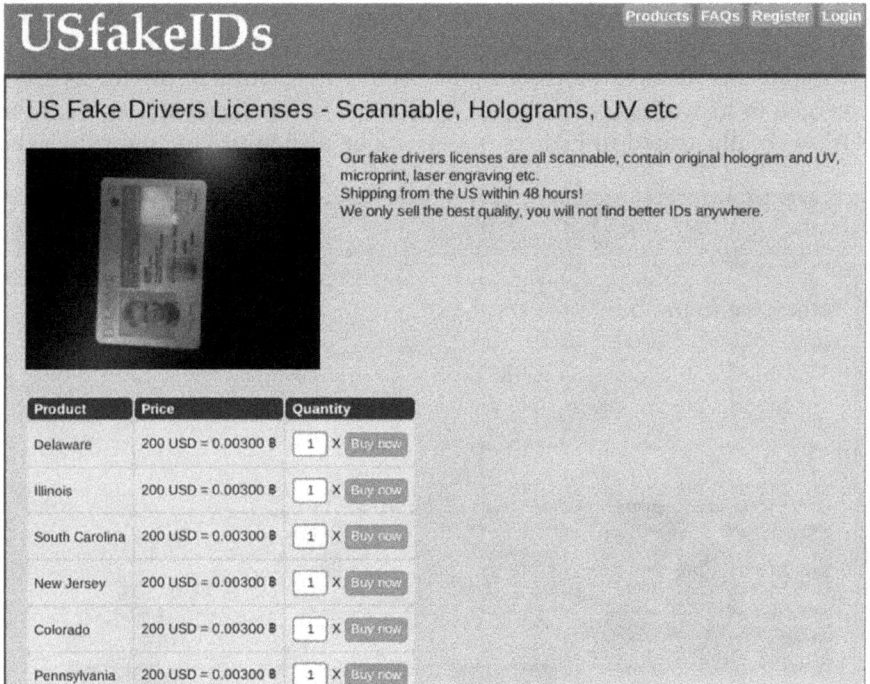

Figure 4.6 US fake IDs.

internet's obscure areas are brought to light by the continuous game of cat and mouse between law enforcement and dark web operators.

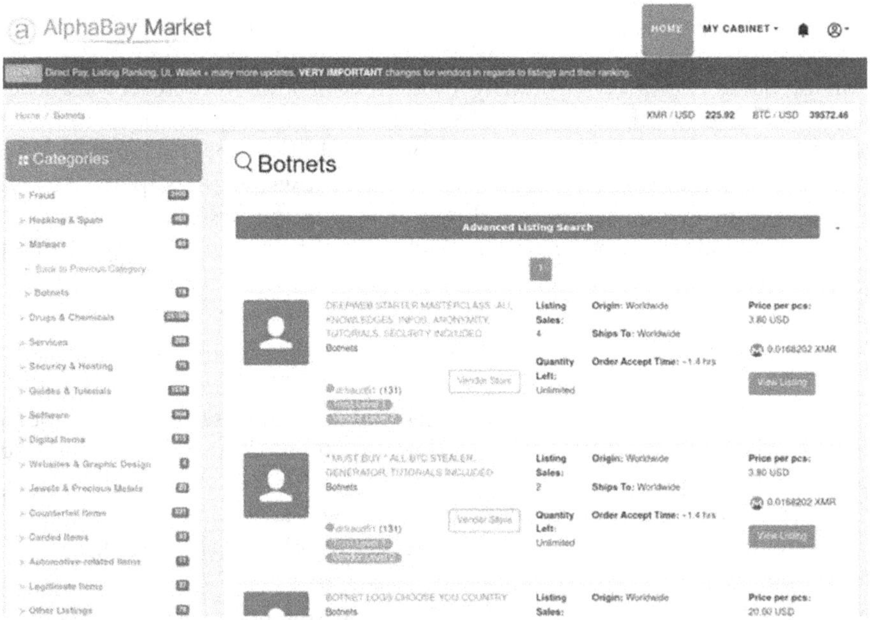

Figure 4.7   AlphaBay dark web site.

4.4.3 AlphaBay

AlphaBay [7] was a prominent dark web marketplace that operated from 2014 until its seizure by law enforcement in July 2017, as illustrated in Figure 4.7. AlphaBay, one of the biggest and most prosperous dark web marketplaces of its day, was well known for offering a wide variety of illegal items and services. It quickly became one of the largest and most popular online marketplaces for illegal goods and services, with estimated revenue of up to $800,000 per day. AlphaBay had a reputation for being more sophisticated and secure than its predecessor Silk Road. It had a reputation for providing a high level of customer service and technical support to its users. The site also had a built-in escrow system to protect buyers and sellers in case of disputes.

Law authorities in the US, Canada, and Thailand shut down AlphaBay in July 2017, and Alexandre Cazes, the company's purported creator, was taken into custody in Thailand. Cazes was found dead in his jail cell shortly after his arrest in what was believed to be a suicide. The takedown of AlphaBay was a major blow to the dark web marketplace ecosystem, and it caused a significant disruption in the illegal online marketplace. The shutdown of AlphaBay demonstrated the ongoing challenge of regulating illegal activity on the dark web, as new marketplaces continue to emerge to fill the void left by its absence. It also emphasizes how crucial law enforcement and international cooperation are to solving the problem.

Like most dark web sites, AlphaBay relied on the Tor network to provide anonymity for its users. Tor encrypts and routes internet traffic across a network of relays, making it challenging to identify the origin or destination of data. AlphaBay primarily used Bitcoin and Monero for transactions. Because of their great level of secrecy, these cryptocurrencies make it difficult to monitor the flow of money. AlphaBay operated similarly to traditional online marketplaces. Users could browse listings, place orders, and leave reviews. The site employed a reputation system to encourage trust and reliability among sellers. AlphaBay offered a vast array of illicit goods and services, including:

- Drugs: A wide range of narcotics, from prescriptions to illegal substances like heroin and cocaine.
- Stolen Data: Login passwords, personal data, and credit card numbers.
- Counterfeit Goods: Luxury items, such as designer clothing and electronics.
- Weapons: Firearms, ammunition, and explosives.
- Hacking Services: Malware, botnets, and other hacking tools.

AlphaBay implemented various security measures to protect its users and operations. These included encryption, multi-factor authentication, and a sophisticated infrastructure designed to resist attacks. Despite its security measures, AlphaBay ultimately fell victim to law enforcement efforts. In 2017, a joint operation involving multiple international agencies led to the seizure of the marketplace's servers and the arrest of its administrators. The takedown of AlphaBay was a significant blow to the dark web ecosystem and demonstrated the ability of law enforcement to target and dismantle major online criminal operations.

4.5 PERFORM DARK WEB SEARCH

Users need specialist browsers, such as Tor browser, which is based on Firefox but adds extra anonymity capabilities, in order to access the dark web. These browsers utilize the Tor network to route traffic and protect user anonymity. Access to dark web sites is typically through specific URLs ending in '.onion,' which are not accessible through traditional browsers. In this hands-on section, I'll be using Kali Linux running on VMware as the virtual environment. The below steps illustrate the process to securely access dark web.

Step 1: Install dark web search tools.

a. Install Onionsearch [8] as shown in Figure 4.8 using $ **sudo pip3 install onionsearch.**

b. Install Tor VPN Service [9] as displayed in Figure 4.9 using $ **sudo apt install tor.**

c. Start the Tor service and check the status as shown in Figure 4.10.

Step 2: Find Tor links.

a. Use the Onion Search to find info/string with one page limit and output to a file as $ **onionsearch 'string to search' –limit 1 – output filesearch.txt.**

b. All links will be saved in a text file as displayed in Figure 4.11.

```
┌──(kali㉿kali)-[~/Documents/Tools/DarkWeb]
└─$ sudo pip3 install onionsearch
DEPRECATION: Loading egg at /usr/local/lib/python3.11/dist-packages/onionsearch-1.3-py3.11.egg is deprecated. pip 24.3
replacement is to use pip for package installation.. Discussion can be found at https://github.com/pypa/pip/issues/123
Requirement already satisfied: onionsearch in /usr/local/lib/python3.11/dist-packages/onionsearch-1.3-py3.11.egg (1.3)
Requirement already satisfied: PySocks in /usr/lib/python3/dist-packages (from onionsearch) (1.7.1)
Collecting argparse (from onionsearch)
  Downloading argparse-1.4.0-py2.py3-none-any.whl (23 kB)
Collecting bs4 (from onionsearch)
  Downloading bs4-0.0.1.tar.gz (1.1 kB)
```

Figure 4.8 Install onionsearch.

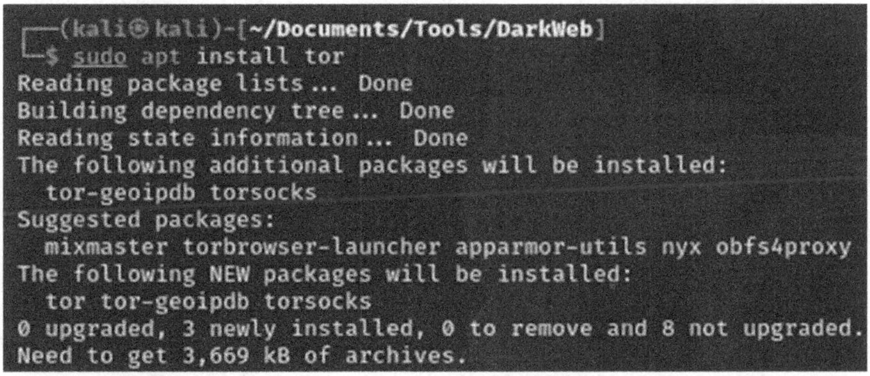

```
┌──(kali㉿kali)-[~/Documents/Tools/DarkWeb]
└─$ sudo apt install tor
Reading package lists ... Done
Building dependency tree ... Done
Reading state information ... Done
The following additional packages will be installed:
  tor-geoipdb torsocks
Suggested packages:
  mixmaster torbrowser-launcher apparmor-utils nyx obfs4proxy
The following NEW packages will be installed:
  tor tor-geoipdb torsocks
0 upgraded, 3 newly installed, 0 to remove and 8 not upgraded.
Need to get 3,669 kB of archives.
```

Figure 4.9 Installing Tor.

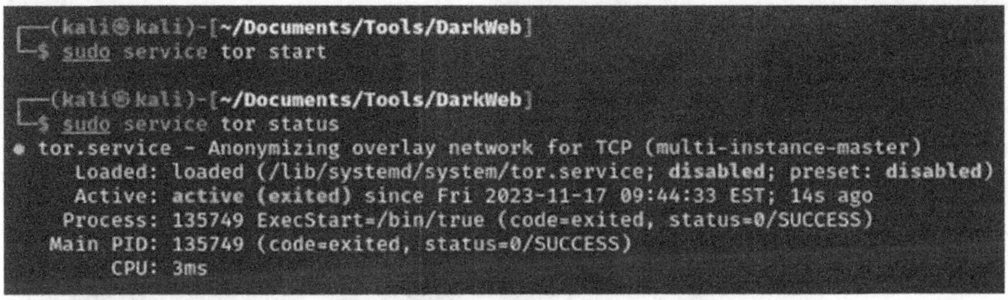

```
┌──(kali㉿kali)-[~/Documents/Tools/DarkWeb]
└─$ sudo service tor start

┌──(kali㉿kali)-[~/Documents/Tools/DarkWeb]
└─$ sudo service tor status
● tor.service - Anonymizing overlay network for TCP (multi-instance-master)
     Loaded: loaded (/lib/systemd/system/tor.service; disabled; preset: disabled)
     Active: active (exited) since Fri 2023-11-17 09:44:33 EST; 14s ago
    Process: 135749 ExecStart=/bin/true (code=exited, status=0/SUCCESS)
   Main PID: 135749 (code=exited, status=0/SUCCESS)
        CPU: 3ms
```

Figure 4.10 Starting and check Tor service status.

```
┌─(kali◎kali)-[~/Documents/Tools/DarkWeb]
└─$ sudo onionsearch "hack webcam" --limit 1 --output 20231117-Hack-Webam.txt
search.py started with 1 processing units...
        Ahmia (#0): 100%|
    OnionLand (#0): 100%|
```

Figure 4.11   Onionsearch links.

Notice these links are randomly generated strings which are unknown and not indexed (searched by Google spiders). The dark web is essentially a bunch of websites accessible by Onion routers and even end in DOT ONION extension. Tor network is designed to resist network traffic analysis and makes it highly challenging to determine the source and destination of communications. Tor uses a system of guard nodes to establish a secure entry point into the dark web network. This involves creating a series of nodes through which the data will pass. This process is managed by the Tor browser. Multiple levels of encryption are employed to anonymize data as it travels via a network of computers run by volunteers (Tor nodes), thus the term 'The Onion Router' (Tor). Each node in the Tor circuit peels back one layer of encryption, hence the name 'Onion Routing'. Tor provides privacy and anonymity, minimizing the risk of exposing identifying user info. Regular browsers (Chrome, Firefox, Edge) are not designed with this focus.

Step 3: Access the searched dark web sites.
   a. For this, we need to first install a specialized dark web browser, the Tor browser [10]. As displayed in Figure 4.12, we need to first install the Tor launcher as $ **sudo apt install -y tor torbrowser-launcher.**
   b. Next, run the install command to download the Tor browser. It will fail the first time, mentioning the system is under attack. Re-run the $ **sudo torbrowser-launcher** command again as shown in Figure 4.13.
   c. Start the Tor browser which establishes connections to route the traffic over tor nodes as displayed in Figure 4.14.

```
┌─(kali◎kali)-[~/Documents/Tools/DarkWeb]
└─$ sudo apt install -y tor torbrowser-launcher
[sudo] password for kali:
Reading package lists... Done
Building dependency tree... Done
Reading state information... Done
tor is already the newest version (0.4.8.9-1).
The following NEW packages will be installed:
  torbrowser-launcher
0 upgraded, 1 newly installed, 0 to remove and 8 not upgraded.
Need to get 54.1 kB of archives.
After this operation, 241 kB of additional disk space will be used.
```

Figure 4.12   Installing Tor launcher.

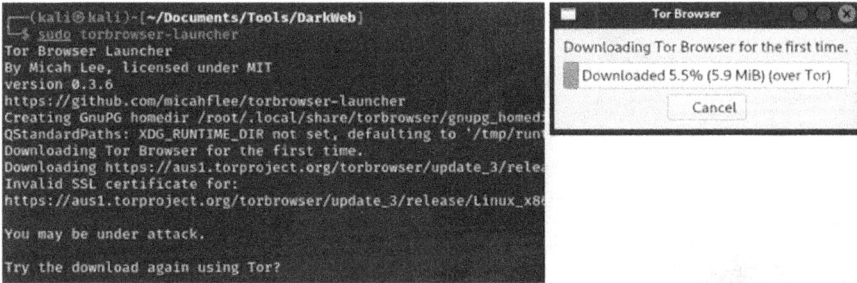

Figure 4.13   Launch the Tor browser.

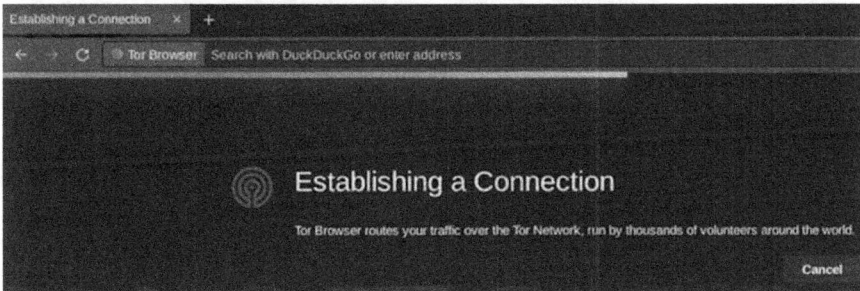

Figure 4.14   Tor browser establishing connections.

Next, plan to access the dark web with increasing security levels.

Level 1 → Open a.ONION link
a. Paste the.ONION URL obtained from Onionsearch into this Tor browser and open. However, this is level 1 for browsing the dark web and not the most secure or recommended way of accessing the dark web.
b. When you use the Tor browser, your ISP can see your connection (your laptop running Tor browser), which has created Tor connections → ISP → the first Onion Router node you are connected to – ISP can see this connection even as further down the line, you are protected. How do we hide this link from the ISP?

Level 2 → Harden your Tor browser
a. Tor Browser → Settings → Privacy and Security → Browser Privacy → initially set to 'Standard'. Change this to 'Safest' option as shown in Figure 4.15.

Level 3 → Use a VPN to then access the dark web
a. Using only the Tor browser, we are anonymous only to a point. You can get detected for accessing the dark web. Use NordVPN

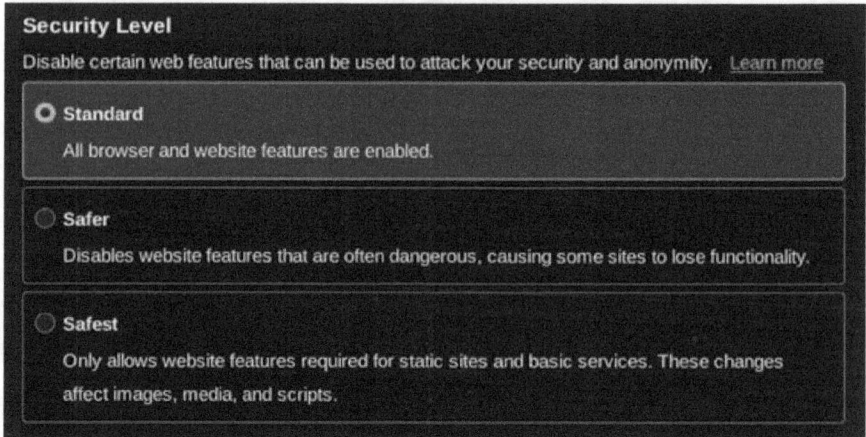

Figure 4.15   Change security level to safest.

[11] from https://github.com/NordSecurity/nordvpn-linux. Nord VPN is a Linux program that offers a straightforward and intuitive command line interface for utilizing all of its functions. The program may either choose the best server for the user or provide a list of server locations worldwide. Additionally, they have the option to change their connection parameters, such as selecting a certain protocol or turning on the kill switch.

b.   In order to install Nord VPN, type the following command line into the terminal and adhere to the prompts to download the Linux VPN client, which is shown in Figure 4.16. command:- **sh <(curl -sSf https://downloads.nordcdn.com/apps/linux/install.sh)**.

c.   Connect to a Nord VPN server as shown in Figure 4.17 using the **$ sudo nordvpn connect** command.

d.   Create an account on https://nordvpn.com and log in for future use as shown in Figure 4.18.

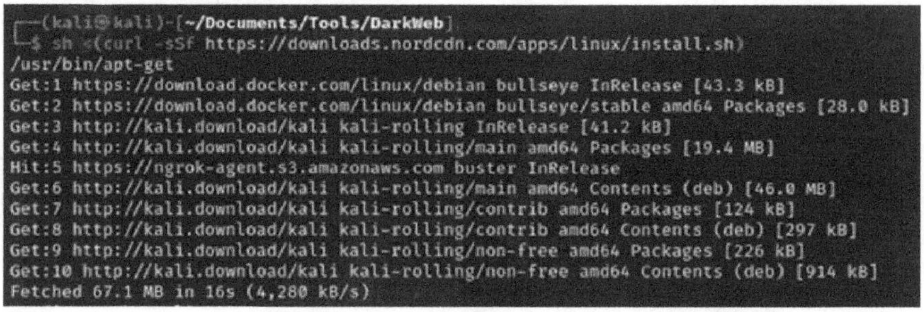

Figure 4.16   Download Linux Nord VPN client.

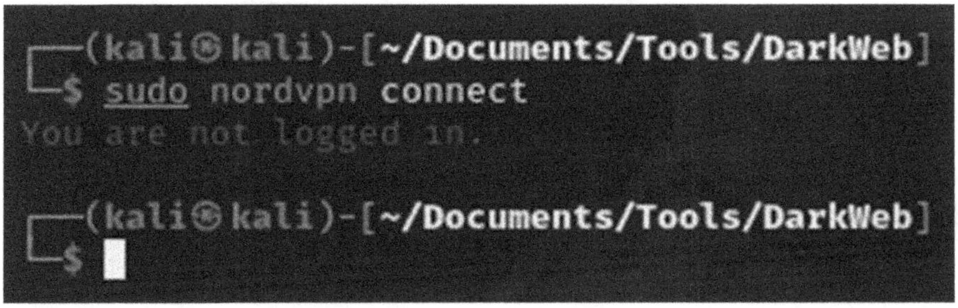

Figure 4.17 Connect to Nord VPN server.

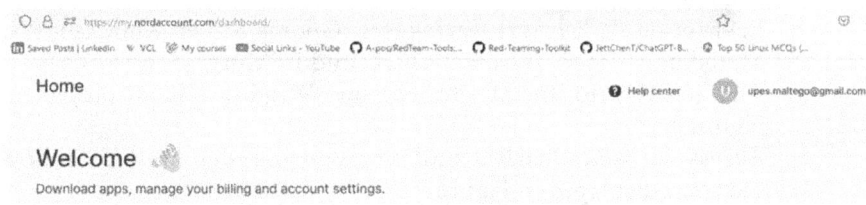

Figure 4.18 Create an account.

e. Now if you access the any.ONION link using the Tor Bowser, your traffic is encrypted from your laptop.

Level 4 → Alternative to Tor browser/VPN installs is using NetworkChuck Cloud Browser

a. Open https://browser.networkchuck.com/ using any surface web browser.
b. Create an account and log in; this is a paid feature.
c. You can be on the dark web using someone's computer in some location, still using your laptop.

Level 5 → Use Tails Linux [12] via a USB drive

Tails [12] is a free, portable Debian 11 operating system that protects against any surveillance, censorship, Advertising, Malware, or any Virus attacks. Tails has Goldfish memory; every time you reboot, it forgets the previous browsing info and starts from a clean slate. Tails has a security toolbox which includes apps to work on sensitive documents and communicate securely, like

• Networking: Tor browser, Stream isolation, Network Manager, Pidgin, Onion Filesharing, Thunderbird Email client, Aircrack NG, Electrum Bitcoin client, and Wget/Curl.

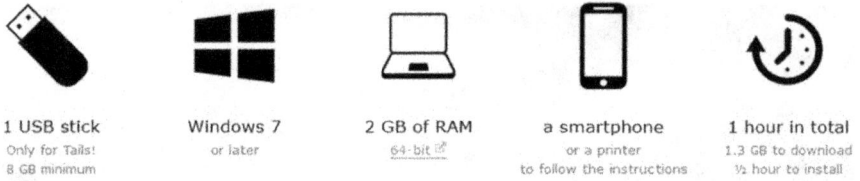

1 USB stick	Windows 7	2 GB of RAM	a smartphone	1 hour in total
Only for Tails!	or later	64-bit ☑	or a printer	1.3 GB to download
8 GB minimum			to follow the instructions	½ hour to install

Figure 4.19   Process to install Tails.

- Desktop: Libre Office, Gimp, Audacity, Doc Scanner, Sound Juicer, Brasero (DVD/CD burner), and Booklet Imposer (PDF to doc converter).
- Encryption & Privacy: Keyloggers, Gnome Screen Kbd, GnuPG, Metadata cleaner, Tesseract OCR, and FFMpeg.
a. The process to install Tails from Windows is displayed in Figure 4.19.
b. Access https://tails.net/install/windows/index.en.html to follow the steps displayed in Figure 4.20.
c. The recommended way is downloading and writing the Tails OS image on a USB. First, download the Tails OS image on a laptop from https://tails.net/install/index.en.html. Plug in your USB into the laptop.
d. Then, download the portable Etcher software on the laptop from https://etcher.balena.io/#download-etcher and run. This will flash the OS images to SD cards and USB drives safely and easily, as displayed in Figure 4.21.
e. Choose the image downloaded on the laptop as shown in Figure 4.22.
f. Select USB → click FLASH so the USB is bootable with Tails OS as illustrated in Figure 4.23.
g. Shutdown the laptop, power up → press F12/F2 (depending on your laptop) → BOIS menu → Change the boot option to use USB as shown in Figure 4.24.
h. Now boot your laptop/PC using this Tails OS on the USB. Connect to your Wifi/Ethernet Lan and access the dark web portals as you would using the Tor browser from your laptop OS.

Download Tails	Verify your download	Download balenaEtcher	Install Tails using balenaEtcher	Restart on your Tails USB stick	Welcome to Tails!

Figure 4.20   Steps to install Tails on USB.

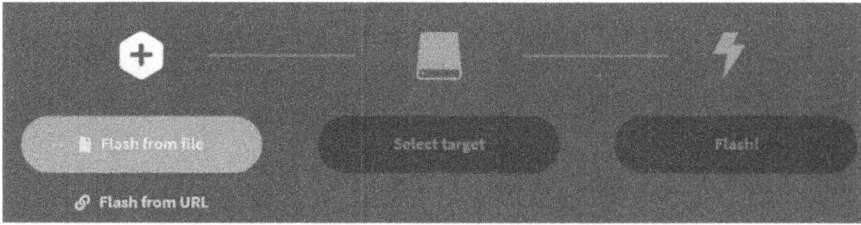

Figure 4.21   Run Etcher app to flash OS images to SD card or USB.

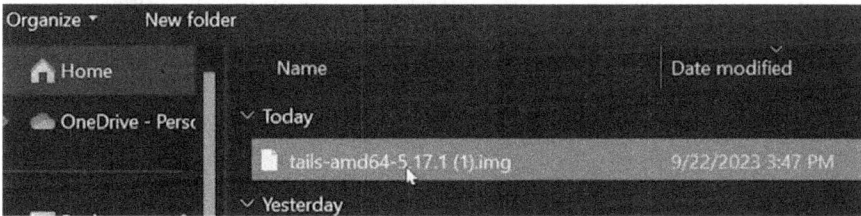

Figure 4.22   Choose Tails OS image.

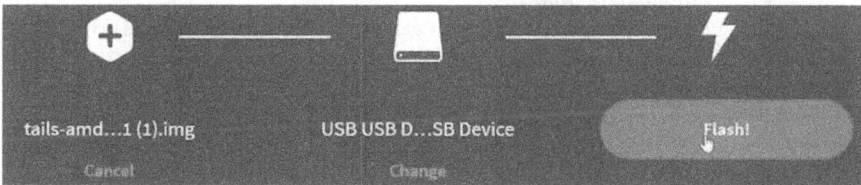

Figure 4.23   Make USB bootable with Tails OS.

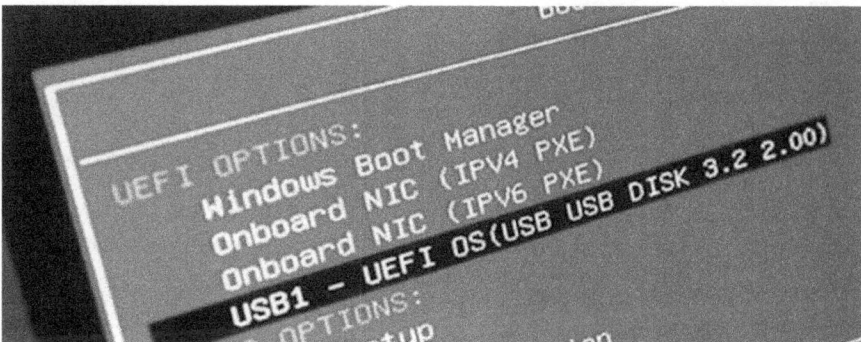

Figure 4.24   Change BIOS Boot options.

Dark web is a complex and multifaceted aspect of the internet that requires careful consideration. By being aware of its potential uses and dangers, individuals can make informed decisions about their online activities and navigate this hidden realm with informed awareness.

4.6 CONCLUSION

The dark web, a hidden realm accessible only through specialized software, presents a unique set of opportunities and challenges. Although it provides privacy and anonymity, it also acts as a haven for illegal activity. Understanding the nature and functionality of the dark web is crucial for individuals to navigate this hidden corner of the internet responsibly. By exploring the dark web using tools like Tails OS, users can gain firsthand experience of its capabilities and limitations. This practical method enables a more thorough comprehension of the possible advantages and dangers of using the dark web.

REFERENCES

1. "Everything You Should Know about the Dark Web | Tulane School of Professional Advancement," https://sopa.tulane.edu/blog/everything-you-should-know-about-dark-web
2. "Deep Web | Definition, Search Engines, & Difference from Dark Web | Britannica," Oct. 12, 2023. https://www.britannica.com/technology/deep-web
3. "Surface Web," authentic8. https://www.authentic8.com/glossary/what-is- surface-web
4. Kaspersky, "What Is Cryptocurrency and How Does It Work?" 2022. https://www.kaspersky.com/resource-center/definitions/what-is-cryptocurrency.
5. "Hidden Wiki | Tor.onion urls directories," 2013. https://thehiddenwiki.org/
6. D. Ghimiray, "A Guide to the Silk Road Dark Web," A Guide to the Silk Road Dark Web, Aug. 19, 2022. https://www.avast.com/c-silk-road-dark-web-market
7. "True Crime Story – AlphaBay," United Nations: Office on Drugs and Crime. https://www.unodc.org/unodc/en/untoc20/truecrimestories/alphabay.html
8. Palenath, "Megadose/OnionSearch," GitHub, Mar. 25, 2024. https://github.com/megadose/OnionSearch
9. Brainf+ck, "Brainfucksec/Kalitorify," GitHub, Nov. 16, 2023. https://github.com/brainfucksec/kalitorify
10. AnandKatariya, "GitHub – AnandKatariya/How-To-Install-Tor-Browser-On-Kali-Linux," GitHub, 2023. https://github.com/AnandKatariya/How-To-Install-Tor-Browser-On-Kali-Linux (accessed Oct. 16, 2024).
11. NordVPN, 2024. https://www.nordvpn.com (accessed Oct. 16, 2024).
12. "Tails – Home," https://tails.net/ (accessed Oct. 16, 2024).

Chapter 5

OSINT search engine techniques

5.1 OSINT SEARCH

In today's interconnected world, information is abundant and readily accessible. The internet has revolutionized the way we access, process, and share data, transforming industries and reshaping societies. As the digital landscape continues to evolve, the ability to effectively navigate and leverage online resources has become increasingly essential. This chapter provides a comprehensive guide to search engine techniques, equipping readers with the tools and knowledge necessary to harness the power of publicly available information. Search engine techniques encompass a wide range of strategies and tools used to gather, analyze, and visualize data from various online sources. By mastering these techniques, individuals can uncover valuable insights, identify trends, and make informed decisions. Whether you are a cybersecurity professional, investigator, intelligence analyst, or simply a curious individual seeking to explore the digital world, understanding search engine techniques is a valuable skill.

By understanding the capabilities and limitations of these tools, individuals can select the most appropriate ones for their specific needs. This chapter will provide step-by-step instructions on how to use each tool effectively, along with real-world examples to illustrate their practical applications. Additionally, we will discuss ethical considerations and best practices for responsible use of these tools to ensure privacy and integrity. This chapter will delve into the tools used for data collection, including search engines, social media platforms, and specialized databases. The third section will focus on data analysis techniques, such as keyword searches, Boolean operators, and data visualization. Finally, the fourth section will explore ethical considerations and best practices for conducting Open-Source Intelligence (OSINT) investigations. Throughout this chapter, we will emphasize the importance of critical thinking and analysis in conjunction with the use of search engine techniques. While tools can provide valuable insights, it is essential to interpret the information critically and consider the context in which it was obtained. By combining technical skills with critical thinking, individuals can make informed judgments and draw meaningful conclusions from the data they gather.

DOI: 10.1201/9781003497615-5

This chapter will delve into the intricacies of using a diverse array of tools and software applications commonly employed in OSINT [1] for data collection, analysis, and visualization. These tools include Maltego, OSINT framework, Shodan, and Google Dorks. Each tool offers unique capabilities and strengths, enabling users to gather information from different sources, such as social media, websites, databases, and networks.

5.2 MALTEGO

In the realm of OSINT, Maltego [2] stands out as a versatile and powerful tool for visualizing and analyzing data. Its graphical interface and extensive data sources make it an indispensable asset for investigators, analysts, and cybersecurity professionals. This section will delve deeper into the technical aspects of Maltego, providing a comprehensive understanding of its capabilities and how to leverage them effectively. Maltego is built upon a client-server architecture. The client-side application provides the user interface for creating entities, applying transforms, and visualizing the results. The server-side component manages the data sources, transforms, and the underlying knowledge base. Key components of Maltego include:

- Entities: Entities represent real-world objects, such as people, organizations, domains, IP addresses, and social media accounts. They serve as the building blocks of Maltego investigations.
- Relationships: Relationships connect entities together, indicating associations or connections between them. For example, a person entity can be related to an organization entity through an employment relationship.
- Transforms: Transforms are the mechanisms used to expand the search and discover related information. They can be categorized into various types, such as social media, Domain Name Server (DNS), WHOIS, and network analysis.
- Data Sources: Maltego integrates with a wide range of data sources, including social media platforms, public records databases, WHOIS information, and DNS records. These data sources provide the raw material for investigations.
- Knowledge Base: The Maltego knowledge base stores the entities, relationships, and associated data. It serves as a central repository for information gathered during investigations.

To install the Maltego Desktop Client, follow the simple steps below.

Step 1: Download and install Maltego Desktop Client that is compatible with your operating system (Windows, Linux, or Mac) from the Maltego portal [3].

Step 2: Launch Maltego Desktop Client on the laptop/desktop as shown in Figure 5.1. On the welcome screen, you will likely see an option to activate the product. Select Maltego One and click 'Activate with Key.' Type in or paste the License key you should have received in your email and click 'Next.'

Step 3: Read and accept the General Terms and Conditions for Software Licenses and Accompanying

Services and click Next, selecting the Maltego Public Transform Server, and wait for Maltego to install the transforms as shown in Figure 5.2.

Maltego offers a powerful scripting language that allows users to create custom transforms. This enables users to extend the tool's capabilities and tailor it to specific use cases. By developing custom transforms, investigators can access specialized data sources or perform complex analysis tasks. Maltego's graphical interface is a key feature that sets it apart from other OSINT tools. The visual representation of entities and relationships allows users to quickly identify patterns, connections, and anomalies within the data. The interface is highly customizable, allowing users to customize the appearance and behavior of the tool to their preferences based on advanced techniques:

- Entity Sets: Entity sets allow users to group entities together for easier management and analysis.
- Entity Templates: Entity templates can be used to define the properties and attributes of entities, ensuring consistency and standardization.

Figure 5.1 Maltego welcome screen.

Figure 5.2 Maltego transforms.

- Custom Entities: Users can create custom entities to represent specific objects or concepts that are not included in Maltego's default entity types.
- Bulk Operations: Maltego supports bulk operations, allowing users to perform actions on multiple entities simultaneously.
- API Integration: Maltego can be integrated with other applications and systems through its API, enabling automation and integration with existing workflows.

Maltego can be used for a wide range of OSINT investigations, including:

- Cybersecurity: Identifying threat actors, tracking cybercrime campaigns, and analyzing vulnerabilities.
- Investigations: Assisting in criminal investigations by identifying suspects, gathering evidence, and understanding criminal networks.
- Intelligence Analysis: Gathering information on foreign governments, organizations, and individuals.
- Corporate Intelligence: Conducting background checks on employees, competitors, and suppliers.
- Risk Assessment: Identifying potential risks and vulnerabilities within an organization.

Conducting an OSINT Investigation with Maltego

- Define the Investigation: Clearly define the scope and objectives of your investigation. Determine the specific information you are seeking, and the entities involved.
- Identify Starting Points: Identify potential starting points for your investigation, such as names, email addresses, phone numbers, or domains.
- Create Entities: Create entities in Maltego corresponding to the starting points you have identified.
- Apply Transforms: Use transforms to expand your search and discover related information. For example, you might transform a person entity to find associated social media profiles or a domain entity to find related IP addresses.
- Analyze Relationships: Examine the relationships between entities to identify patterns, connections, and potential anomalies.
- Visualize the Data: Use Maltego's graphical interface to visualize the relationships between entities and understand the overall picture of your investigation.

Use Case #1 Find a leaked or publicly available ID number from a person's image.

⊗ ⊘ Whoryo... ⬆ Ⓐ Open with Preview ⬆

Figure 5.3 TinEye image search.

Step 1: Assuming you have the person's image, upload to Google, Yandex Image search, or PimEyes, which often does not give good results, so we tried using TinEye [4] as illustrated in Figure 5.3.

Step 2: This provides several URLs and images, one of which reveals interesting data points as some details like name of the person (Roberto Sandoval Castañeda), designation (Former Nayarit Governor in Mexico), and date (May 23, 2019) [5], as illustrated in Figure 5.4.

Step 3: To begin the investigation using Maltego, open an empty graph to search 'entities' which are the data points, select 'Phrase' entity and rename it to 'Roberto Sandoval.' Maltego provides transforms to run on this, which are essentially algorithms to organize data and an API call to bring in new data from external data sources. This provides the

Brief

Ex-Governor Bribed by Jalisco Cartel Tests Mexico's Anti-Corruption Resolve

by *Chris Dalby*   23 May 2019

Former Nayarit governor, Roberto Sandoval Castañeda, has been accused by the US of receiving bribes from Mexico's Jalisco Cartel New Generation

Figure 5.4 Name of the person revealed from the InsightCrime portal.

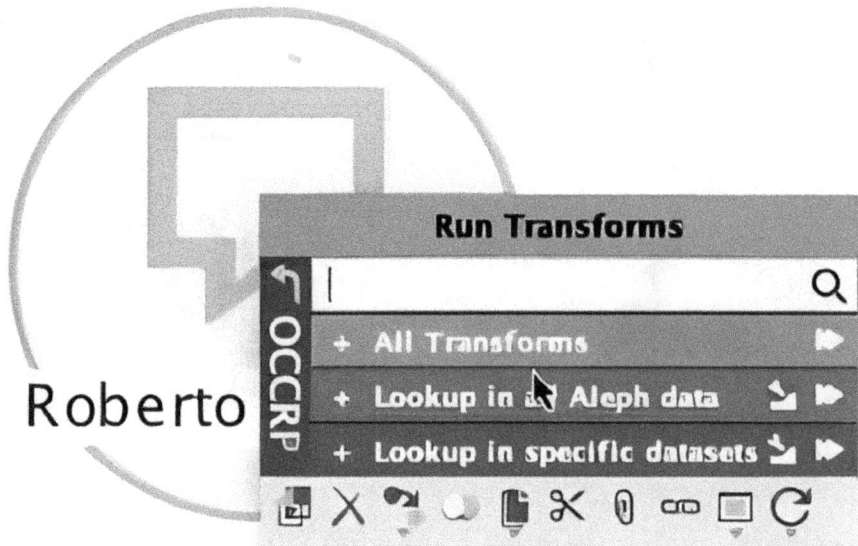

Figure 5.5 Maltego Aleph persons of interest search.

ability to take any data point and pivot using a series of transforms to take a single data point and turn that into potentially many different leads. For this investigation, we select 'Aleph data' to query for 'Persons of interest' search as presented in Figure 5.5.

Step 4: Maltego reveals hits with links and document as illustrated in Figure 5.6, one of which is 'US OFAC Sanctions List' which is the US Office of Foreign Asset Control, and since the person was inducted in a corruption case, this could be a vital link.

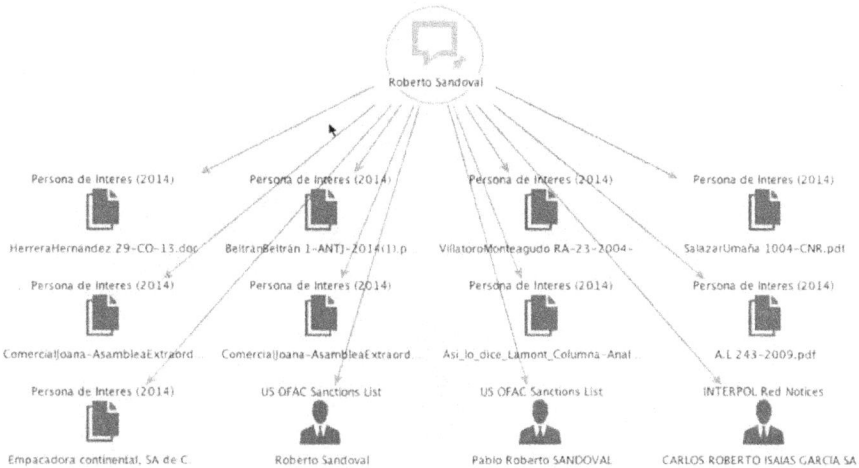

Figure 5.6 Maltego entity hits.

Step 5: From the properties of that link, we find a URL which reveals personal details about the target entity – city, country, data, and place of birth as illustrated in Figure 5.7.

Step 6: Examining further, we found an identification mentioning the passport number of the target as shown in Figure 5.8.

Figure 5.7 Personal details about the target entity found.

Passport number	Country	Document type
⌄ SACR691115HNTNSB06	Mexico	C.U.R.P.

(Passports **1**   Sanctions 1   Similar 79)

Figure 5.8 Passport number of the target entity found.

Step 7: This is validated by running another transform query as displayed in Figure 5.9 for 'All Relationships' which reveals the person, the US OFAC Sanctions List, and that number (which could be some ID number if not the passport number).

Checking on the Aleph CCRP Database [6] also confirms that the target entity name exists on the data source as presented by Figure 5.10.

Reviewing the US department report from the database, Figure 5.11 confirms that the target entity is a true positive match that was revealed by Maltego initially in this search.

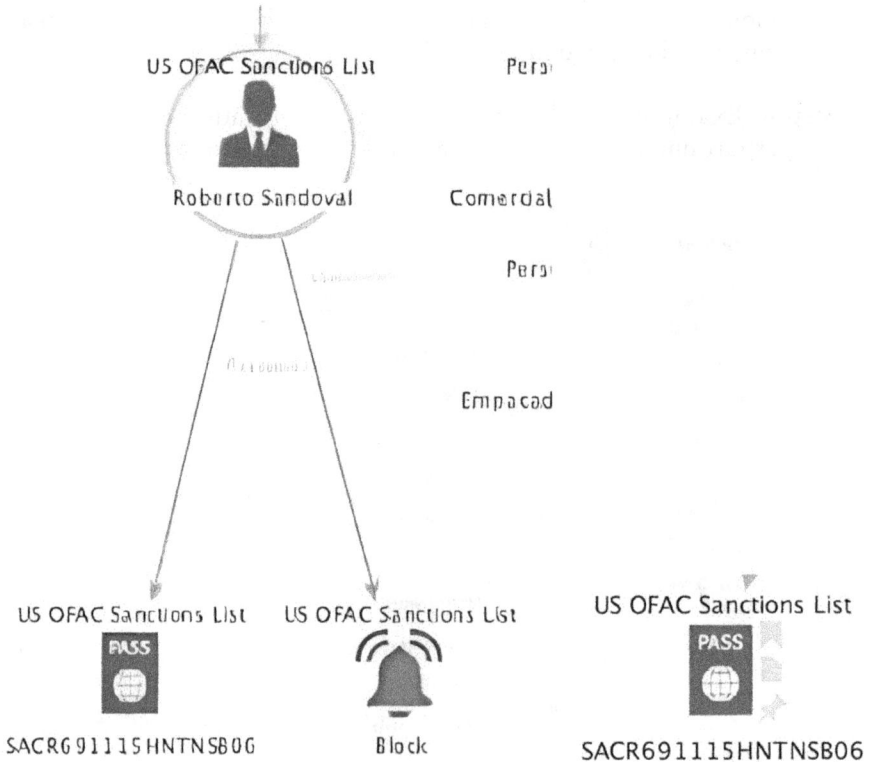

Figure 5.9 Validating passport number.

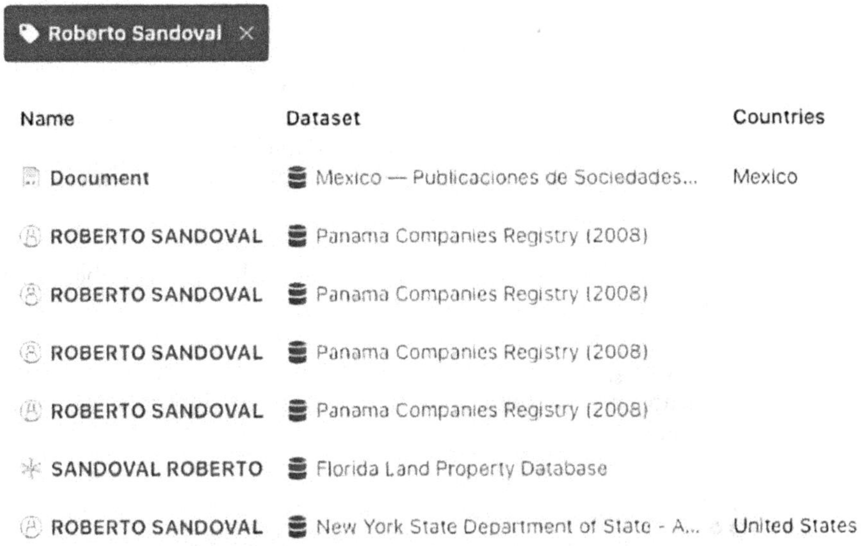

Name	Dataset	Countries
📄 Document	🗄 Mexico — Publicaciones de Sociedades...	Mexico
🅐 ROBERTO SANDOVAL	🗄 Panama Companies Registry (2008)	
🅐 ROBERTO SANDOVAL	🗄 Panama Companies Registry (2008)	
🅐 ROBERTO SANDOVAL	🗄 Panama Companies Registry (2008)	
🅐 ROBERTO SANDOVAL	🗄 Panama Companies Registry (2008)	
✳ SANDOVAL ROBERTO	🗄 Florida Land Property Database	
🅐 ROBERTO SANDOVAL	🗄 New York State Department of State - A...	United States

Figure 5.10 Aleph OCCRP database search.

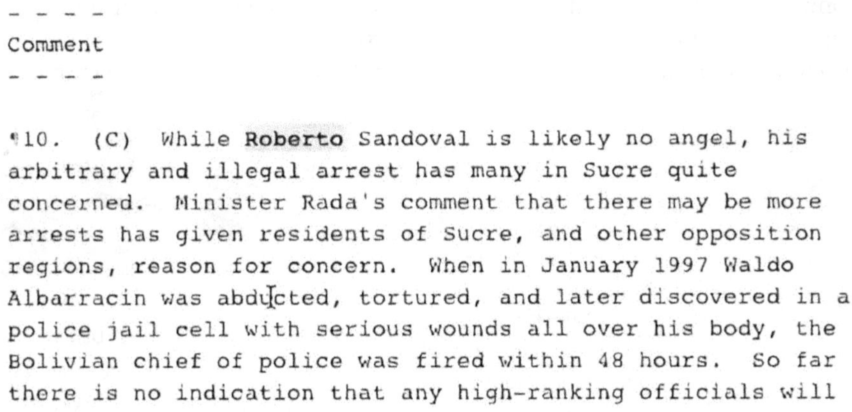

```
- - - -
Comment
- - - -
```

```
¶10. (C)  While Roberto Sandoval is likely no angel, his
arbitrary and illegal arrest has many in Sucre quite
concerned.  Minister Rada's comment that there may be more
arrests has given residents of Sucre, and other opposition
regions, reason for concern.  When in January 1997 Waldo
Albarracin was abducted, tortured, and later discovered in a
police jail cell with serious wounds all over his body, the
Bolivian chief of police was fired within 48 hours.  So far
there is no indication that any high-ranking officials will
```

Figure 5.11 US department report on the target.

Best Practices for Using Maltego are to start with a clear objective, so define the investigation goals before starting. Combine information from various sources to get a more complete picture. OSINT investigations can be time-consuming, so be patient and persistent in your search. Always use Maltego ethically and responsibly. Respect the privacy of individuals and organizations. Always stay up to date with the latest tools, techniques, and data sources in the field of OSINT.

5.3 OSINT FRAMEWORK

Information collection from free tools and resources is the main goal of OSINT framework [7] portal. This site is designed to assist in locating free OSINT resources. While some of the websites may need registration or provide information for commercial service accounts, OSINT personnel can access at least some of the material for free, related to various criteria as illustrated in Figure 5.12.

The portal has the following legends:

- (T) - indicates a Github link to a resource tool that needs to be downloaded, installed to run locally
- (D) - Google Dork focusing on Google search
- (R) - requires registration, and typically uses a fake or dummy account
- (M) - indicates a link containing the search term, and the URL needs to be tweaked and edited manually.

5.4 SHODAN

Shodan [8] is referred to as the 'Google for the Internet of Things (IoT)', and this is a specialized search engine designed to discover and catalog devices connected to the internet. Unlike traditional search engines that index web pages, Shodan indexes the services and protocols running on these devices, providing a unique perspective into the digital landscape. Shodan employs a

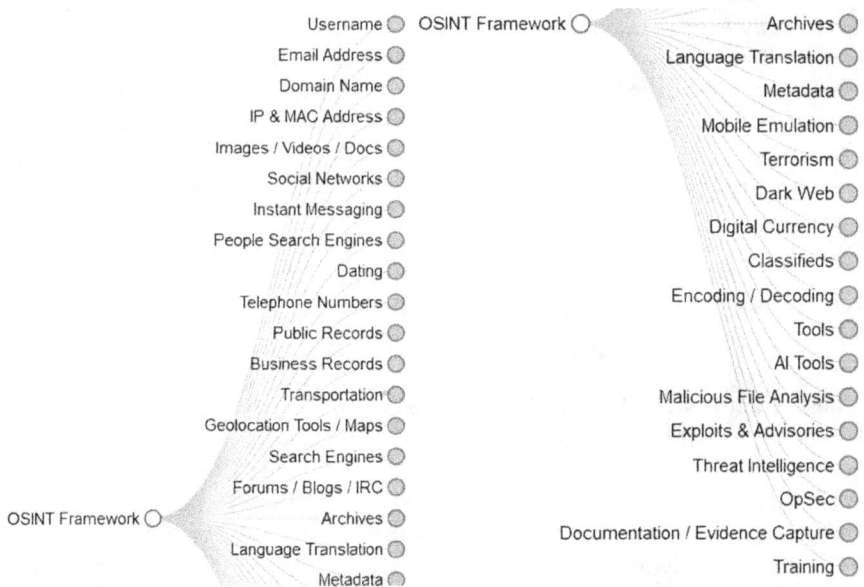

Figure 5.12 OSINT framework portal.

sophisticated set of techniques to scan the internet, identifying devices and their associated services. This involves:

- Port Scanning: Shodan systematically probes devices on various ports to determine which services are running.
- Banner Grabbing: Once a service is identified, Shodan attempts to retrieve the banner, a piece of text that often reveals the software version and configuration details.
- Fingerprinting: By analyzing the responses from devices, Shodan can fingerprint them, classifying them based on their characteristics.
- Keyword Search: Shodan allows users to search for specific keywords or phrases within the banners or metadata associated with devices.

Shodan's ability to reveal the details of connected devices makes it a powerful tool for identifying potential vulnerabilities. By understanding the software versions and configurations of devices, security researchers and hackers can:

- Discover Exposed Services: Shodan can uncover services that are running on default or weak credentials, making them prime targets for exploitation.
- Identify Vulnerable Systems: By searching for specific software versions known to have vulnerabilities, Shodan can help researchers prioritize their efforts.
- Locate Critical Infrastructure: Shodan can be used to map critical infrastructure, such as power plants, water treatment facilities, and industrial control systems, providing valuable intelligence to attackers.
- Uncover Hidden Devices: Shodan can reveal devices that are not explicitly advertised on the internet, such as home routers, security cameras, and smart appliances.

Pseudocode for Shodan Search is presented below for reference, even as Shodan's algorithm includes factors such as network latency, data storage efficiency, and security considerations for output.

```
function ShodanSearch (query):
# 1. Break down the query into keywords or patterns.
keywords = extractKeywords(query)
# 2. Search the inverted index for matching devices.
deviceIds = searchInvertedIndex(keywords)
# 3. Retrieve device details from the database.
deviceDetails = fetchDeviceDetails(deviceIds)
# 4. Filter results based on additional criteria (e.g., location, services).
filteredResults = filterResults(deviceDetails, query)
# 5. Return the filtered results.
return filteredResults
```

Some of the Shodan search techniques employed are:

- Distributed (P2P) network scanning as distributed agents scan different parts of the internet, reducing the overall time and load on a single server. However, coordinating agents, ensuring data consistency, and managing network traffic are complex.
- Port scanning is performed using SYN Scan, which involves sending SYN packets to target devices to establish connections and analyze the responses to determine open ports. But excessive scanning can be detected and blocked by firewalls.
- Banner Grabbing and Fingerprinting uses regular expressions to identify patterns to extract specific information from banners and identify device types. But handling diverse banner formats and evolving device characteristics can be challenging.
- Data Indexing and search is performed like traditional search engines, using inverted indexes to efficiently search for specific devices or services. However, scaling the index to handle the vast amount of data generated by internet scanning can be computationally intensive.

5.4.1 Hands-on: explore critical infrastructure

Security professionals use Shodan to search for specific devices, software versions, or known vulnerabilities, allowing them to identify potential risks and prioritize remediation efforts. This hands-on presents the use of Shodan to identify and assess vulnerabilities in critical infrastructure. By scanning the internet for open ports and services, Shodan reveals exposed systems and devices that are vulnerable to exploitation. However, it's important to note that Shodan should be used responsibly and ethically, as unauthorized access or exploitation of critical infrastructure can have severe consequences.

Supervisory Control and Data Acquisition [9], Programmable Logic Controller [10], and Industrial Control Systems [11] infrastructures use 'Modbus 502' [12] as a communication protocol due to its simplicity, reliability, and widespread adoption. This protocol provides a standard way for devices to communicate over various networks, such as Serial, Ethernet, or TCP/IP. The protocol is designed to be robust and fault-tolerant, ensuring reliable communication even in challenging environments. Modbus is an open standard, meaning it is freely available and not controlled by any single company, which promotes interoperability and competition. Modbus is used to control various devices, such as pumps, valves, motors, and sensors, in critical infrastructure systems. This allows collection of data from devices, such as temperature, pressure, and flow measurements. Modbus enables remote monitoring and control of critical infrastructure systems, improving efficiency and reducing downtime. Modbus can be integrated with other systems and protocols to create comprehensive solutions.

5.4.1.1 Shodan query #1: Modbus 502

Step 1: Log in to Shodan and search for the keyword **Modbus 502** reveals 139 critical infrastructure devices as illustrated in Figure 5.13.

Step 2: Figure 5.14 presents the details on reviewing one such device (IP address).

Step 3: Port 21 access is validated live for two such devices as illustrated in Figure 5.15, which shows organizations still using legacy, clear text protocols for data transfers. Trying to access the IP on the File Transfer Protocol (FTP) port 21 has the system prompting for a User ID and Password; most brute force tools can break this in few minutes.

5.4.1.2 Shodan query #2: Prismview Player

Step 1: Shodan search query for another critical infrastructure for **Prismview Player** identifies devices on the internet that have the 'Prismview Player' server application which is used in digital signage and video wall displays. By searching for this specific server, users can potentially identify devices that are vulnerable to known security vulnerabilities associated with the software as displayed in Figure 5.16.

Step 2: Review of Shodan details for one such IP reveals open ports 80 and 81 using HTTP/1.1 as shown in Figure 5.17. HTTP/1.1 was the second major version of the Hypertext Transfer Protocol, which is the foundation of the World Wide Web and introduced several improvements over HTTP/1.0.

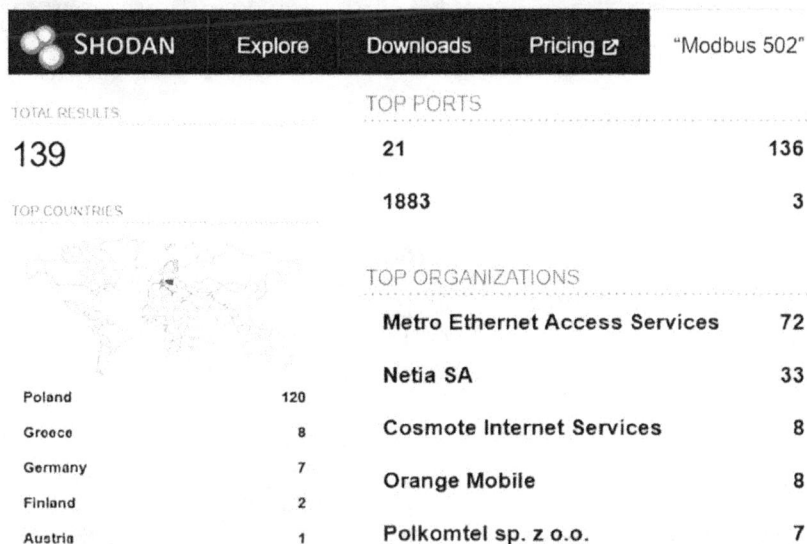

Figure 5.13 Shodan 'Modbus 502' search.

Figure 5.14 Details of the IP address & open port.

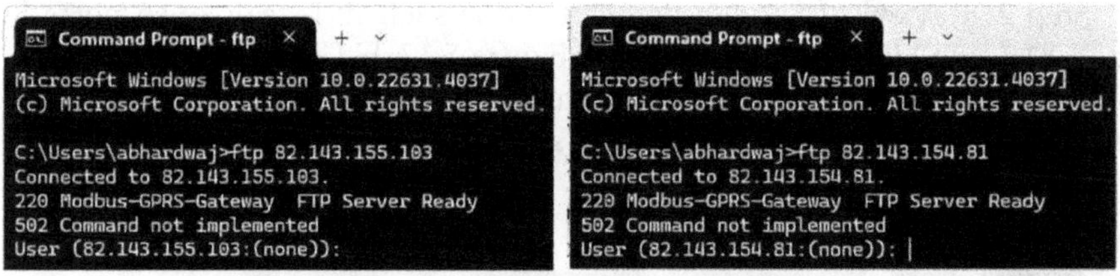

Figure 5.15 Live FTP access.

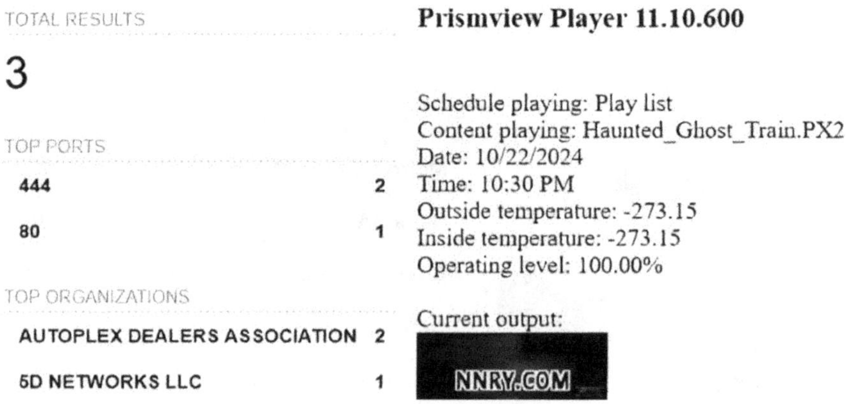

TOTAL RESULTS

3

Prismview Player 11.10.600

TOP PORTS

444	2
80	1

Schedule playing: Play list
Content playing: Haunted_Ghost_Train.PX2
Date: 10/22/2024
Time: 10:30 PM
Outside temperature: -273.15
Inside temperature: -273.15
Operating level: 100.00%

TOP ORGANIZATIONS

AUTOPLEX DEALERS ASSOCIATION	2
5D NETWORKS LLC	1

Current output:

NNRY.COM

Figure 5.16 Shodan search for Prismview Player search.

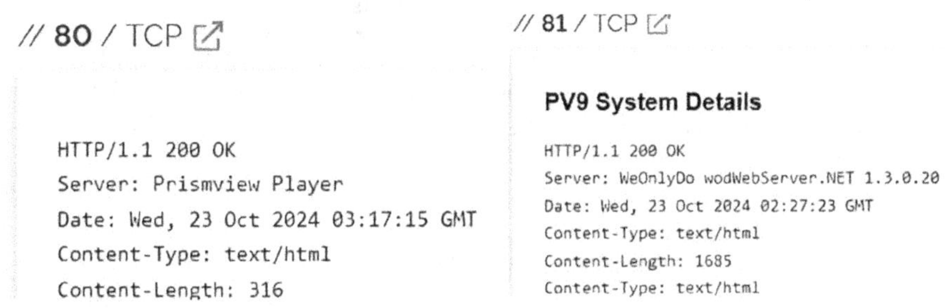

// 80 / TCP ☐

// 81 / TCP ☐

PV9 System Details

HTTP/1.1 200 OK
Server: Prismview Player
Date: Wed, 23 Oct 2024 03:17:15 GMT
Content-Type: text/html
Content-Length: 316

HTTP/1.1 200 OK
Server: WeOnlyDo wodWebServer.NET 1.3.0.20
Date: Wed, 23 Oct 2024 02:27:23 GMT
Content-Type: text/html
Content-Length: 1685
Content-Type: text/html

Figure 5.17 Open port information for Prismview Player.

While HTTP/1.1 is an efficient and robust protocol, it is not without its vulnerabilities. Some of the vulnerabilities that can be exploited in HTTP/1.1 include:

- Cross-Site Scripting: This occurs when malicious code is injected into a web page and executed by the user's browser.
- Cross-Site Request Forgery: This occurs when a malicious website tricks a user into performing an unwanted action on a trusted site.
- SQL Injection: This occurs when malicious code is injected into a SQL query, allowing an attacker to access or modify data.
- Directory Traversal: This occurs when an attacker is able to access files or directories outside of the intended scope.
- HTTP Response Splitting: This occurs when an attacker is able to inject additional HTTP headers into a response, potentially leading to various attacks.

There are several CVEs (Common Vulnerabilities and Exploits) associated with HTTP/1.1 including:

- CVE-2014–3566: This vulnerability allows an attacker to bypass security restrictions and access unauthorized data.
- CVE-2017–5638: This vulnerability allows an attacker to execute arbitrary code on a vulnerable server.
- CVE-2018–12037: This vulnerability allows an attacker to bypass authentication and gain unauthorized access to a web application.

These are just a few examples, and there are many other HTTP/1.1 vulnerabilities that can be exploited. It is essential for web developers and system administrators to be aware of these vulnerabilities and take steps to protect their applications and systems.

5.4.1.3 Shodan query #3: Network cameras

Step 1: Yet another Shodan search query for **Network Camera VB-M600** reveals 16 camera devices live on the internet, as shown in Figure 5.18. This query searches for cameras on the internet having the 'VB-M600' model name listed as the device description and metadata.

Step 2: This query reveals Canon VB-M600 cameras having open ports 9000 and 9001 with the camera accessible without any ID/password on a factory floor, as illustrated in Figure 5.19.

Step 3: Querying another Canon device IP address reveals open ports 1723, 5000, and 5001, with the camera revealing a store video stream with no ID/password validation as displayed in Figure 5.20.

5.4.1.4 Shodan query #4: Server: GeoHTTPServer

Step 1: Shodan search query **Server: GeoHTTPServer** is designed to identify devices on the internet that have the GeoHTTPServer software, as shown in Figure 5.21. This application is used in geographic information systems applications and found on devices such as web servers, network cameras, and sensors. By searching for this server, users can potentially identify devices that may be vulnerable to known security vulnerabilities associated with the GeoHTTPServer software. This information can be useful for security researchers, system administrators, and others who need to identify and assess the security posture of devices running the GeoHTTPServer software.

Step 2: Figure 5.22 reveals these servers running live on the internet with several apps accessible easily.

TOTAL RESULTS		TOP ORGANIZATIONS	
16		IIJ Internet	5
		NTT PC Communications,Inc.	3
TOP PORTS			
8081	7	ARTERIA Networks Corp.	2
8083	3	INTERLINK Co.,LTD.	2
50000	2		
5001	1	ARTERIA Networks Corporation	1
8085	1	More...	

Figure 5.18 Shodan query for network camera VB-M600.

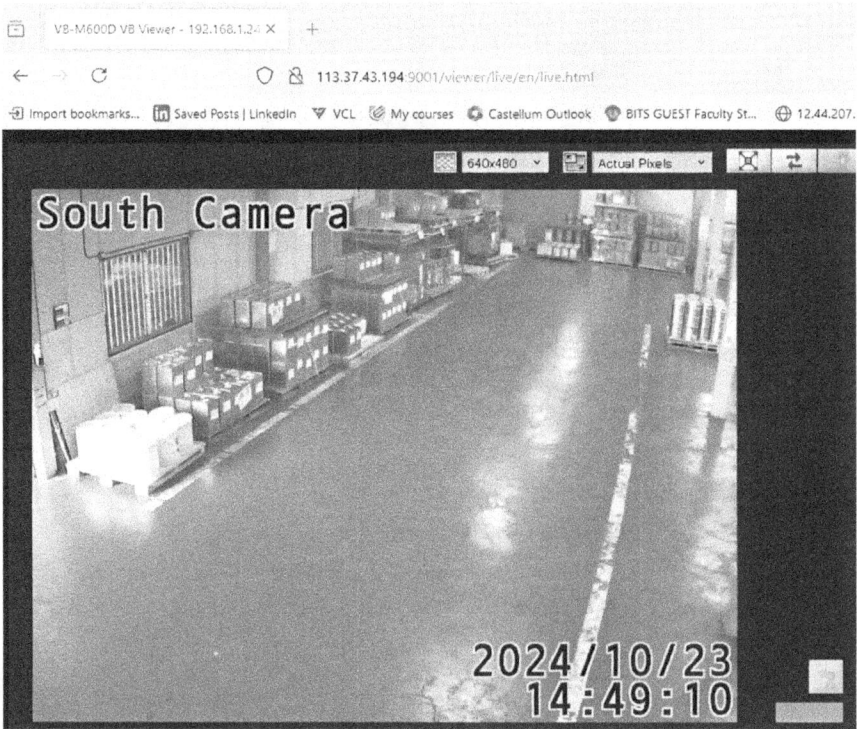

Figure 5.19 Live camera access of the factory floor.

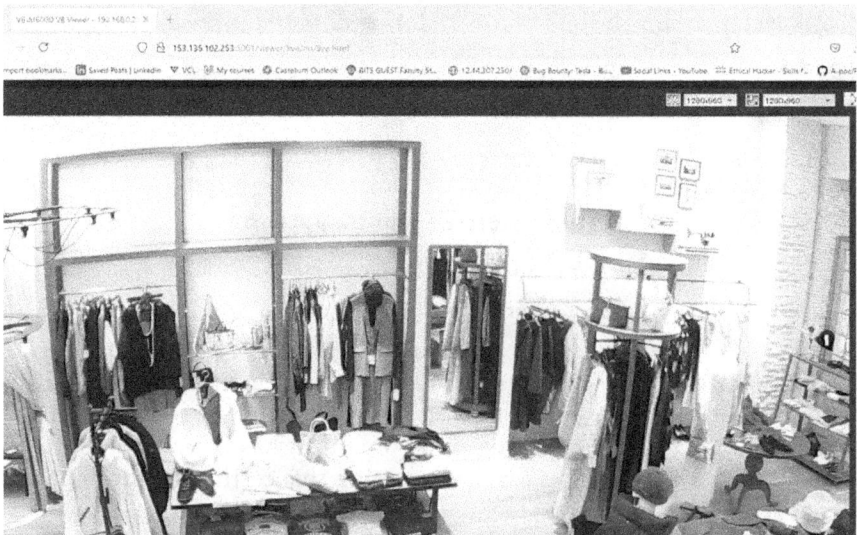

Figure 5.20 Live camera access of a shopping store.

TOTAL RESULTS

29,144

TOP COUNTRIES

TOP PORTS	
80	12,851
81	2,748
8080	1,239
8081	646
8000	555

United States	12,108
Germany	3,287
Canada	1,308
Taiwan	957
Japan	824

TOP PRODUCTS

GeoVision GeoHttpServer for w...	20,595
NETGEAR DGN2200	11
nginx	2

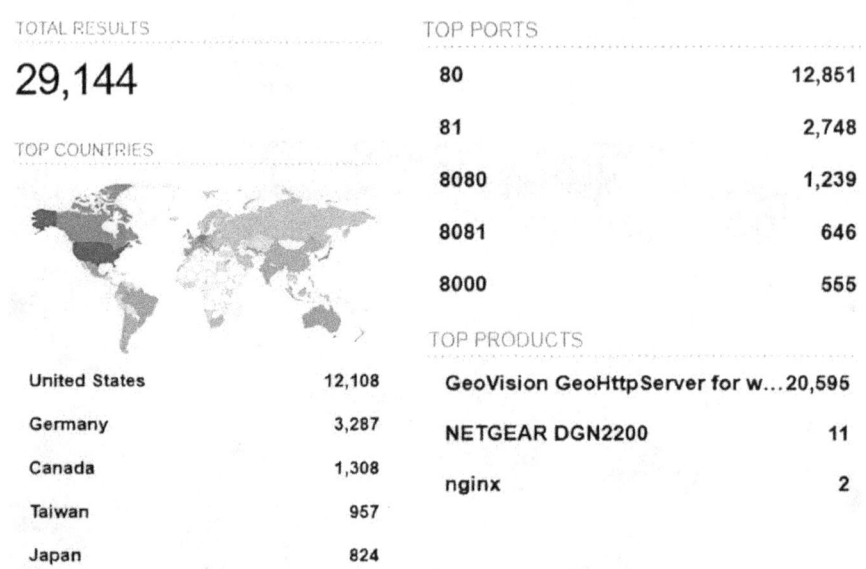

Figure 5.21 Shodan query for GeoHTTPServer.

Figure 5.22 GeoHTTPServers on internet.

5.4.2 Hands-on: explore enterprise systems

5.4.2.1 Shodan query #1: SSL:"Xerox Generic Root

Step 1: Shodan search query **SSL:"Xerox Generic Root"** is used to identify devices on the internet that are configured to use the 'Xerox Generic Root' certificate for SSL/TLS encryption, as displayed in Figure 5.23. This certificate is a root certificate issued by Xerox, which verifies the authenticity of other certificates issued by Xerox or by organizations that trust the Xerox Generic Root. By searching for devices using this certificate, investigators identify devices that are vulnerable to man-in-the-middle attacks. This information can be useful for security researchers, system administrators, and others who need to identify and assess the security posture of devices using the Xerox Generic Root certificate.

TOTAL RESULTS

304

TOP COUNTRIES

United States	145
Canada	18
Italy	16
India	14
Czechia	13

TOP PORTS

443	287
8443	5
4443	2
8083	2
444	1

TOP ORGANIZATIONS

University of Hawaii	36
Charter Communicat...	13
Comcast Cable Com...	11
Bharti Infotel Ltd. (BB...	5
Instituto Politecnico ...	5

Figure 5.23 Shodan query for Xerox printer certificates.

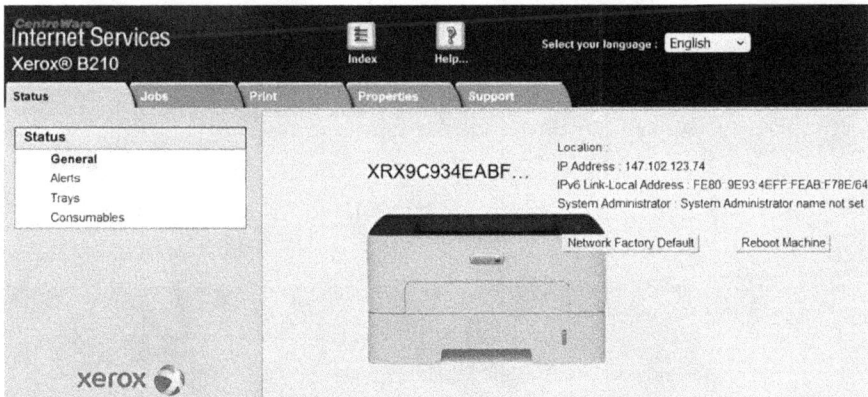

Figure 5.24 Xerox printer available online.

Step 2: Accessing one of the devices as revealed by this Shodan query displays a Xerox B210 printer with self-signed certificates. Anyone with the IP link to the print device can easily reboot or reset the configuration to default as illustrated in Figure 5.24.

Figure 5.25 Shodan query Xerox multifunction printer.

Step 3: Another device on live public IP is accessible online as displayed in Figure 5.25 as Xerox AltaLink C8145 with no administrator password set.

Step 4: Printer notifications are accessible as displayed in Figure 5.26, which is information disclosure in Cyber terms and leaves the print device highly vulnerable.

Step 5: Yet another device was found with no administrator password accessible online as displayed in Figure 5.27. This is a Xerox AltaLink C8055 multifunction printer.

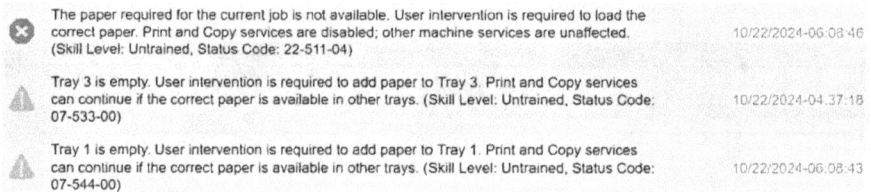

Figure 5.26 Printer notifications.

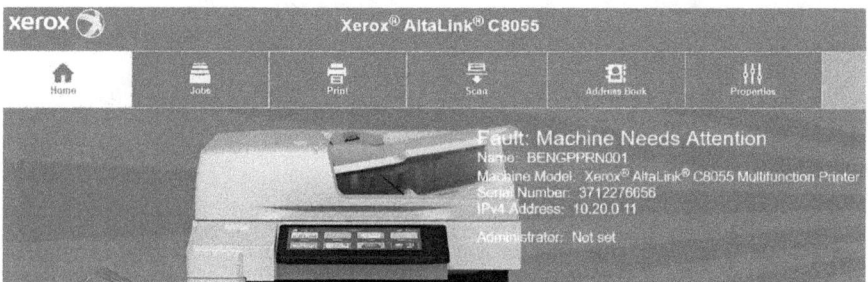

Figure 5.27 Xerox multifunction printer.

Active Jobs

Delete ⌄   Go

Job Name	Owner	Status	Type	Copy Count
Job 5553	Remote User	Waiting for printer	print	1
Job 5576	Remote User	Held - resources not available	print	1
Job 5604	Remote User	Held - resources not available	print	1
Job 5607	Remote User	Held - resources not available	print	1
Job 5644	Remote User	Held - resources not available	print	1
Job 5679	Remote User	Held - resources not available	print	1
Job 5689	Remote User	Held - resources not available	print	1
Job 5697	Remote User	Held - resources not available	print	1
Job 5700	Remote User	Held - resources not available	print	1

Figure 5.28 Printer active jobs.

Step 6: Browsing this device further reveals active jobs as displayed in Figure 5.28, which are pending to be printed due to a system fault.

5.4.2.2 Shodan query #2: "230 login successful." port:21

Step 1: Shodan search query "230 **Login successful.**" **port:21** is designed to identify devices on the internet that are running an FTP server on port 21 and have recently logged in successfully. Figure 5.29 reveals 46,860 FTP Servers still utilizing the clear text file transfer protocol.

Step 2: The '230 Login successful' indicates the search looks for devices that have recently logged in successfully to their FTP server and the '230 Login successful.' message is typically sent by an FTP server in response to a successful login attempt. Trying to access the FTP systems as an anonymous user was successful, as shown in Figure 5.30.

Step 3: Furthermore, information disclosure reveals use of VSFTPD app version 3.0.2 for FTP, for which there are several CVEs and exploit tools like Metasploit that can easily provide backdoor access into the server. This information can be useful for security researchers, system administrators, and others who need to identify and assess the security posture of FTP servers.

5.4.3 Hands-on: explore home devices

5.4.3.1 Shodan query #1: Find Yamaha Stereos

Step 1: Using Shodan search query **Server: AV_Receiver** identifies devices on the internet that are acting as AV receivers and are responding with a specific HTTP status code. The first part of the query specifies that the server software running on the device is identified as an AV receiver. This could indicate that the device is a home theater receiver or a similar device that can decode audio and video signals, and the second part of the query specifies that the device is responding to HTTP requests with a status code of 406. This status code means that the server is unable to fulfill the request

TOTAL RESULTS

46,860

TOP COUNTRIES

TOP ORGANIZATIONS

Aliyun Computin...	1,871
Hosting Servers	1,684
Chunghwa Teleco...	1,357
Korea Telecom	1,322
Linode	1,244

TOP PRODUCTS

vsftpd	105
pyftpdlib	25
Microsoft ftpd	20
Serv-U ftpd	17
bftpd	17

United States	7,801
China	5,524
Japan	3,615
Korea, Republic of	3,288
Poland	3,065

Figure 5.29 Shodan query for FTP servers.

```
Command Prompt - ftp    ×    +  ˅
Microsoft Windows [Version 10.0.22631.4037]
(c) Microsoft Corporation. All rights reserved.

C:\Users\abhardwaj>ftp 149.28.41.53
Connected to 149.28.41.53.
220 (vsFTPd 3.0.2)
200 Always in UTF8 mode.
User (149.28.41.53:(none)): anonymous
331 Please specify the password.
Password:

230 Login successful.
ftp>
```

```
Command Prompt - ftp    ×    +  ˅
C:\Users\abhardwaj>ftp 40.78.109.46
Connected to 40.78.109.46.
220 (vsFTPd 3.0.2)
200 Always in UTF8 mode.
User (40.78.109.46:(none)): anonymous
331 Please specify the password.
Password:

230 Login successful.
ftp>
```

Figure 5.30 Successful anonymous login to FTP servers.

due to an unacceptable media type. This could happen, for example, if the client sends a request for a specific media type that the AV receiver does not support. Figure 5.31 displays 126 devices and the breakup.

		TOP PORTS		TOP ORGANIZATIONS	
Sweden	26	80	113	Korea Telecom	14
United States	26	9100	4	Telia Network Services	12
Germany	21	81	1	Charter Communicati...	9
Korea, Republic of	15	90	1	Deutsche Telekom AG	8
Finland	10	1025	1	1&1 Versatel Deutschl...	5

Figure 5.31 Audio video receivers breakup.

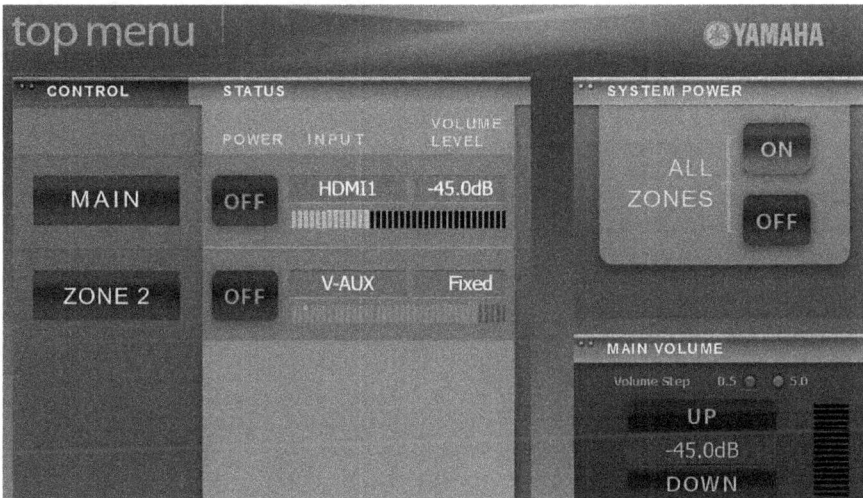

Figure 5.32 Yamaha AV receiver control menu.

Step 2: Reviewing one such device presents an AV receiver system with open port 80 (HTTP), displaying the Control panel with status, power, and volume as displayed in Figure 5.32.

5.4.3.2 Shodan query #2: Find Network Attached Storage (NAS)

Step 1: Shodan query **Authentication: disabled** search criteria identify devices or systems that lack any form of authentication mechanism, so anyone can potentially access and manipulate these systems, posing a significant security risk. These include servers, routers, IoT devices, or other networked systems that have not been configured with proper security measures, as revealed in Figure 5.33.

TOP PORTS		TOP PRODUCTS		TOP OPERATING SYSTEMS	
445	239,158	Samba	170,428	Unix	156,304
5900	2,403	VNC	4,250	Windows 6.1	14,234
4800	1,218	Moxa Nport	1,218	Windows Server 2012 R2 Standa...	1,307
5901	807	Alfresco CIFS Server 6.0.0	81	Windows Server 2016 Standard ...	1,246
5910	56	win6	26	Windows 7 Professional 7600	906

Figure 5.33 Devices with 'authentication disabled.'

Step 2: Accessing one of the devices (IP address), we find a device with authentication disabled, having multiple open ports. Usually, such devices are honeypots, set up online to capture logs of the attacker behavior and browsing or attack process (Figure 5.34).

Step 3: We reviewed a few ports and were able to access the NAS device on port 9000, revealing the list of video albums stored on the NAS as displayed in Figure 5.35.

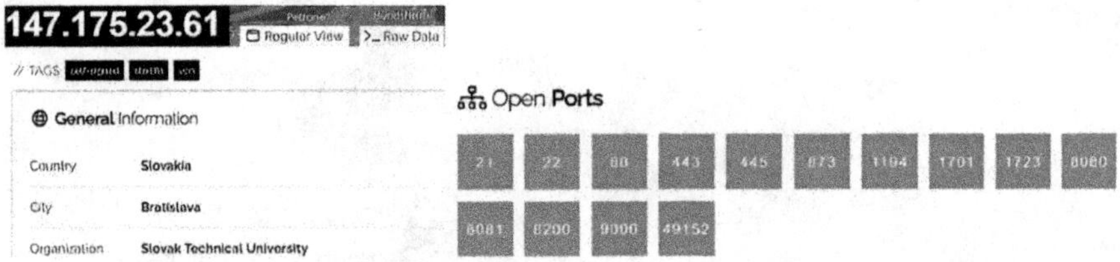

Figure 5.34 Found NAS with multiple ports.

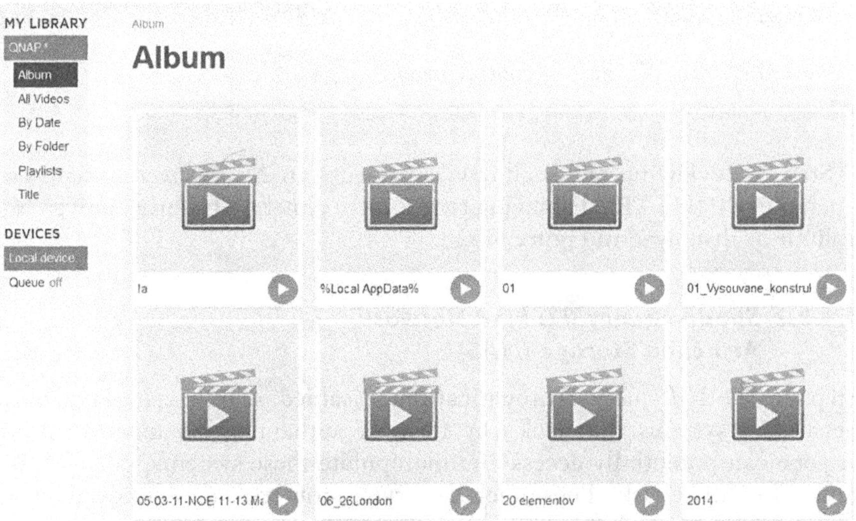

Figure 5.35 NAS video contents revealed.

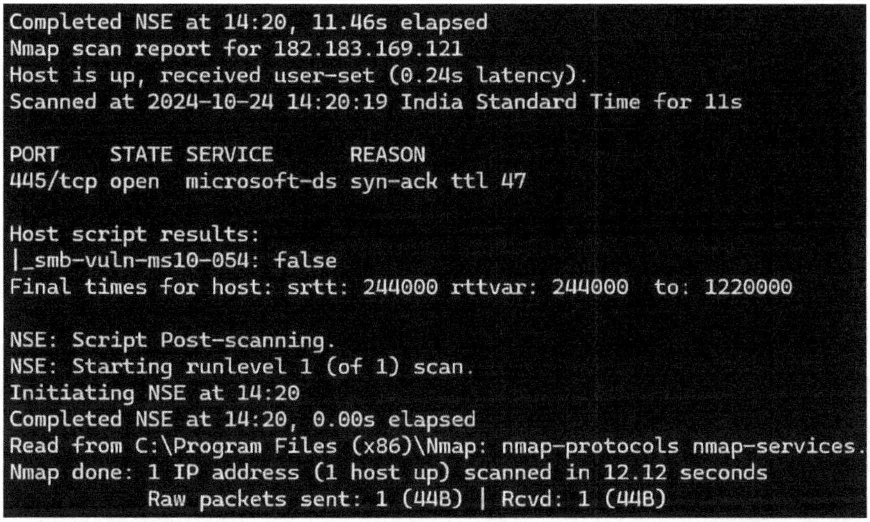

```
Completed NSE at 14:20, 11.46s elapsed
Nmap scan report for 182.183.169.121
Host is up, received user-set (0.24s latency).
Scanned at 2024-10-24 14:20:19 India Standard Time for 11s

PORT     STATE SERVICE       REASON
445/tcp open  microsoft-ds syn-ack ttl 47

Host script results:
|_smb-vuln-ms10-054: false
Final times for host: srtt: 244000 rttvar: 244000  to: 1220000

NSE: Script Post-scanning.
NSE: Starting runlevel 1 (of 1) scan.
Initiating NSE at 14:20
Completed NSE at 14:20, 0.00s elapsed
Read from C:\Program Files (x86)\Nmap: nmap-protocols nmap-services.
Nmap done: 1 IP address (1 host up) scanned in 12.12 seconds
          Raw packets sent: 1 (44B) | Rcvd: 1 (44B)
```

Figure 5.36 Microsoft SMB services found on the device.

Step 4: Scanning another IP address using the NMAP tool on port 445, reveals the device running Microsoft SMB application as displayed in Figure 5.36, which an attacker can exploit.

5.4.3.3 Shodan query #3: Find Webcam7 or WebcamXP

Step 1: Running the search query **Webcam7** or **WebcamXP** identifies devices using legacy Webcam7 or WebcamXP software. Figure 5.37 reveals the below-mentioned ports, products, and OS.

Step 2: Accessing one of the devices presents the device home page for User ID and Password as displayed in Figure 5.38.

Step 3: Reviewing one of the devices presents the Webcam 7 video stream without authentication as displayed in Figure 5.39.

5.4.3.4 Shodan query #4 Devices from Cobham SATCOM

Step 1: Shodan Dork **Cobham SATCOM** identifies devices such as satellite modems, antennas, and ground stations, manufactured by Cobham SATCOM that are connected to the internet. Probing one such device revealed by Shodan presents three open ports, one of which is FTP which is validated by Figure 5.40.

5.4.3.5 Shodan query #5: Refrigeration units

Step 1: Figure 5.41 presents the result of Shodan search query "**Server: CarelDataServer**" "**200 Document follows**". This is designed to find devices

TOP PORTS		TOP PRODUCTS		TOP OPERATING SYSTEMS	
8080		219 Yawcam webcam viewer httpd	140	Windows	88
8081		216 Apache httpd	120	Ubuntu	5
443		158 webcam 7 httpd	80	QTS 5.1.3	4
80		92 nginx	46	Synology DiskStation Manager (DSM...4	
8085		38 Netwave IP camera http config	32	Windows (build 10.0.19041)	4

Figure 5.37 Webcam 7 or XP devices.

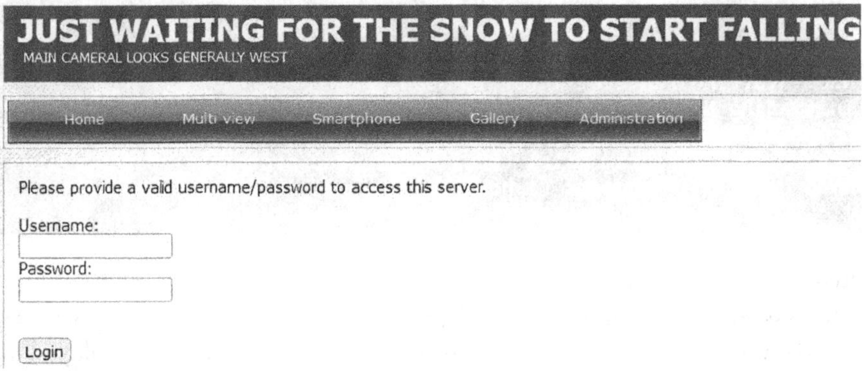

JUST WAITING FOR THE SNOW TO START FALLING
MAIN CAMERA1 LOOKS GENERALLY WEST

Home   Multi view   Smartphone   Gallery   Administration

Please provide a valid username/password to access this server.

Username:

Password:

Login

Figure 5.38 Webcam device seeking ID/password.

running the Carel DataServer software that respond to HTTP requests with a 200 status code indicating a successful request and requested document found.

Step 2: Carel DataServer software has known vulnerabilities that are exploited by malicious actors, presenting a risk to an organization as displayed in Figure 5.42.

5.4.3.6 Shodan query #6: Servers using CherryPy web framework

Step 1: Figure 5.43 presents the Shodan search query **"CherryPy/5.1.0" "/ home"** to identify servers running Python-based CherryPy web framework version 5.1.0 with URL page accessible at "/home".

Step 2: This is the home page, a directory listing, or any other type of content served at that specific URL as displayed in Figure 5.44.

Step 3: CherryPy has several security vulnerabilities as confirmed in Figure 5.45.

5.4.3.7 Shodan query #7: Find Linksys Web Cams

Step 1: Shodan search query **"+tm01+"** identifies Linksys Webcam devices as Shodan sends out network probes to devices on the internet to extract

Figure 5.39 Webcam 7 video stream.

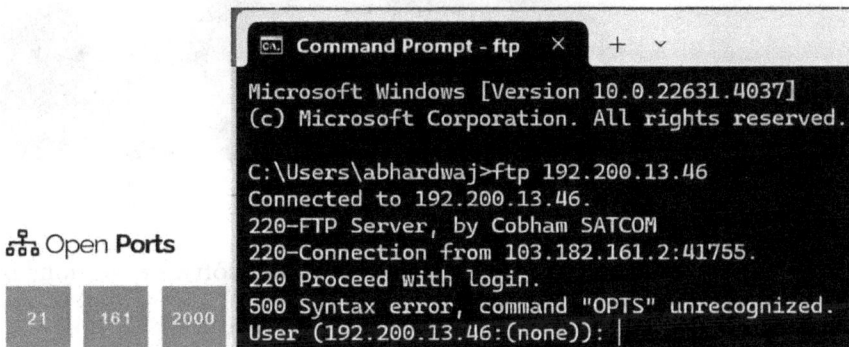

Figure 5.40 Cobham satellite device FTP port.

Frig◉impianti
SUPERVISORY SYSTEM
version 3.3

Login   Guest ⌄
Password [   ]
Ok   Kbd

Figure 5.41 Carel data server.

Carel : Security Vulnerabilities, CVEs

Published in: ≡ ▾ 2024 January February March April May June July August September October

CVSS Scores Greater Than: 0 1 2 3 4 5 6 7 8 9   In CISA KEV Catalog

Sort Results By : Publish Date ↓↑ Update Date ↓↑ CVE Number ↓↑   CVE Number ↑↓   CVSS Score ↓↑   EPSS Score ↓↑

Figure 5.42 Carel server known security vulnerabilities.

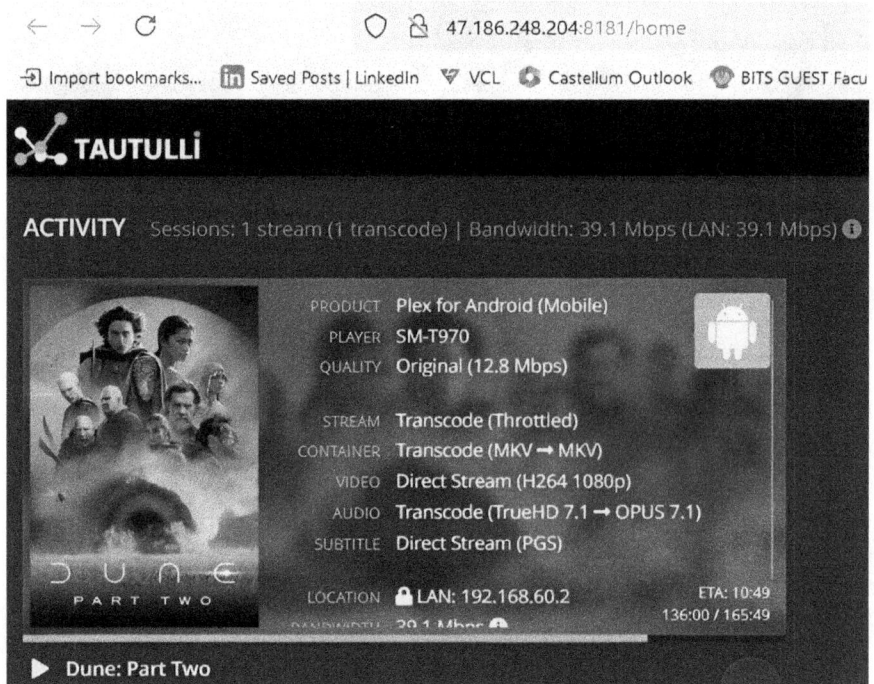

← → C   ○ 🔒 47.186.248.204:8181/home

⤓ Import bookmarks... in Saved Posts | LinkedIn ▽ VCL 🜨 Castellum Outlook 🌐 BITS GUEST Facu

✖ TAUTULLI

ACTIVITY Sessions: 1 stream (1 transcode) | Bandwidth: 39.1 Mbps (LAN: 39.1 Mbps) ⓘ

PRODUCT Plex for Android (Mobile)
PLAYER SM-T970
QUALITY Original (12.8 Mbps)

STREAM Transcode (Throttled)
CONTAINER Transcode (MKV → MKV)
VIDEO Direct Stream (H264 1080p)
AUDIO Transcode (TrueHD 7.1 → OPUS 7.1)
SUBTITLE Direct Stream (PGS)

LOCATION 🔒 LAN: 192.168.60.2   ETA: 10:49
                                      136:00 / 165:49

▶ Dune: Part Two

Figure 5.43 Home page for the CherryPy web framework system.

device information such as name, model number, software version, or unique identifier and signatures associated with Linksys webcams as shown in Figure 5.46.

Step 2: Reviewing a few of the device IP addresses displays device access as illustrated in Figure 5.47.

Developed by

A*xelor*) & Tiny

Welcome to OpenERP

Ope*ñ*ERP
Made by Tiny & Axelor

Database:
User:
Password:
Login

MAIN MENU   SHORTCUTS   Could not connect to server!

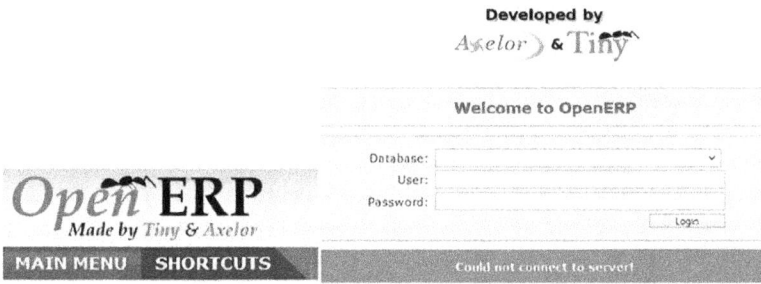

Figure 5.44 Home page interface found.

Cherrypy : Security Vulnerabilities, CVEs

Published in: ≡ ▾ 2024 January February March April May June July August September October

CVSS Scores Greater Than: 0 1 2 3 4 5 6 7 8 9   in CISA KEV Catalog

Sort Results By : Publish Date ⇅ Update Date ⇅ CVE Number ⇅ CVE Number ⇵ CVSS Score ⇅ EPSS Score ⇅

CVE-2008-0252   Max CVSS   7.5

Directory traversal vulnerability in the _get_file_path function in (1) lib/sessions.py in CherryPy 3.0.x up to 3.0.2, (2) filter/   EPSS Score   0.00%
sessionfilter.py in CherryPy 2.1, and (3) filter/sessionfilter.py in CherryPy 2.x allows remote attackers to create or delete   Published   2008-01-12
arbitrary files, and possibly read and write portions of arbitrary files, via a crafted session id in a cookie.   Updated   2018-10-15
Source: MITRE

CVE-2006-0847   Max CVSS   5.0

Directory traversal vulnerability in the staticfilter component in CherryPy before 2.1.1 allows remote attackers to read   EPSS Score   0.84%
arbitrary files via "." sequences in unspecified vectors.   Published   2006-02-22
Source: MITRE   Updated   2017-07-20

Figure 5.45 CherryPy security vulnerabilities.

TOP ORGANIZATIONS		TOP PRODUCTS		TOP OPERATING SYSTEMS	
Verizon Business	6	thttpd	25	MikroTik RouterOS 6.44	3
INCUBATEC GmbH - Srl	5	Mosquitto	5	Synology DiskStation Manager (DSM...	2
Interac Corp.	4	Postfix smtpd	3	Debian	1
Bell Canada	3	Remote Desktop Protocol	3	Linux	1
Dynamic IP assignment for broadba...	3	ClickHouse	2	Mac OS X	1

Figure 5.46 Linksys Webcam search.

LINKSYS®
A Division of Cisco Systems, Inc.   WVC54GCA

Wireless-G Internet Home Monitoring Camera   Home | View Video | Setup | Linksys Web | Help | Exit

View Video

Advanced Configuration

Figure 5.47 Linksys device.

5.5 GOOGLE DORKING

Google Dorking [13] or Google hacking is a technique that leverages Google's search engine to discover information that may not be readily accessible through standard search queries. It involves using advanced search operators, known as Dorks, to refine search results and uncover specific types of information. These Dorks can be used to find files of a particular type, search within a specific website, look for certain keywords in the title or content of a webpage, or even find pages that link to a particular URL. By exploiting the vast index of webpages that Google maintains, Dorks allow users to find information that might not be easily discoverable otherwise. This technique can be used for various purposes, including ethical hacking, cybersecurity research, competitive intelligence, and general information gathering. It is important to use Dorks responsibly and ethically, as it can potentially reveal sensitive information if it's publicly accessible, and crucial to respect the privacy and security of others and to avoid using Dorks for malicious purposes.

5.5.1 Uncover sensitive documents

- Open Google and type in the Dork **intext:confidential intitle:filetype:xls OR filetype:xlsx OR filetype:csv** to view confidential Excel sheets as displayed in Figure 5.48.

- Googe **intitle:classified OR intitle:top secret intext:password filetype:pdf** to find secret PDF files as illustrated in Figure 5.49.

- Use Google Dork **intext:"client data" OR intext:"customer details" intitle:"confidential" filetype:docx** to find Microsoft Word documents with content and keywords like Client data, Customer details, as shown in Figure 5.50.

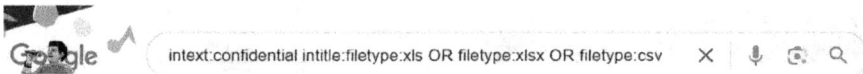

Figure 5.48 Finding confidential Excel files.

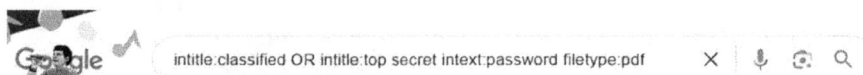

Figure 5.49 Searching secret PDF files.

intext:"client data" OR intext:"customer details" intitle:"confidential" file ✕

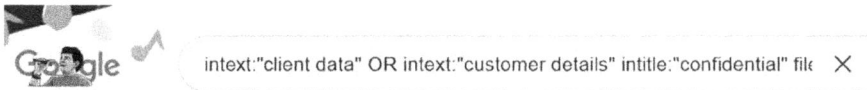

Figure 5.50 Finding confidential word documents.

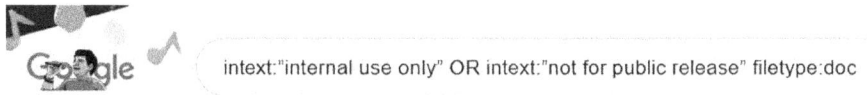

intext:"internal use only" OR intext:"not for public release" filetype:doc

Figure 5.51 Searching documents meant for internal company use.

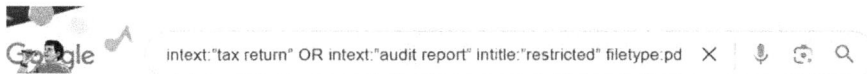

intext:"tax return" OR intext:"audit report" intitle:"restricted" filetype:pd ✕   🎤 📷 🔍

Figure 5.52 Find documents related to tax or audit.

- Google **intext:"internal use only" OR intext:"not for public release" filetype:doc** to search Word documents meant for only internal company use as displayed in Figure 5.51.

- Use Dork **intext:"tax return" OR intext:"audit report" intitle:"restricted" filetype:pdf** to search for PDF documents related to tax or audit, as shown in Figure 5.52.

5.5.2 Search location-specific targets

- This Dork targets business directories, seeking mentions of a person with location-related terms, potentially revealing business affiliations or address information associated with the individual. Figure 5.53 displays links when using the Google Dork **site:yellowpages.com OR site:yelp.com OR site:businessdirectory.com intext:"John Doe" intext:"USA" OR intext:"NEw York" OR intext:"map"**.

- This Dork scans for online classifieds in specific location with mentions of 'John Doe' alongside location-related terms, potentially revealing postings, listings, or advertisements with location-specific details. Google Dork **site:craigslist.org OR site:gumtree.com intext:"John Doe" intext:"location" OR intext:"address" OR intext:"map"** is shown in Figure 5.54.

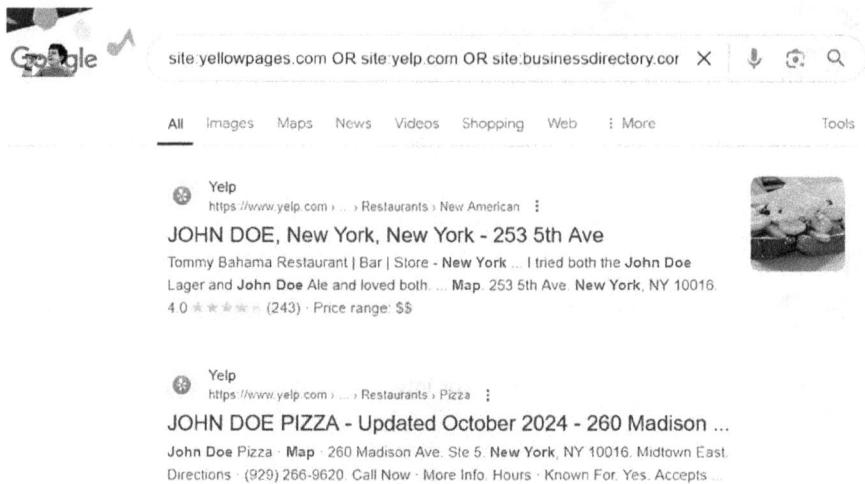

Figure 5.53 Dork to find a businessperson at a location.

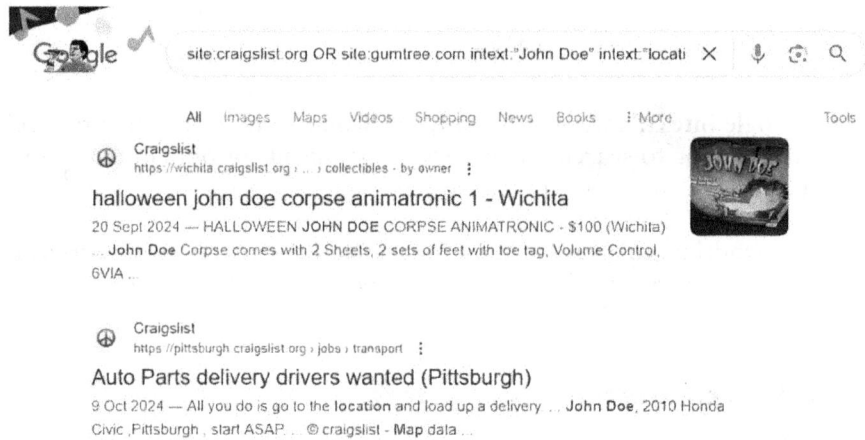

Figure 5.54 Search classifieds for specific locations.

- This Dork scans documents for metadata in online document repositories, seeking content mentioning 'John Doe' alongside terms related to location or geotagging, potentially revealing location metadata within documents or presentations. Google Dork **site:slideshare. net OR site:scribd.com intext:"John Doe" intext:"location" OR intext:"coordinates" OR intext:"geotag"** (Figure 5.55).

Figure 5.55 Dork to find metadata in documents.

5.6 OSINT EMAIL IDENTIFICATION

- To identify email in corporate reports or proposals looking for the specific email format within the document content (intext) and restrict the search to documents titled as 'corporate report' or 'proposal.,' use Dork **intext:"email: username@domain.com" intitle:"corporate report" OR intitle:"proposal" filetype:pdf OR filetype:docx** as shown in Figure 5.56.

- To find email references of say Elon Musk via his X email ID for sensitive contracts or agreements, use Dork as displayed in Figure 5.57 as **intext:"username@domain.com" intitle:"sensitive contract" OR intitle:"restricted agreement" filetype:pdf OR filetype:docx**.

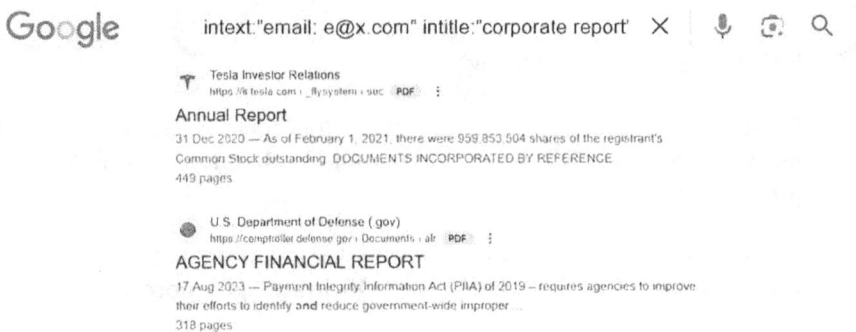

Figure 5.56 Identify corporate email reports.

Google   intitle:"index of intext:"database.sql" OR intext:"(✕ ⬇ ⊙ ᴏ

Exploit-DB
https://www.exploit-db.com › ghdb ⋮

"index of" "database.sql.zip" - Sensitive Directories GHDB ...

4 Sept 2018 — "index of" "database.sql.zip" This Google Dork discovers servers with open directories exposing database backup files.

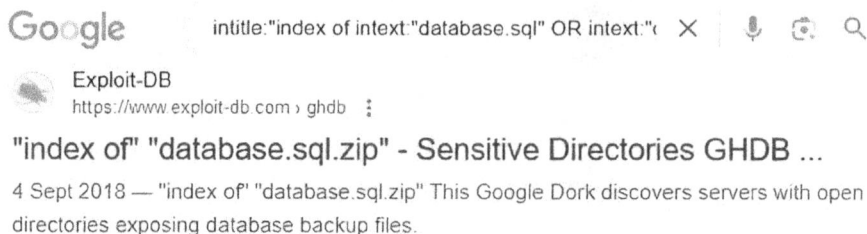

Figure 5.57 Search email references in sensitive contracts or agreements.

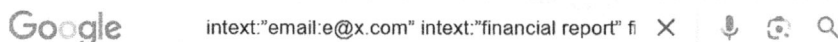

Google   intext:"email:e@x.com" intext:"financial report" fi ✕ ⬇ ⊙ ᴏ

Figure 5.58 Search emails in financial reports.

- Google dock to locate emails in financial report document containing both the specific email format and references to 'financial report' is presented in Figure 5.58 as **intext:"email: username@domain.com" intext:"financial report" filetype:pdf OR filetype:docx.**

5.7 NETWORK SECURITY ASSESSMENT DORKS

- Dork for searching exposed Network Devices is displayed in Figure 5.59 and is listed as **intitle:"index of" AND ("router login" OR "device settings") AND ext:(txt OR cfg OR conf).**

- Google Dork to find exposed Configuration Files is presented in Figure 5.60 as **intitle:"index of" intext:"config.yml" OR intext:"database.yml" OR intext:"settings.py".**

- Google dock to find vulnerable webcams is presented in Figure 5.61 as **intitle:webcam" inurl:"/view'.**

- Google dock to find sensitive server log files is **intitle:"index of intext:"access.log' OR intext: "error.log"' OR intext:"server.log"** as presented in Figure 5.62.

- Figure 5.63 illustrates Google Dork for exposed Git Repositories using **intitle: "index of" inurl:".git" OR inurl:".gitignore".**

Google   intitle:"index of" AND ("router login" OR "device   ✕ ⬇ ⊙ ᴏ

Figure 5.59 Search exposed network devices.

Google   intitle:"index of" intext:"config.yml" OR intext:"da   X   🎤   📷   🔍

All   Videos   Images   Shopping   Web   News   Books   ⋮ More   Tools

บริษัท วินเนอร์กรุ๊ป เอ็นเตอร์ไพรซ์ จำกัด (มหาชน)
https://www.winnergroup.co.th › files › www-database   ⋮

Index of /files/cache/system/db/www-database.yml

Index of /files/cache/system/db/www-**database.yml**. [ICO], Name · Last modified · Size ·
Description. [PARENTDIR], Parent Directory, -

Figure 5.60 Exposed configuration files.

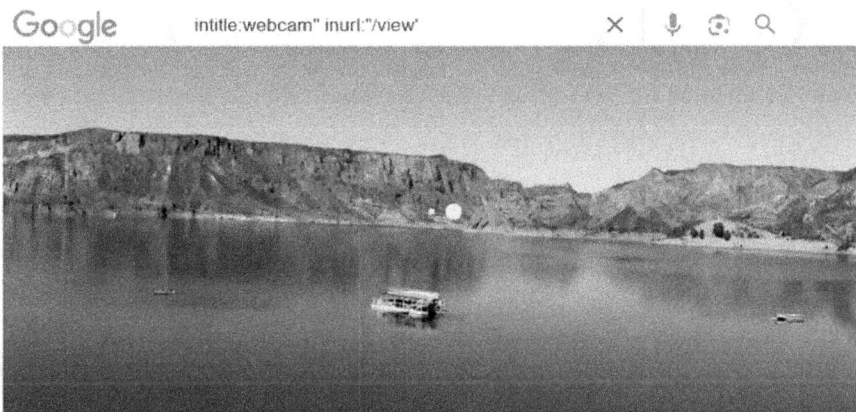

Google   intitle:webcam" inurl:"/view'   X   🎤   📷   🔍

Figure 5.61 Vulnerable webcams.

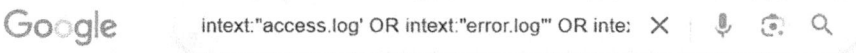

Google   intext:"access.log' OR intext:"error.log'" OR inte: X   🎤   📷   🔍

Figure 5.62 Finding sensitive server log files.

- Dork for finding open network devices is presented in Figure 5.64 as intitle:"index of" intext: "config.xml OR intext:"status.xml" OR intext: "network.xml".

- Google dock to find exposed cloud storage as presented in Figure 5.65 as intitle: "index of" intext: "aws_access_key" OR intext: "gcp_credentials.json" OR intext: "azure_storage_account".

- Dork for insecure API endpoints is displayed in Figure 5.66 as intitle:"index of" inurl:"/api" OR inurl:"/api/v1".

Google   intitle:"index of" inurl:".git" OR inurl:".gitignore"

GitHub
https://github.com › jonschlinkert › index-of › blob ›   ⋮

index-of/.gitignore at master · jonschlinkert/index-of

Get the index of the first element in an array that returns truthy for the given value, using strict equality for comparisons. - index-of/.gitignore at ...

GitHub
https://github.com › stdlib-js › utils-index-of › blob ›   ⋮

utils-index-of/.gitignore at main

Return the first index at which a given element can be found. - utils-index-of/.gitignore at main stdlib-js/utils-index-of.

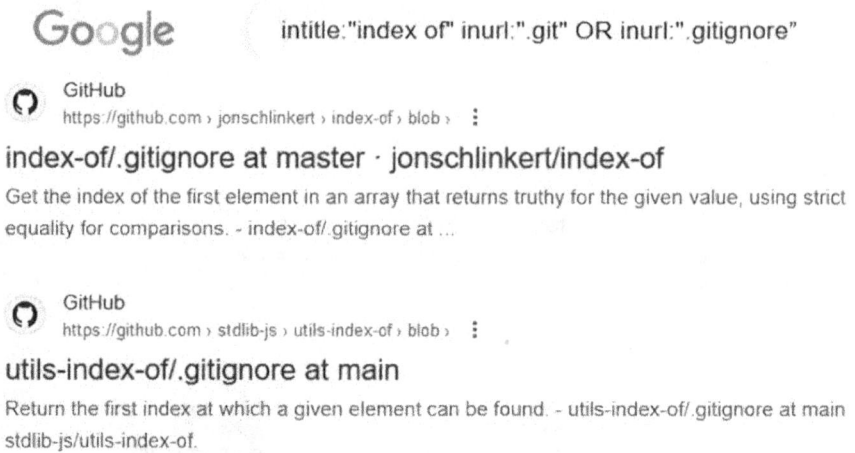

Figure 5.63 Exposed Git Repositories.

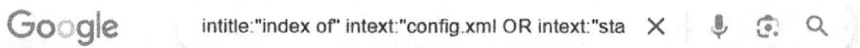

Google   intitle:"index of" intext:"config.xml OR intext:"sta   ✕   🎤   📷   🔍

Figure 5.64 Finding open network devices.

Google   intitle:"index of" intext:"aws_access_key" OR inl   ✕   🎤   📷   🔍

GitHub Pages
https://ansible-collections.github.io › main › collections   ⋮

Index of all Collection Environment Variables

The profile option is mutually exclusive with the **aws_access_key**, aws_secret_key and security_token options. The boto_profile alias has been deprecated and will ...

Ansible Documentation
https://docs.ansible.com › ansible › latest › collections   ⋮

Index of all Collection Environment Variables

AWS_ACCESS_KEY . See the documentations for the options where this environment variable is used. Used by: amazon.aws.aws_account_attribute lookup plugin ...

Figure 5.65 Exposed cloud storage.

- Google Dork to find exposed databases is presented in Figure 5.67 as **intitle: index of intext: "database.sql" OR intext: "dump.sql" OR intext: "backup.sql"**.

Google intitle:"index of" inurl:"/api" OR inurl:"/api/v1" ✕ 🎤 📷 🔍

OpenStack
https://docs.openstack.org › api-ref ⋮

Index of /api-ref

Index of /api-ref ; [PARENTDIR], Parent Directory ; [DIR], accelerator/, 2024-10-17 02:35 ; [DIR], admin-logic/, 2024-07-11 00:42 ...

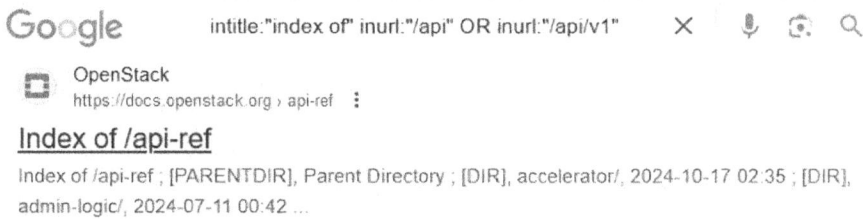

Figure 5.66 Insecure API endpoints.

Google intitle:"index of intext:"database.sql" OR intext:" ✕ 🎤 📷 🔍

Exploit-DB
https://www.exploit-db.com › ghdb ⋮

"index of" "database.sql.zip" - Sensitive Directories GHDB ...

4 Sept 2018 — "index of" "database.sql.zip" This Google Dork discovers servers with open directories exposing database backup files.

Figure 5.67 Exposed databases.

Google intitle:"error message' intext:"stack trace' OR int ✕ 🎤 📷 🔍

Figure 5.68 Information disclosure in error messages.

Google intitle:"index of" inurl:".php' OR inurl:".asp" OR ii ✕ 🎤 📷 🔍

Figure 5.69 Exposed web application source code.

- Dork for information disclosure in error messages is displayed in Figure 5.68 as intitle:"error message' intext:"stack trace' OR intext:"exception details".

- Google Dork for exposed Web Application source code is presented in Figure 5.69 as intitle: "index of" inurl: ".php' OR inurl:".asp" OR inurl:".js' OR inurl:".html".

- Dork for leaked security configuration files is displayed in Figure 5.70 as intitle: "index of" intext: "security.yml" OR intext: "secrets. properties".

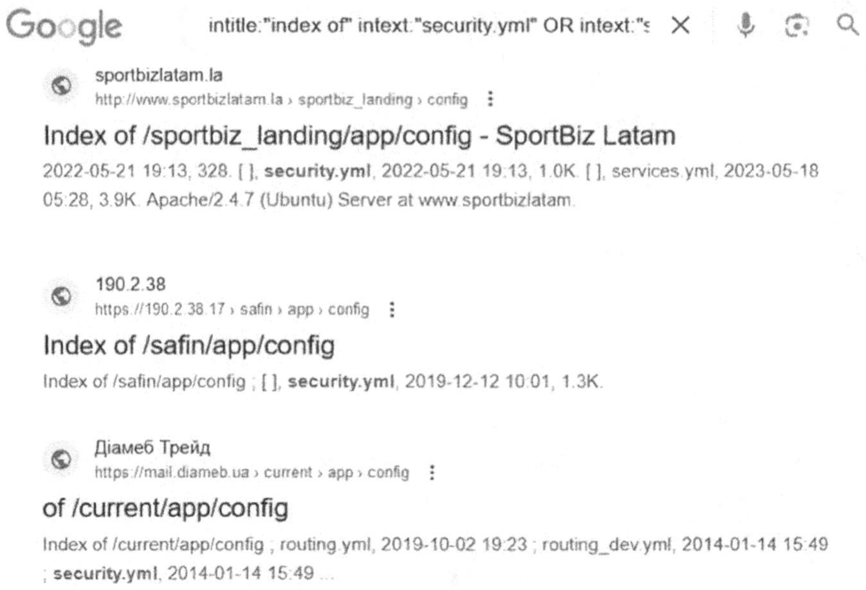

Google   intitle:"index of" intext:"security.yml" OR intext:"s   ✕   🎤   📷   🔍

⊙   sportbizlatam.la
     http://www.sportbizlatam.la › sportbiz_landing › config   ⋮

Index of /sportbiz_landing/app/config - SportBiz Latam

2022-05-21 19:13, 328. [ ], **security.yml**, 2022-05-21 19:13, 1.0K. [ ], services.yml, 2023-05-18
05:28, 3.9K. Apache/2.4.7 (Ubuntu) Server at www.sportbizlatam.

⊙   190.2.38
     https://190.2.38.17 › safin › app › config   ⋮

Index of /safin/app/config

Index of /safin/app/config ; [ ], **security.yml**, 2019-12-12 10:01, 1.3K.

⊙   Діамеб Трейд
     https://mail.diameb.ua › current › app › config   ⋮

of /current/app/config

Index of /current/app/config ; routing.yml, 2019-10-02 19:23 ; routing_dev.yml, 2014-01-14 15:49
; **security.yml**, 2014-01-14 15:49 ...

Figure 5.70 Leaked security configuration files.

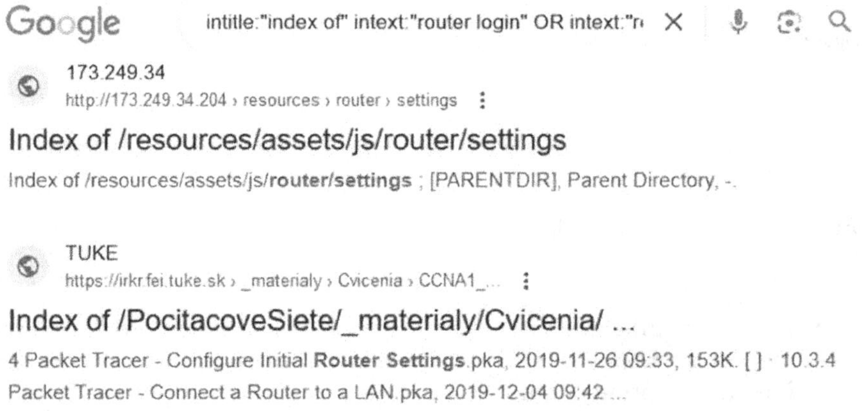

Google   intitle:"index of" intext:"router login" OR intext:"r   ✕   🎤   📷   🔍

⊙   173.249.34
     http://173.249.34.204 › resources › router › settings   ⋮

Index of /resources/assets/js/router/settings

Index of /resources/assets/js/**router/settings** ; [PARENTDIR], Parent Directory, -.

⊙   TUKE
     https://irkr.fei.tuke.sk › _materialy › Cvicenia › CCNA1_...   ⋮

Index of /PocitacoveSiete/_materialy/Cvicenia/ ...

4 Packet Tracer - Configure Initial **Router Settings**.pka, 2019-11-26 09:33, 153K. [ ] · 10.3.4
Packet Tracer - Connect a Router to a LAN.pka, 2019-12-04 09:42 ...

Figure 5.71 Exposed network devices.

- Dork for exposed network router and switches is presented in Figure 5.71 as **intitle: "index of" intext: "router login" OR intext: "router settings"**.

Google   intitle:"index of" intext:".s3.amazonaws.com' OR   ✕   🎤   📷   🔍

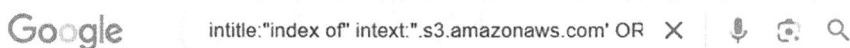

Figure 5.72 Open Amazon Web services $3 Buckets.

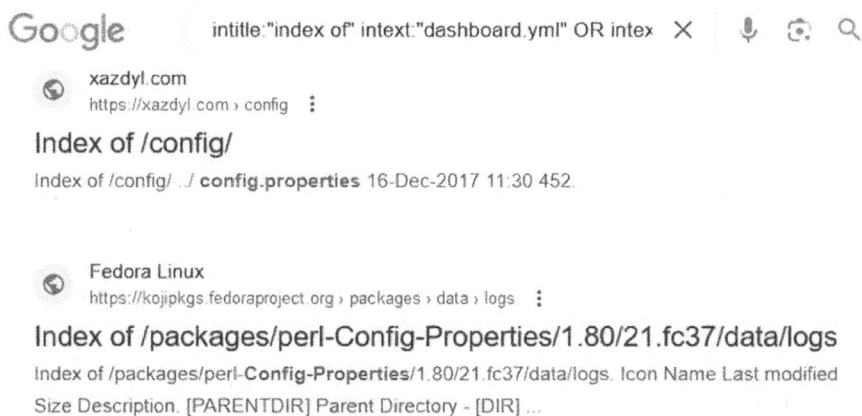

Google   intitle:"index of" intext:"dashboard.yml" OR intex   ✕   🎤   📷   🔍

◎   xazdyl.com
https://xazdyl.com › config   ⋮

Index of /config/

Index of /config/ ../ **config.properties** 16-Dec-2017 11:30 452.

◎   Fedora Linux
https://kojipkgs.fedoraproject.org › packages › data › logs   ⋮

Index of /packages/perl-Config-Properties/1.80/21.fc37/data/logs

Index of /packages/perl-**Config-Properties**/1.80/21.fc37/data/logs. Icon Name Last modified
Size Description. [PARENTDIR] Parent Directory - [DIR] ...

Figure 5.73 Exposed configuration dashboards.

- Google Dork for open Amazon Web services $3 Buckets is displayed in Figure 5.72 as **intitle: "index of" intext:".s3.amazonaws.com' OR intext:".s3-eu-west-1.amazonaws.com"**.

- Dork to find exposed configuration dashboards is displayed in Figure 5.73 as **intitle: "index of" intext:"dashboard.yml" OR intext:"settings.conf" OR intext:"config.properties"**.

- Dork to search for exposed API documentation as displayed in Figure 5.74 as **intitle:"index of" intext:"api-docs.json" OR intext:"swagger.json.**

- Google Dork for vulnerable WordPress Plugins is displayed in Figure 5.75 as **intitle:"index of" inurl:" wp-content/plugins"**.

- Dork for performing OSINT on company employees is presented in Figure 5.76 as **intext:"site:linkedin.com/in/" OR intext:"site:twitter. com/ OR intext:"site:github.com/*.**

- Dork for searching vulnerable IoT Devices on the internet is listed in Figure 5.77 as **intitle:"IoT device" OR intitle:"smart home" AND ext:(xml OR json OR cfg).**

Google   intitle:"index of" intext:"api-docs.json" OR intext: ✕   🎤   📷   🔍

Apache Pulsar
https://pulsar.apache.org › swagger   ⋮

Index of /swagger/2.3.2

Index of /swagger/2.3.2 ; [PARENTDIR], Parent Directory ; [ ], **swagger.json**, 2022-05-17 03:12 ;
[ ], swaggerfunctions.json, 2022-05-17 03:12 ...

Apache Pulsar
https://pulsar.apache.org › swagger   ⋮

Index of /swagger/3.2.2

Index of /swagger/3.2.2 ; [PARENTDIR], Parent Directory ; [ ], **swagger.json**, 2024-04-02 06:42 ;
[ ], swaggerfunctions.json, 2024-04-02 06:42 ...

Figure 5.74 Exposed API documentation.

Google   intitle:"index of" inurl:" wp-content/plugins"   ✕   🎤   📷   🔍

MOYCOR
https://moycor.com › wp-content › plugins   ⋮

Index of /wp-content/plugins

Index of /wp-content/plugins ; [PARENTDIR], Parent Directory ; [DIR], Basic-Auth-master/,
2018-11-08 16:03 ; [DIR], advanced-custom-fields/, 2019-04-17 11:45 ...

MGM University
https://mgmu.ac.in › wp-content › plugins   ⋮

Index of /wp-content/plugins

Index of /wp-content/plugins. Parent Directory · js_composer/ · porto-functionality/ · revslider/

Figure 5.75 List of vulnerable WordPress Plugins.

- Dork for finding exposed CCTV Cameras or video feeds is presented in Figure 5.78 as **intitle:"WJ-NT104 Main" OR intitle:"webcamXP 5" inurl:8080.**

- Google Dork for vulnerable FTP Servers or Credentials is presented in Figure 5.79 as **intitle:"index of" AND ("ftp" OR "credentials") AND ext:(txt OR ini OR cfg OR log).**

- Dork for finding open RDP Connections or Instances is presented in Figure 5.80 as **intitle:"index of" AND ("rdp" OR "remote desktop connection") AND ext:(ini OR cfg OR conf).**

Google   intext:"site:linkedin.com/in/" OR intext:"site:twitte   ✕   🎤   📷   🔍

Figure 5.76 OSINT on employees.

Google   intitle:"IoT device" OR intitle:"smart home" AND   ✕   🎤   📷   🔍

Figure 5.77 Vulnerable IoT devices.

Figure 5.78 Exposed CCTV camera and video feeds.

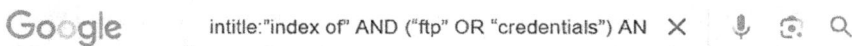

Google   intitle:"index of" AND ("ftp" OR "credentials") AN   ✕   🎤   📷   🔍

Figure 5.79 Vulnerable FTP servers or credentials.

These tools collectively contribute to the OSINT lifecycle, from data collection and analysis to visualization. It's essential for OSINT practitioners to be familiar with a variety of tools and choose the ones that best suit their specific investigative needs. Additionally, ethical considerations and adherence to legal boundaries should always be prioritized in OSINT activities.

Google   intitle:"index of" AND ("rdp" OR "remote desktop   ✕   🎤   📷   🔍

217.160.255
http://217.160.255.254 › landingpage › etc › supervisor ⋮

of /backup_github/08_2024/landingpage/alpine_xfce_rdp/etc ...

Index of /backup_github/08_2024/landingpage/alpine_xfce_rdp/etc/supervisor.d. Parent
Directory · 00-system.conf · 01-rdp.conf.

FreeRDP
https://pub.freerdp.com › repositories › deb › buster ⋮

Index of /repositories/deb/buster/

Index of /repositories/deb/buster/ ../ conf/ 27-Jul-2017 10:14 - db/ 10-Oct-2023 02:34 - dists/ 13-
Aug-2018 06:42 - pool/ 27-Jul-2017 13:38 -

Figure 5.80 Open RDP connections or instances.

5.8 CONCLUSION

OSINT search engine techniques are essential for navigating the vast landscape of online information. By mastering the tools and techniques presented in this chapter, individuals can effectively gather, analyze, and visualize data from various sources. The tools and search portals discussed in this chapter, including Maltego, OSINT framework, Shodan, and Google Dorking, offer powerful capabilities for conducting OSINT investigations. By understanding the strengths and limitations of each tool, individuals can select the most appropriate ones for their specific needs. It is important to remember that while these tools provide valuable insights, they should be used responsibly and ethically. Privacy and integrity should always be top priorities when conducting OSINT investigations. By following best practices and adhering to ethical guidelines, individuals can leverage the power of search engine techniques to gain valuable intelligence while respecting the rights of others. By the end of this chapter, readers will have developed a strong foundation in search engine techniques and gained the skills necessary to conduct effective OSINT investigations. Armed with this knowledge, individuals can confidently navigate the digital landscape and uncover valuable information from publicly available sources.

REFERENCES

1. "OSINT," 2025. https://www.maltego.com/categories/osint/
2. Maltego, "What Is Maltego?" 2019. https://docs.maltego.com/support/solutions/articles/15000019166-what-is-maltego-
3. "Downloads," 2019. https://www.maltego.com/downloads/

4. Tineye, "TinEye Reverse Image Search," 2019. https://tineye.com/
5. C. Dalby, "Ex-Governor Bribed by Jalisco Cartel Tests Mexico's Anti-Corruption Resolve," May 23, 2019. https://insightcrime.org/news/brief/governor-bribed-jalisco-cartel-mexico-anti-corruption (accessed Oct. 28, 2024).
6. OCCRP Aleph, 2024. https://aleph.occrp.org/ (accessed Oct. 28, 2024).
7. J. Nordine, "OSINT Framework," 2019. https://osintframework.com/ (accessed Jan. 29, 2024).
8. Shodan, 2013. https://www.shodan.io/ (accessed Jan. 29, 2024).
9. "What Is Supervisory Control and Data Acquisition (SCADA)?" Spiceworks. https://www.spiceworks.com/tech/tech-general/articles/what-is-supervisory- control-and-data-acquisition-scada/
10. UNITRONICS, "What is PLC? Programmable Logic Controller," 2023. https://www.unitronicsplc.com/what-is-plc-programmable-logic-controller/
11. "Industrial Control System – Definition," https://www.trendmicro.com/vinfo/in/security/definition/industrial-control-system
12. "IndMALL Automation," Aug. 30, 2024. https://www.indmall.in/faq/what-is-the-502-port-used-for/
13. RecordedFuture, "What Are Google Dorks?" May 28, 2024. https://www.recordedfuture.com/threat-intelligence-101/threat-analysis-techniques/google-Dorks

Chapter 6

Email address intelligence

6.1 INTRODUCTION

Email address intelligence has emerged as a powerful tool in the digital age, enabling businesses to unlock the potential of data. By analyzing and interpreting data associated with email addresses, businesses can gain valuable insights into customer preferences, behaviors, and online activities. This information can be leveraged to enhance customer experiences, improve marketing effectiveness, and mitigate fraud risks. One of the key benefits of email address intelligence is its ability to enhance customer understanding. By analyzing email addresses, businesses can create detailed customer profiles, including demographics, interests, and purchase history. This information can be used to segment customers into specific groups, allowing for targeted marketing campaigns and personalized experiences. Additionally, tracking email interactions, such as open rates and click-through rates, can provide insights into customer behavior and preferences.

Email address intelligence also plays a crucial role in improving marketing effectiveness. By understanding customer preferences, businesses can deliver highly targeted marketing campaigns that resonate with specific audience segments. This personalized approach can increase engagement and conversion rates. Furthermore, analyzing historical data can help predict future customer behavior, allowing for proactive marketing strategies. Fraud prevention and risk mitigation are other important applications of email address intelligence. By identifying suspicious activity, such as fraudulent account creation or identity theft, businesses can take proactive measures to protect their systems and customers. Additionally, real-time verification of email addresses can help prevent fraudulent transactions and chargebacks.

Email address intelligence contributes to data enrichment and cleansing. By identifying and correcting errors in email databases, businesses can ensure data accuracy and integrity. Furthermore, by enriching email addresses with additional information, such as full names, job titles, and company names, businesses can gain a more comprehensive view of their

 DOI: 10.1201/9781003497615-6

audience. While email address intelligence offers significant benefits, it is essential to use it responsibly and ethically. Businesses must comply with data privacy regulations to protect customer data. Transparency and consent are crucial when collecting and using personal information. By striking a balance between leveraging the power of data and respecting individual privacy, businesses can harness the full potential of email address intelligence.

Use of Email Intelligence:

- Strategic Insights: Email address intelligence offers a deeper understanding of individual behavior by analyzing email interactions and associated data. By examining how people engage with content, their device usage, and demographic information, businesses can tailor their messaging to resonate with specific audiences. This personalized approach not only enhances customer experiences but also strengthens brand loyalty and drives higher response rates.
- Deeper Understanding: Email address intelligence distills vast amounts of raw data into actionable insights. By collecting, cleaning, analyzing, and interpreting data from various online sources, businesses can gain a deeper understanding of customer behavior across multiple websites. This transformation from raw data to meaningful information empowers organizations to make informed decisions, personalize marketing efforts, and strengthen customer relationships.
- Identity Linkage and Refinement: Email address intelligence enhances customer profiles by linking and verifying multiple identifiers like email addresses, names, and postal addresses. By resolving incomplete information and ensuring data consistency, businesses can create a unified view of their customers across different channels. This comprehensive understanding enables organizations to deliver seamless omnichannel experiences and personalized interactions.
- Foundation for Analytics: Leveraging email address intelligence to gain a deeper understanding of your audience is crucial for future-proofing your business. By utilizing advanced technologies like analytics, data science, machine learning, and AI, organizations can build on this foundation to adapt to evolving customer needs and market trends. This proactive approach ensures that marketing and engagement strategies remain effective and relevant.
- Enhanced Security and Protection: Email address intelligence goes beyond data analysis to provide a crucial layer of security. By verifying and validating email identities, businesses can strengthen their defenses against fraud and protect their databases from malicious actors. This proactive approach ensures data integrity, minimizes the risk of phishing attacks and regulatory fines, and ultimately provides peace of mind knowing that insights and strategies are built upon reliable and secure data.

6.2 ANALYZING USE CASES

This section presents multiple use case steps based on portals and tools to enumerate email address and phone numbers to gather details and provide the bigger picture. This covers the following:

- Uncovers the user's full name and phone linked to the email address on online public sources.
- Detects invalid emails with unusual string composition or spam traps with checks deliverability.
- Presents the list of accounts linked to an email address across a vast range of digital services.
- Detects maturity of email addresses, including free, disposable or newly registered domains.
- Reviews email composition and domain checks for unusual patterns, placeholders, and redirects.
- Accesses insights into the company linked to a business email (e.g. employees, annual revenue).
- Leverages AI-powered analysis of users' profile pictures, including age and gender estimation.
- Accesses a vast library of known data breaches in which the assessed email address was found.
- Flags negative news related to a specific user's email on media sources and official records.

6.2.1 Use case #1: email address analysis of valid ID

Step 1: Lookup for a valid, demo email ID using 'Trustful' portal [1] as illustrated in Figure 6.1; this displays a poor score highlighted with two risks: data breaches and no vowels in email address. The email address has four trust signals: email is in use, email not from a newly created domain, associated with a company, and email has image of a person related with this email address.

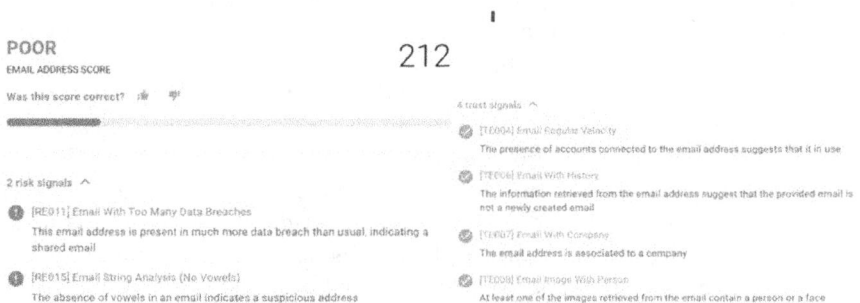

POOR
EMAIL ADDRESS SCORE

212

Was this score correct?

4 trust signals

[TE004] Email Regular Velocity
The presence of accounts connected to the email address suggests that it in use

2 risk signals

[TE006] Email With History
The information retrieved from the email address suggest that the provided email is not a newly created email

[RE011] Email With Too Many Data Breaches
This email address is present in much more data breach than usual, indicating a shared email

[TE007] Email With Company
The email address is associated to a company

[RE015] Email String Analysis (No Vowels)
The absence of vowels in an email indicates a suspicious address

[TE008] Email Image With Person
At least one of the images retrieved from the email contain a person or a face

Figure 6.1   Email address lookup.

Step 2: Further analysis reveals the full name, mobile, and connected profile having this email address as displayed in Figure 6.2. This also reveals the status, first seen (way back in 2016), and the email domain associated with this email.

Step 3: There are multiple mobile numbers and names associated with this email address, indicating that the user has changed mobile numbers and his/her names. The first and last breach dates are also revealed as illustrated in Figure 6.3.

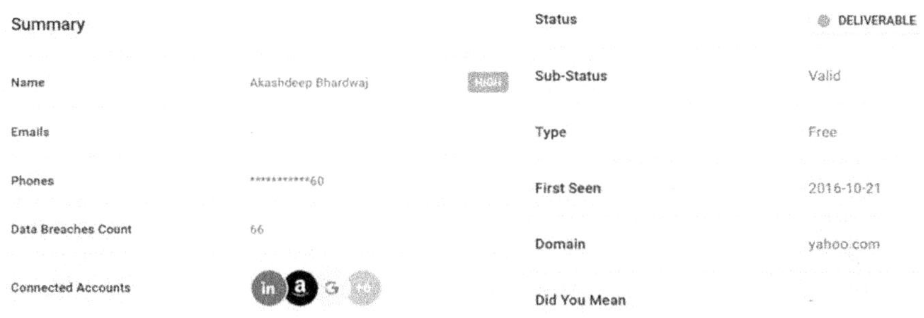

Summary			Status	DELIVERABLE
Name	Akashdeep Bhardwaj	HIGH	Sub-Status	Valid
Emails			Type	Free
Phones	***********60		First Seen	2016-10-21
Data Breaches Count	66		Domain	yahoo.com
Connected Accounts	(in) (a) G		Did You Mean	-

Figure 6.2 Email address related details found.

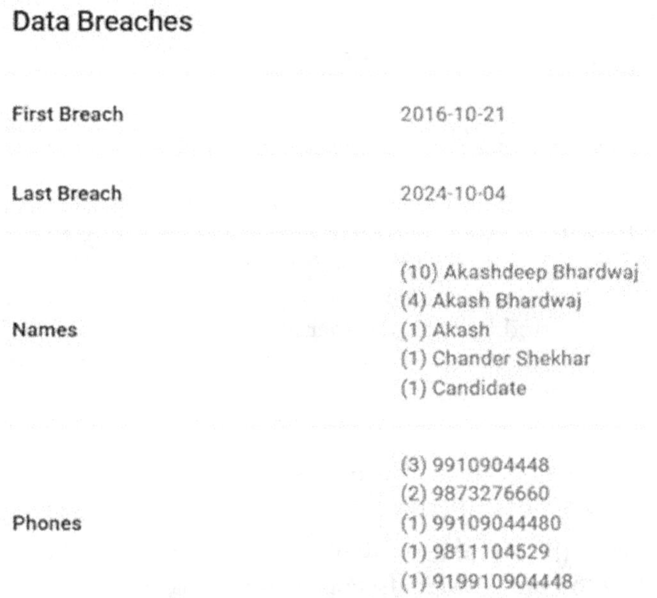

Data Breaches

First Breach	2016-10-21
Last Breach	2024-10-04
Names	(10) Akashdeep Bhardwaj (4) Akash Bhardwaj (1) Akash (1) Chander Shekhar (1) Candidate
Phones	(3) 9910904448 (2) 9873276660 (1) 99109044480 (1) 9811104529 (1) 919910904448

Figure 6.3 Mobiles associated with email found.

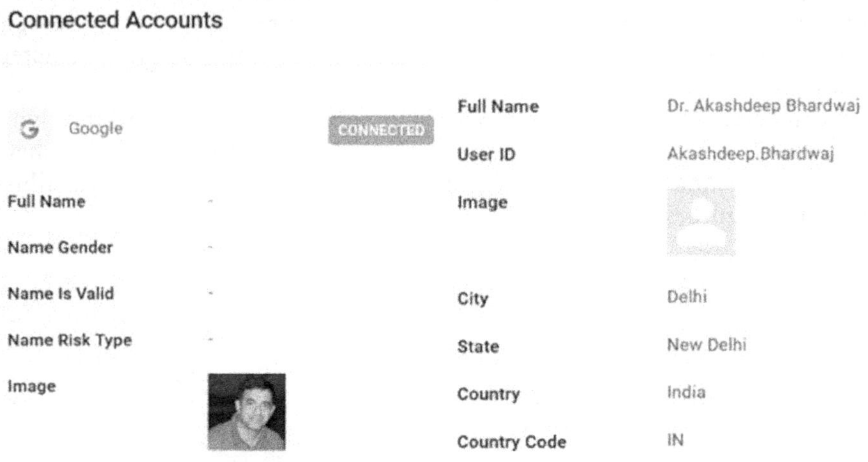

Connected Accounts

		Full Name	Dr. Akashdeep Bhardwaj
G Google	CONNECTED	User ID	Akashdeep.Bhardwaj
Full Name	-	Image	
Name Gender	-		
Name Is Valid	-	City	Delhi
Name Risk Type	-	State	New Delhi
Image		Country	India
		Country Code	IN

Figure 6.4   Email associated with Gmail.

Step 4: This account is also associated with Gmail; the full name is also revealed along with the city, state, and country where it was initially created as shown in Figure 6.4.

Step 5: There is a 99% face similarity match from Google for this email address user's face as illustrated in Figure 6.5.

6.2.2 Use case #2: email address analysis of potential spammers

Step 1: Lookup for the potential spammer email ID is illustrated in Figure 6.6; results in a poor score of 69 are highlighted with four risk signals and 1 trust signal.

Step 2: Analyzing further reveals the spammer's full name along with the number of breaches and connected social media and other portal accounts as shown in Figure 6.7. This email address is disposable and was first seen in 2021.

Step 3: Manual lookup also reveals the different names and phones changed over a period by the spammer as presented in Figure 6.8.

Step 4: This email address is connected to few web portals like Pinterest, Office 265, and Disney Plus but not to others as revealed in Figure 6.9.

6.2.3 Use case #3: email address analysis of spammers

Step 1: Lookup the spammer's email reveals a 'bad' score as illustrated in Figure 6.10 with four risk signals: email containing suspicious characters or numbers, absence of any connected accounts which indicates that the email address is probably used only for spamming and not connected to any web

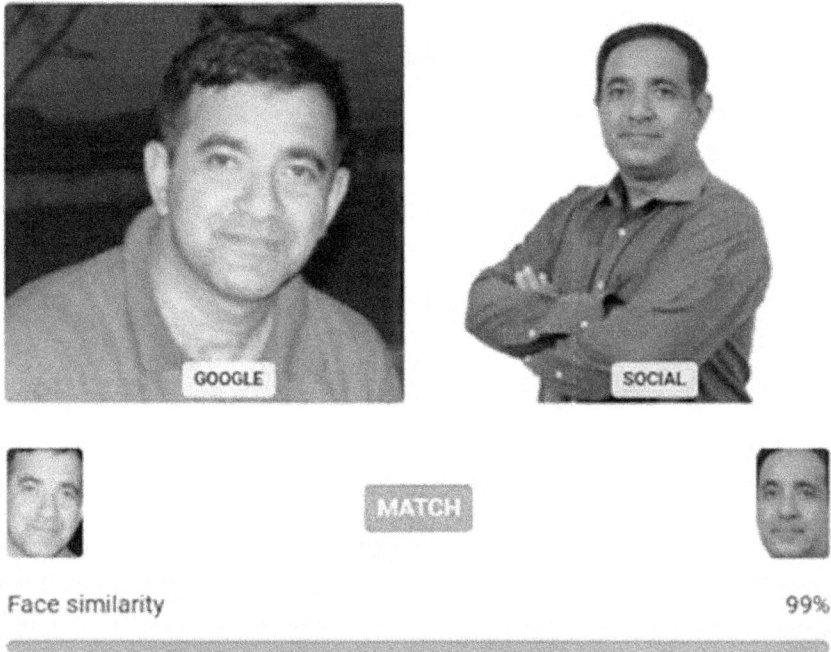

Figure 6.5   Face similarity found.

or social media portal accounts, and has a valid secondary email with limited engagement and no profile picture.

Step 2: Figure 6.11 reveals a name with a recent creation date.

Step 3: Investigating the email domain 'Mail.Ru' on WHOIS [2] reveals the country as Russia, created in 1997 by organization 'Moskva' using two name servers (ns1.mail.ru and ns2.mail.ru) as displayed in Figure 6.12.

Figure 6.13 further reveals this domain as a 'BAD' reputation score with email users also running a VPN to probably conceal their actual location.

6.2.4 Use case #4: TheHarvester

TheHarvester [3] is a powerful Python-based tool designed for gathering Open-Source Intelligence (OSINT) during the initial stages of a penetration test or red team engagement. It leverages various search engines and public databases to collect information about a target organization, including email addresses, subdomains, virtual hosts, open ports, banners, and employee names. By automating the process of searching multiple sources, TheHarvester significantly accelerates the reconnaissance phase of a security assessment.

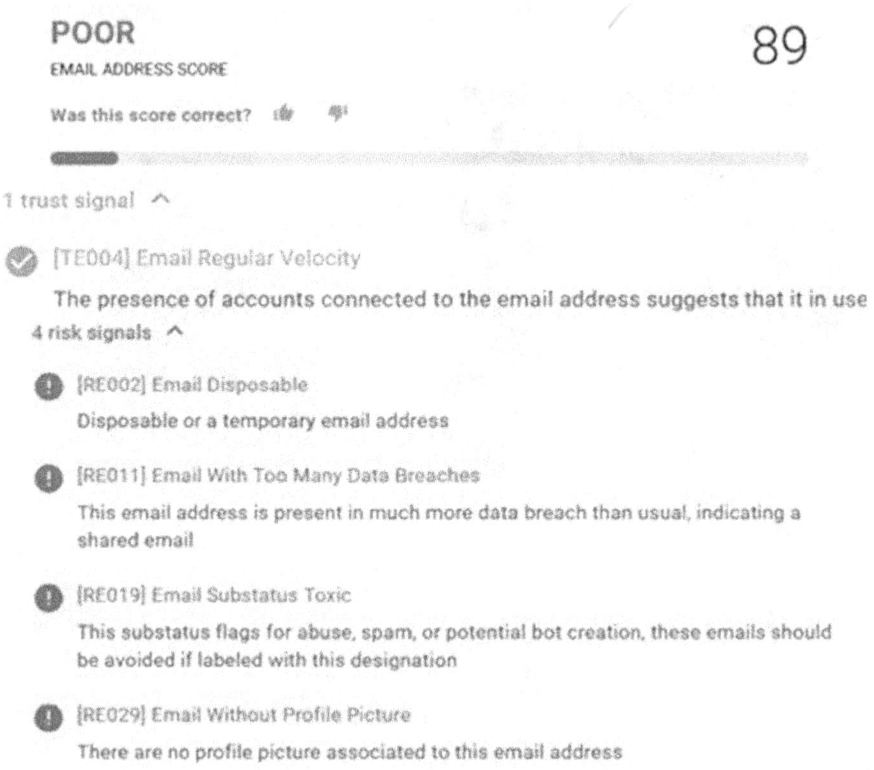

POOR

EMAIL ADDRESS SCORE

Was this score correct?   👍   👎

89

1 trust signal ∧

✓ [TE004] Email Regular Velocity

The presence of accounts connected to the email address suggests that it in use

4 risk signals ∧

! [RE002] Email Disposable

Disposable or a temporary email address

! [RE011] Email With Too Many Data Breaches

This email address is present in much more data breach than usual, indicating a shared email

! [RE019] Email Substatus Toxic

This substatus flags for abuse, spam, or potential bot creation, these emails should be avoided if labeled with this designation

! [RE029] Email Without Profile Picture

There are no profile picture associated to this email address

Figure 6.6   Email analysis of potential spammer.

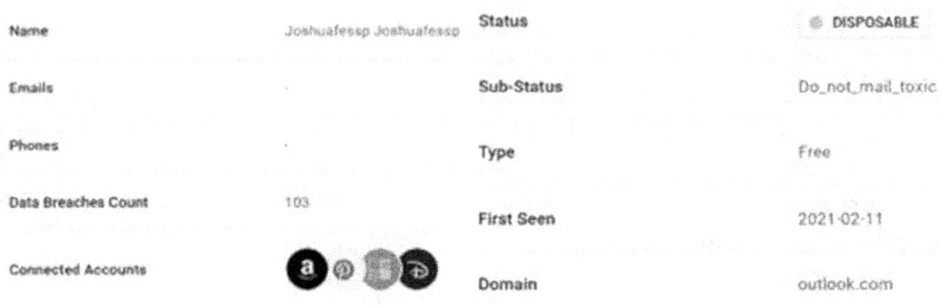

Name	Joshuafessp Joshuafessp	Status	⊚ DISPOSABLE
Emails	.	Sub-Status	Do_not_mail_toxic
Phones	.	Type	Free
Data Breaches Count	103	First Seen	2021-02-11
Connected Accounts	a ⊚ 🔵🔴	Domain	outlook.com

Figure 6.7   Spammer's full name, breached count, and connected accounts found.

The tool's core functionality revolves around its ability to query multiple search engines and databases simultaneously. These sources include popular search engines like Google, Bing, and Yahoo, as well as specialized platforms like Shodan, Censys, and Hunter.io. By utilizing these diverse sources, TheHarvester can uncover a wealth of information that might otherwise be difficult to obtain manually.

Names		Phones	
(2) Justinvef			(2) 85755833713
(2) Joshuades			(1) 87881219823
(2) Averillriz Averillriz			(1) 83681142183
(2) Joshuarer Joshuarer			(1) 83847636393
(2) Justintum Justintum			(1) 87829559323
(2) Joshuabut Joshuabut			(1) 84585449669
(2) Marianodob Marianodob			(1) 89652113634
(2) Marianobxu Marianobxu			(1) 85579188113
(1) Frankrew Frankrew			(1) 85574229899
(1) Calvinrourf			(1) 86212923945

Figure 6.8   Multiple names and phone numbers associated with spammer's email address.

Figure 6.9   Social media and web portals associated with spammer's address.

One of the key strengths of TheHarvester lies in its flexibility and customization options. Users can fine-tune the search parameters by specifying the target domain, search engine, number of results, and other relevant criteria. This allows for tailored reconnaissance efforts based on specific needs and objectives. Additionally, the tool supports various output formats, including plain text, CSV, and JSON, making it easy to analyze and process the gathered information. While TheHarvester is a valuable tool for ethical hackers and security professionals, it's important to use it responsibly and ethically. Misusing this tool for malicious purposes can have

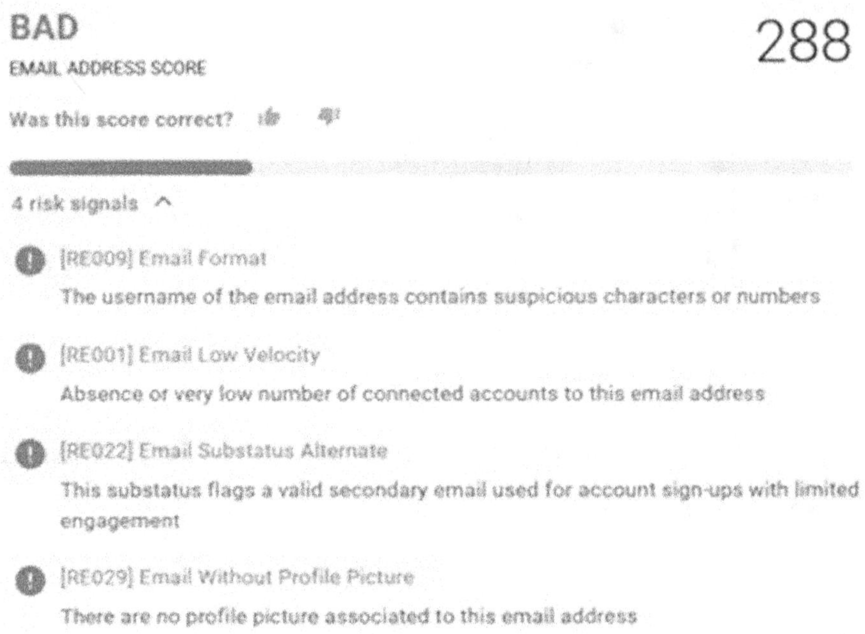

BAD

EMAIL ADDRESS SCORE

288

Was this score correct?

4 risk signals ∧

🔴 [RE009] Email Format

The username of the email address contains suspicious characters or numbers

🔴 [RE001] Email Low Velocity

Absence or very low number of connected accounts to this email address

🔴 [RE022] Email Substatus Alternate

This substatus flags a valid secondary email used for account sign-ups with limited engagement

🔴 [RE029] Email Without Profile Picture

There are no profile picture associated to this email address

Figure 6.10 'BAD' score email address confirmed.

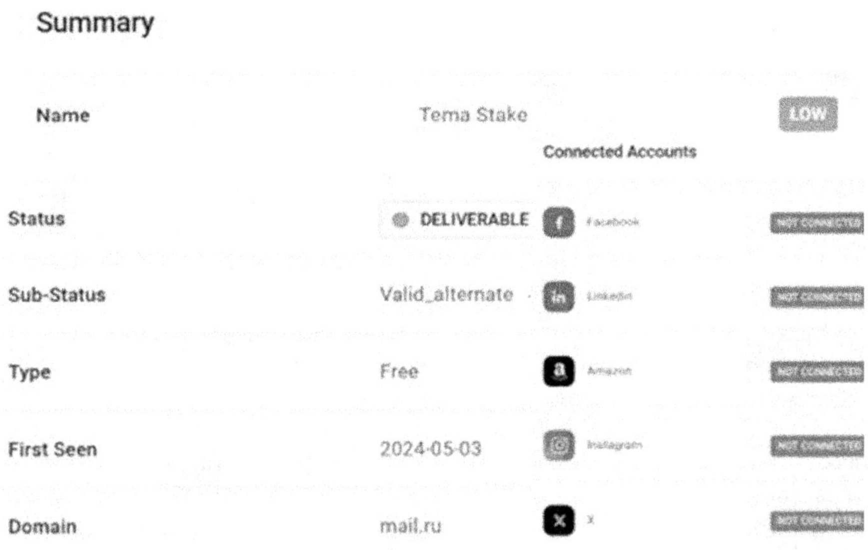

Summary

Name	Tema Stake			LOW
		Connected Accounts		
Status	● DELIVERABLE	f	Facebook	NOT CONNECTED
Sub-Status	Valid_alternate	in	Linkedin	NOT CONNECTED
Type	Free	a	Amazon	NOT CONNECTED
First Seen	2024-05-03	◉	Instagram	NOT CONNECTED
Domain	mail.ru	X	X	NOT CONNECTED

Figure 6.11 Spammer name, recent creation, and no connected accounts confirmed.

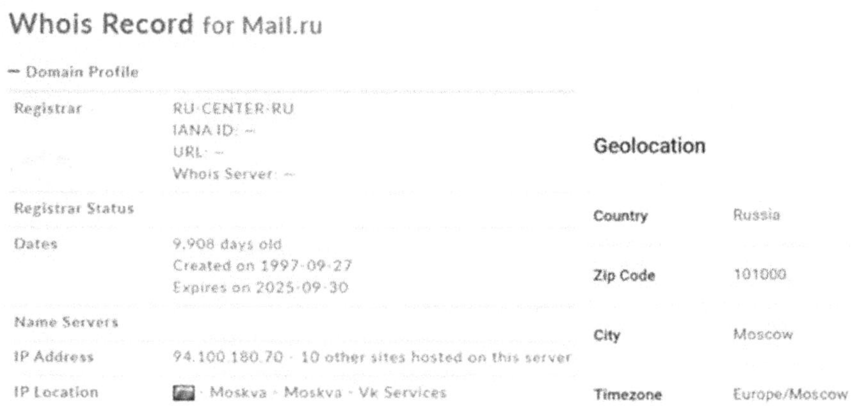

Whois Record for Mail.ru

— Domain Profile

Registrar	RU-CENTER-RU IANA ID: — URL: — Whois Server: —		**Geolocation**	
Registrar Status			**Country**	Russia
Dates	9,908 days old Created on 1997-09-27 Expires on 2025-09-30		**Zip Code**	101000
Name Servers			**City**	Moscow
IP Address	94.100.180.70 · 10 other sites hosted on this server			
IP Location	Moskva · Moskva · Vk Services		**Timezone**	Europe/Moscow

Figure 6.12   Investigating spammer's email domain.

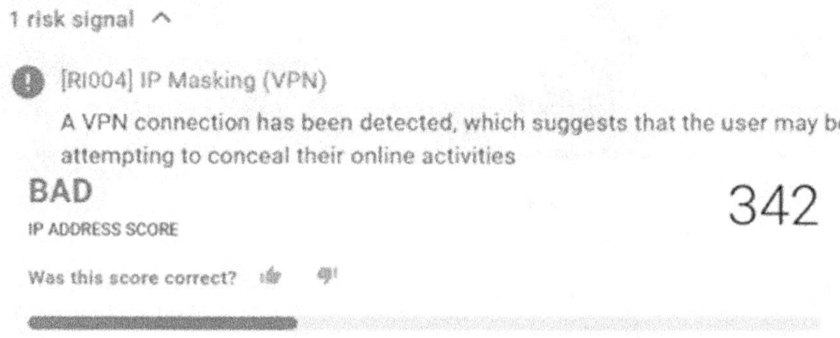

1 risk signal ∧

[RI004] IP Masking (VPN)

A VPN connection has been detected, which suggests that the user may be attempting to conceal their online activities

BAD

IP ADDRESS SCORE

Was this score correct?

342

Figure 6.13   Domain confirmed with 'BAD' reputation.

serious legal consequences. It's crucial to always adhere to ethical hacking principles and obtain proper authorization before conducting any reconnaissance activities.

Step 1: This tool is preinstalled in Kali Linux OS which I am using for this use case demo, else you can refer to the Laramies Github link as displayed in Figure 6.14.

Step 2: To install, simply Git clone and install this on Kali or Linux OS as shown in Figure 6.15.

Step 3: Figure 6.16 presents the result of attempt to get domain and email information for a specific target, in our case 'Tesla.com.' The search did not find any Emails of IP address but found forty-five subdomains using 'DNSDumpster' as the source.

Steo 4: Using 'URLScan' as the source, Figure 6.17 provides a lot more information.

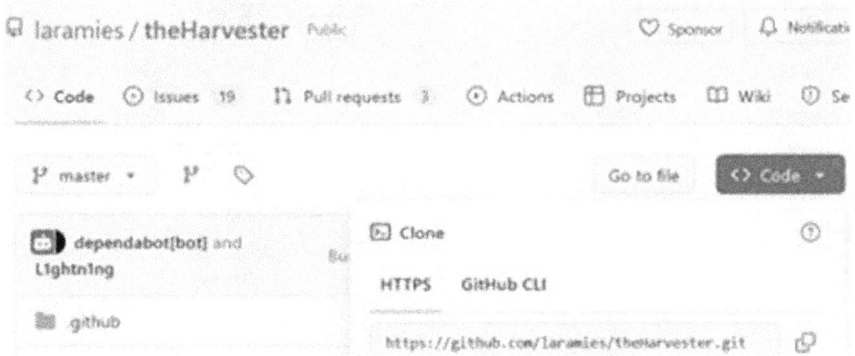

Figure 6.14   Github link for TheHarvester.

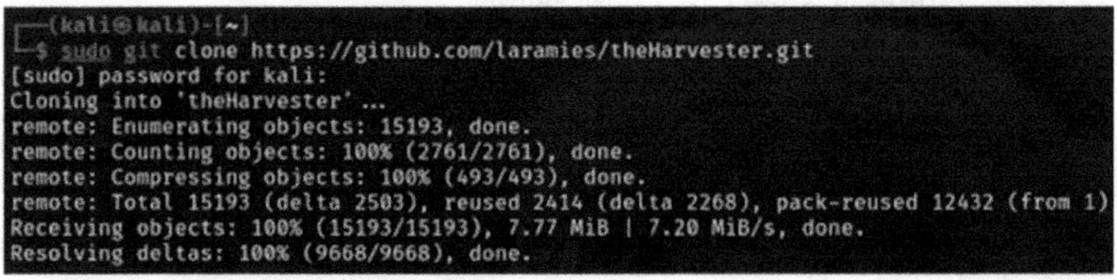

Figure 6.15   Installation process for TheHarvester.

6.2.5 Use case #5: Holehe

The Holehe [4] tool is a Python script to check if an email address is associated with social media and more than 120 other sites and runs seeking an email as the target as shown in Figure 6.18.

Step 2: This tool can be used to verify results from other OSINT tools as shown in Figure 6.19.

This process is known as information disclosure by Google and any attacker can utilize these steps to perform information gathering on social media for that user's Facebook and other accounts by filtering for the mobile numbers.

6.2.6 Use case #6: gather Gmail account information

Step 1: The objective for this use case is to find information associated with a Gmail account. Imagine you obtain someone's Gmail ID (say 'markus-brown'), head over to the Gmail Login page as shown in Figure 6.20.

Step 2: Click 'Next' option which confirms if that Gmail ID is Gmail Address or not as shown in Figure 6.21.

```
[*] Target: tesla.com

[*] Searching Dnsdumpster.

[*] No IPs found.

[*] No emails found.

[*] Hosts found: 45

apacvpn1.tesla.com
click.emails.tesla.com
cnvpn.tesla.com
cnvpn1.tesla.com
email1.tesla.com
emails.tesla.com
events.tesla.com
external-3pl-prd.tesla.com
external-automation.tesla.com
```

Figure 6.16   Attempts to get domain and email info.

```
[*] Target: tesla.com                    [*] IPs found: 47
[*] Searching urlscan.
                                         104.18.23.89
[*] ASNS found: 9                        104.76.100.49
                                         13.35.93.39
AS13335                                  148.66.136.57          [*] Hosts found: 14
AS16376                                  151.101.1.195
AS16509                                  162.159.137.83         asigateway-message-center-ownership.tesla.com
AS26625                                  172.66.44.60           business-ui-ownership.tesla.com
AS394695                                 172.66.46.225          cx-api-apac.tesla.com
AS30948                                  172.67.142.131         engage.tesla.com
AS32612                                  172.67.152.239         feedback.tesla.com
AS394496                                 172.67.218.68          logcollection.tesla.com
AS6A133                                  188.114.96.3           logcollector-ext.tesla.com
                                         188.114.97.3           api-supplier-gfo-stg.tesla.com
[*] Interesting Urls found: 10           198.54.116.25          secure-static-assets.tesla.com
                                         23.197.252.107         shop.tesla.com
https://asigateway-message-center-ownership.tesla.com/                         sso.tesla.com
https://business-ui-ownership.tesla.com/                                       toolbox.tesla.com
https://cx-api-apac.tesla.com/                                                 vantage-alerts.tesla.com
https://engage.tesla.com/static/mdfjs/web/viewer.html?
https://feedback.tesla.com/?ke=foru/SV_1XRJrRImyS1CarA8
https://logcollection.tesla.com/
```

Figure 6.17   Result with 'URLScan' as the source.

```
┌──(kali㉿kali)-[~]
└─$ sudo holehe
[sudo] password for kali:
usage: holehe [-h] [--only-used] [--no-color] [--no-clear] [-NP] [-C] [-T TIMEOUT] EMAIL [EMAIL ...]
holehe: error: the following arguments are required: EMAIL
```

Figure 6.18   Holele email.

Figure 6.19 'Holehe' validates for email existence.

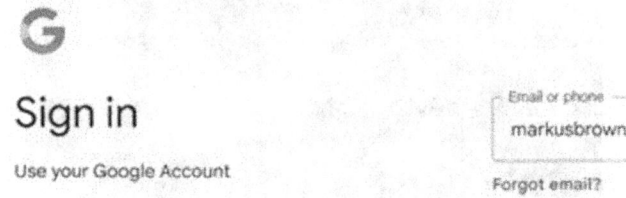

Figure 6.20 Gmail login page.

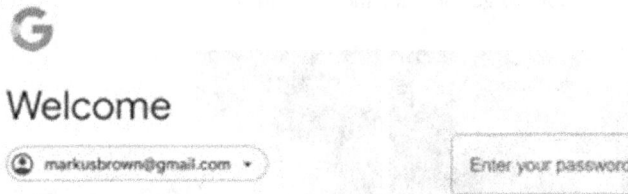

Figure 6.21 Gmail ID confirmation.

Step 3: Click 'Forgot Password' option to check options to recover that account as illustrated in Figure 6.22, which reveals that this user has an iPhone.

Step 4: Trying this process with another account (say 'markus.james') as shown in Figure 6.23.

Step 5: Click 'Next' option which confirms that the Gmail ID is an account on Google with the Gmail address as displayed in Figure 6.24.

Step 6: Clicking the 'Forgot Password' option reveals a US mobile number ending with '77' associated with this email address as illustrated in Figure 6.25

Google

Account recovery

To help keep your account safe, Google wants to
make sure it's really you trying to sign in

ⓐ markusbrown@gmail.com ⌄

**Use the Camera app on your iPhone to scan this
QR code:**

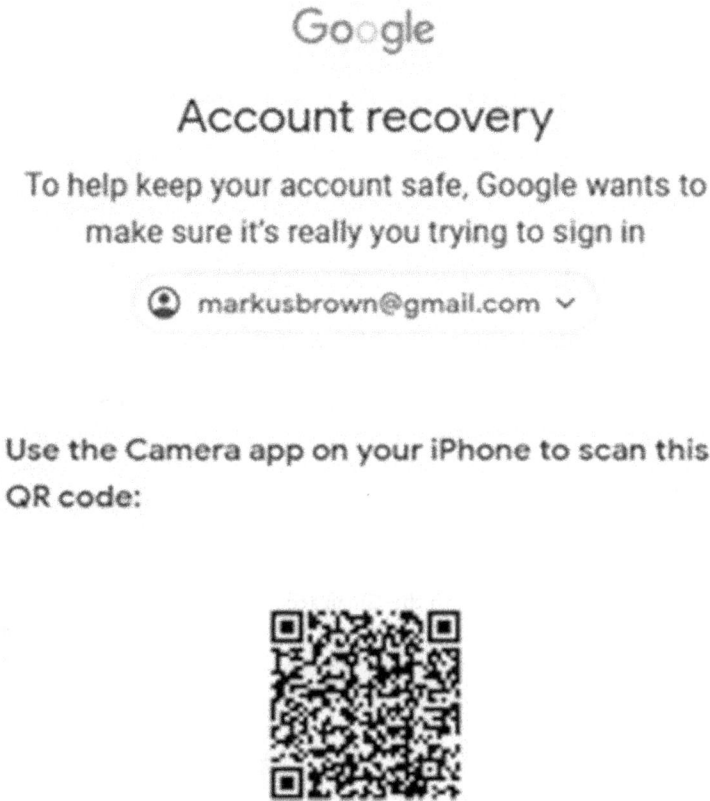

Figure 6.22 Check option to recover account.

G

Sign in

Use your Google Account

Email or phone
markus.james

Forgot email?

Figure 6.23 Check for another Gmail ID.

Step 7: Clicking the 'Try Another Way' option reveals another US mobile ending with '54' associated with this Gmail account, as displayed in Figure 6.26.

Step 8: Trying with another Gmail ID (say 'saadsarraj') as shown in Figure 6.27 confirms that Gmail ID is a Gmail address, but clicking the 'Forgot Password' option provides a different result mentioning that the phone cannot locate the device.

G

Welcome

markus.james@gmail.com ▾   Enter your password

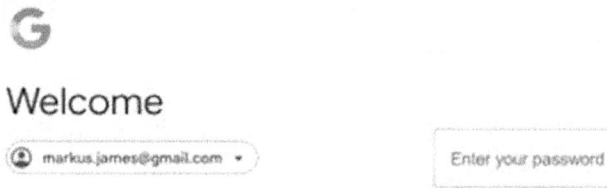

Figure 6.24   Gmail address confirmed.

G

Account recovery

To help keep your account safe, Google wants to
make sure it's really you trying to sign in

markus.james@gmail.com ▾

Confirm the phone number you provided in your security
settings: (•••) •••-••77

▓ ▾   Phone number

Figure 6.25   Mobile associated with the Gmail account.

G

Account recovery

To help keep your account safe, Google wants to
make sure it's really you trying to sign in

markus.james@gmail.com ▾

Confirm the phone number you provided in your security
settings: (•••) •••-••54

▓ ▾   Phone number

Figure 6.26   Second mobile associated with this Gmail account.

Google

Account recovery

To help keep your account safe, Google wants to
make sure it's really you trying to sign in

saadsarraj@gmail.com ▾

G

Sign in

Use your Google Account

Email or phone
saadsarraj

Forgot email?

Your phone can't locate your device

Move your phone closer to the device where you're signing
in, and then try again

Try another way ▷   Try again

Figure 6.27   Information gathering third account.

Google

Account recovery

To help keep your account safe, Google wants to
make sure it's really you trying to sign in

(•) saadsarraj@gmail.com ∨

Confirm the phone number you provided in your security
settings: ·· ·· ·· ·· 6d[

▇ ▾   Phone number

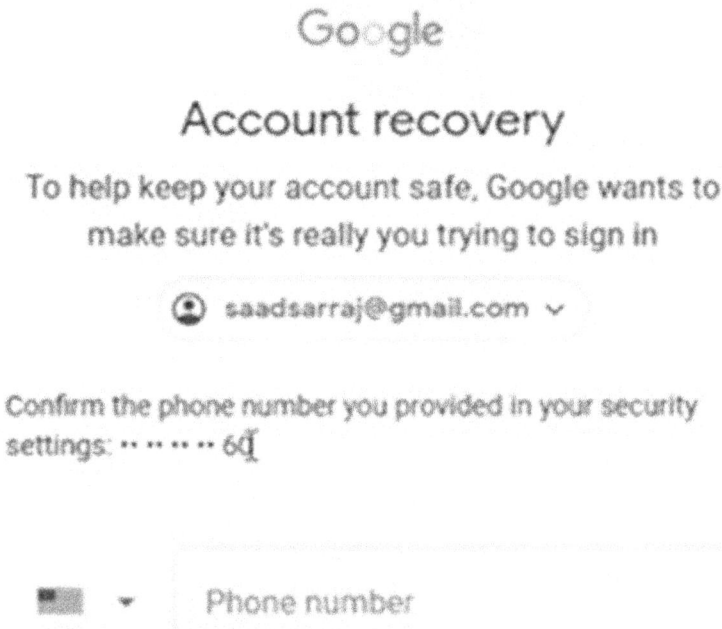

Figure 6.28   Associated mobile number found.

Step 8: Clicking 'Try Another Way' option reveals a US mobile number ending in '60' associated with this email account as displayed in Figure 6.28.

Step 9: Again clicking 'Try Another Way' reveals a recovery account associated with this email account as probably 'Saad...@Outlook.com' as displayed in Figure 6.29.

Step 10: Finding the language being used in the Gmail account reveals that most likely the user speaks that language and could be a native of a country having that as the local language. As proof of concept, I changed the original language from English to Spanish for a demo account. After few minutes, only by entering the Gmail ID (not login), the Login page reflects the new language as shown in Figure 6.30.

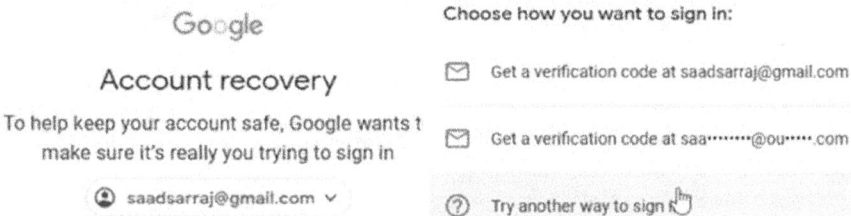

Google

Account recovery

To help keep your account safe, Google want t
make sure it's really you trying to sign in

(•) saadsarraj@gmail.com ∨

Choose how you want to sign in:

✉   Get a verification code at saadsarraj@gmail.com

✉   Get a verification code at saa·········@ou·····.com

⑦   Try another way to sign 🖑

Figure 6.29   Found recovery email ID associated with this email.

Preferred language   Idioma preferido

English   Español
India   Filipinas

Other languages   →   Otros idiomas   Español (España)   ▾

Figure 6.30   Change preferred language of the Gmail account.

Step 11: Here, we try to get the Google ID of a Gmail account used internally by Google (also known as GAIA ID); this helps view any archived pictures or Google map reviews posted anytime. This reveals the user's location – live or visit places. For this login to your Google Hangouts account, add the Gmail account of the target you wish to reconnaissance as shown in Figure 6.31.

Step 12: I am using Firefox web browser, right click selecting 'Inspect' and move to 'Network' tab as shown in Figure 6.32.

Step 13: Refresh the page, wait for the network rows to settle down and then filter to search for the keyword 'GetassistiveFeature'. You should get an entry with the POST method as shown in Figure 6.33.

Step 14: Highlight that row, click 'Response,' and open the down-arrow tabs. These will reveal a number ('104142479148802913985' in my case), which is the internal Google ID as shown in Figure 6.34.

Step 15: This Google ID can be posted to Google Maps link to gather information about the reviews posted by that user and geolocation as shown in Figure 6.35, which indicates that the user (Markus Brown) most probably lives in this area. Also from the reviews, it seems like the user is associated with architecture or building designs.

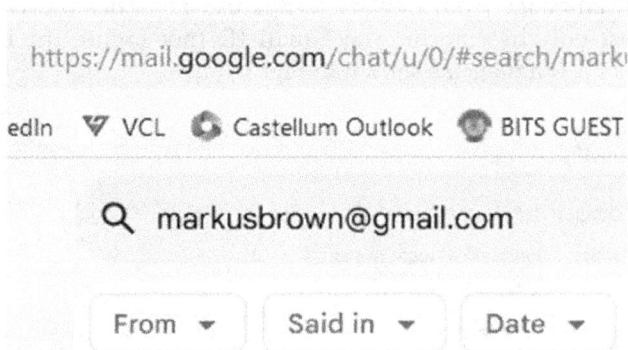

https://mail.google.com/chat/u/0/#search/mark

edln   ☒ VCL   ⦿ Castellum Outlook   ⦿ BITS GUEST

🔍 markusbrown@gmail.com

From ▾   Said in ▾   Date ▾

Figure 6.31   Recon Gmail using Google Hangouts.

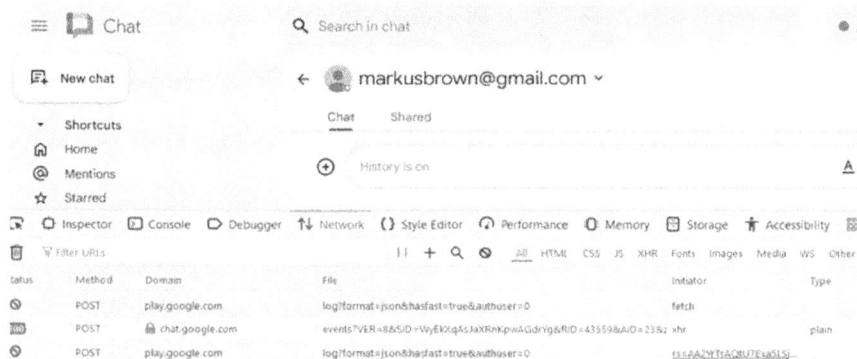

Figure 6.32   Use inspect → network.

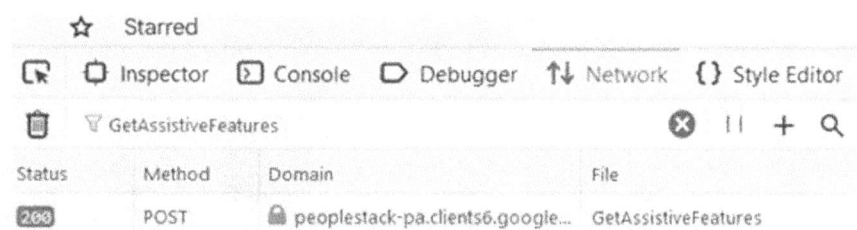

Figure 6.33   Search for 'GetassistiveFeature.'

Figure 6.34   Network → response reveals the internal Google ID.

6.3 FIND EMAIL ADDRESS FROM FACEBOOK ID

Email address is a unique identifier, so one email typically belongs to one person only even as there might be several users with the same name. By having someone's email address using OSINT, we can gather a lot of online

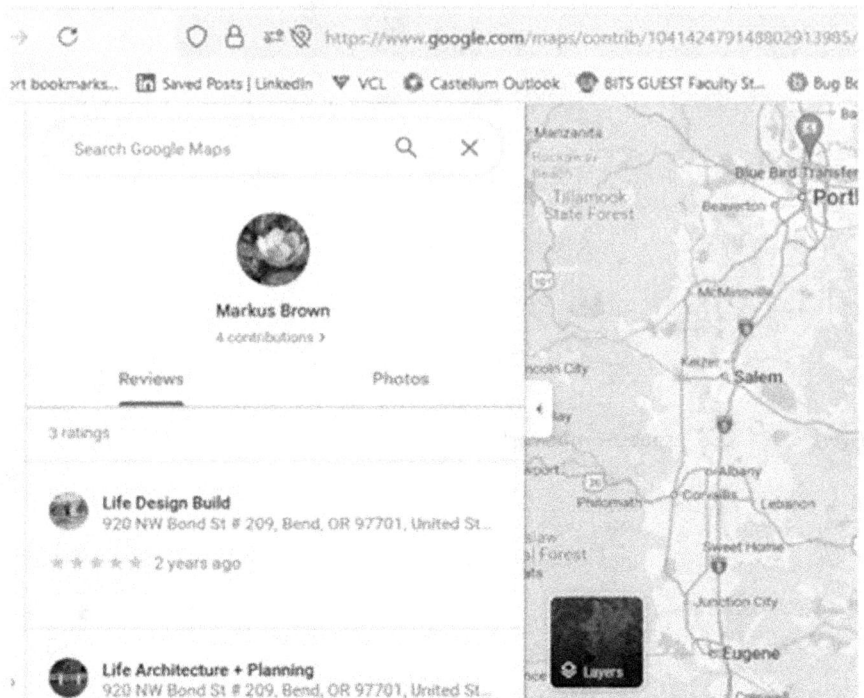

Figure 6.35   Information revealed from Google Maps.

information – social media accounts, reviews performed on Google Maps, portals they are registered on, or may have leaked passwords.

Step 1: Select a target (say 'Charlotte Lang') to check social media accounts associated with that name, so initially checking Google for the user's name, displays LinkedIn, Twitter (X), and Facebook account as shown in Figure 6.36.

Step 2: From Facebook portal, we can see the target's Id or username (charlotte.lang3), and by opening an incognito Firefox tab, selecting the 'Forgot Password' option reveals three email IDs associated with that Facebook ID as shown in Figure 6.37.

Step 3: Copy the three partially hidden email IDs, paste into Notepad, and try to add the full name, adjusting the character count as shown in Figure 6.38. The partially hidden first email has 24 characters, while first-name.lastname@hotmail has 27 characters. The third email has 27 characters, which can be guessed by the attackers who would manipulate the characters to reach 27 characters to find the hidden email.

Step 4: The second partially hidden email has 17 characters and seems to be a non-Hotmail or Gmail email ID belonging to an organization. For this, refer to the All_Email_Provider_Domains link [5] as shown in Figure 6.39 to check on 'All Email Provider Domains.'

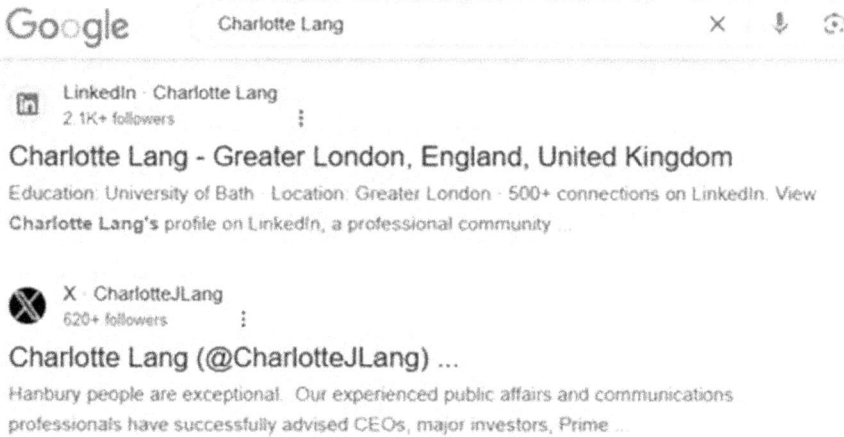

Figure 6.36 Google user's name.

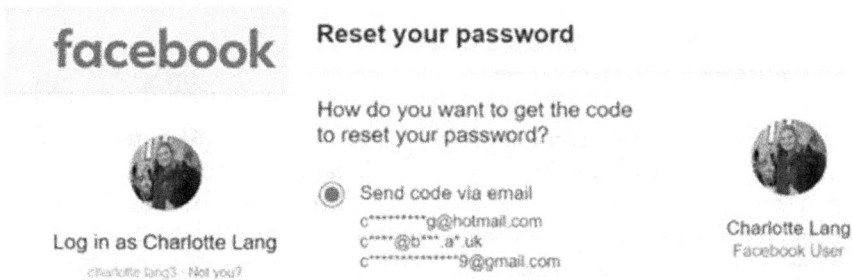

Figure 6.37 Facebook information disclosure.

Figure 6.38 Adjusting email characters.

Step 5: Copying this list to an Excel sheet or Notepad, eliminating anything not starting with 'B,' and then removing those not ending with 'UK,' we can get few domains which could be the third hidden email ID.

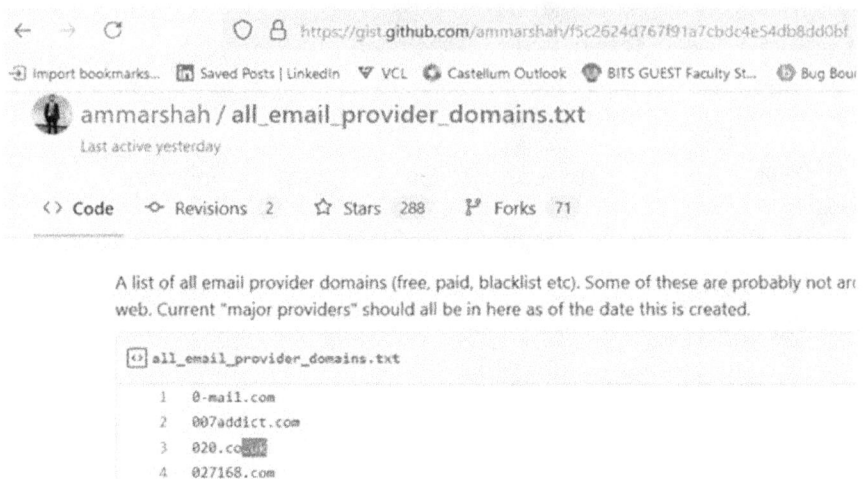

Figure 6.39   Check all email provider domains.

6.4 FIND EMAIL ADDRESS USING CHROME EXTENSION

Step 1: Use Google Chrome and install 'ContactOut' [6] extension from Chrome Store. This helps find emails for 75% of LinkedIn or any website. Open the target's LinkedIn page in Google Chrome as shown in Figure 6.40 which displays the target's organization and education details.

Step 2: Create a free account in 'ContactOut' and check the extension to view the Emails and Mobile associated with the LinkedIn account as shown in Figure 6.41. Notice one of the emails that we were trying earlier is displayed as 'Charlottelang89@gmail.com.' Copy all emails to a Notepad which reveal the company business email IDs and are validated from the LinkedIn profile.

Step 3: From the LinkedIn profile, notice the target went to 'University of Bath' and searching on Google displays the domain name as 'www.bath. ac.uk.' We can confirm the second partially hidden email address is most likely 'Clang@bath.ac.uk' as shown in Figure 6.42.

Step 4: To ensure that the target is working with Hanbury Strategy, we can validate the email address using online services like 'verify-email' or 'Hunter' [7] as illustrated in Figure 6.43. These confirm that the email address has the correct format and it is not gibberish; the email server DNS (MX records) is valid and present for the domain, so anyone can send emails to that email address. The domain name is not used for web emails or disposable/temporary email addresses.

Step 5: Assuming with target's first and last name we were not able to find the stars from one of the LinkedIn revealed email address (say c*********g@ hotmail.com → 23 characters); then, the objective is to use Google to find

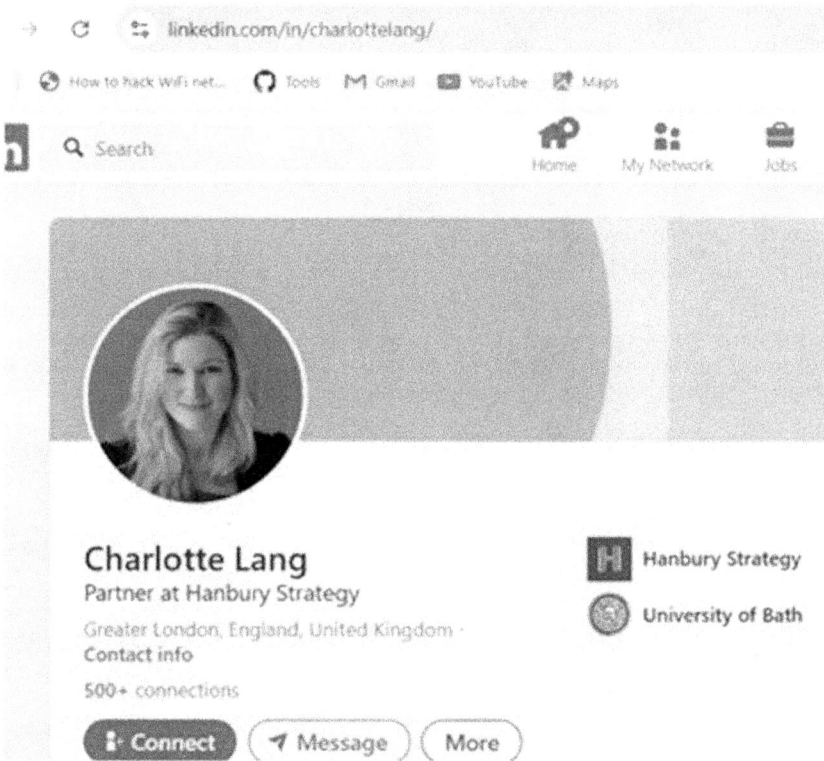

Figure 6.40 Open target's LinkedIn in Google Chrome with 'Contact Out' extension.

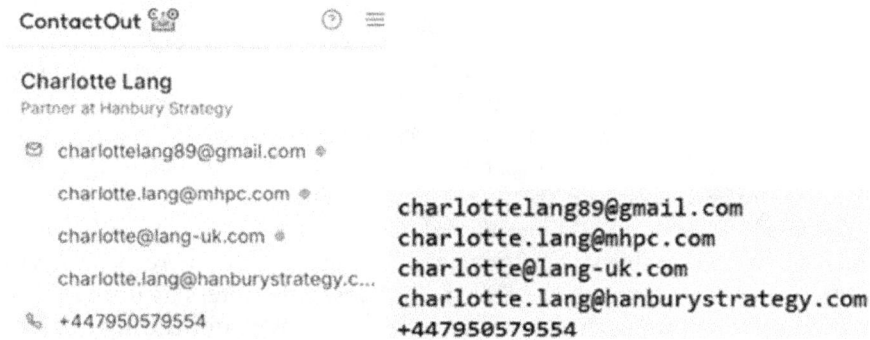

Figure 6.41 Email & mobile associated with the LinkedIn account.

social media account like Twitter or X as illustrated in Figure 6.44. This reveals that the X profile ID is 'charlottejlang,' and using this, we can try to find the missing characters on Pinterest.

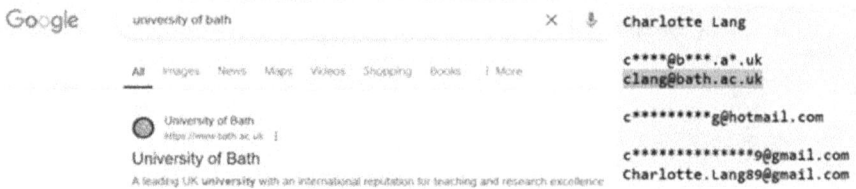

Figure 6.42   Domain name found.

Figure 6.43   Validate email address.

Step 6: In case this does not work, we can use Metric Sparrow's Email Permutator service [8] to permutate email addresses using the first and last name along with the domain. In our case, using first name 'Charlotte' and last name 'Lang' with email address 'c*********g@hotmail.com', Figure 6.45 shows the 34 email addresses created.

Step 7: To refine this information, we can sort the 34 email addresses shortest to the longest as displayed in Figure 6.46.

Step 7: Now counting the number of characters (or stars) in the partially hidden Hotmail address (27 characters), we select only the relevant email address that would match the star in the Hotmail address as displayed in Figure 6.47. We know that the email starts with a 'c' and end with 'g,' so we can use an email validator (like Hunter) to confirm the valid address as 'charlotte_g@hotmail.com.'

Step 8: Finally, using the phone number found earlier (+447950579554), we can use Facebook's Forgot Password option to verify if any email addresses exist. Figure 6.48 confirms two email addresses are linked with the user's Facebook account.

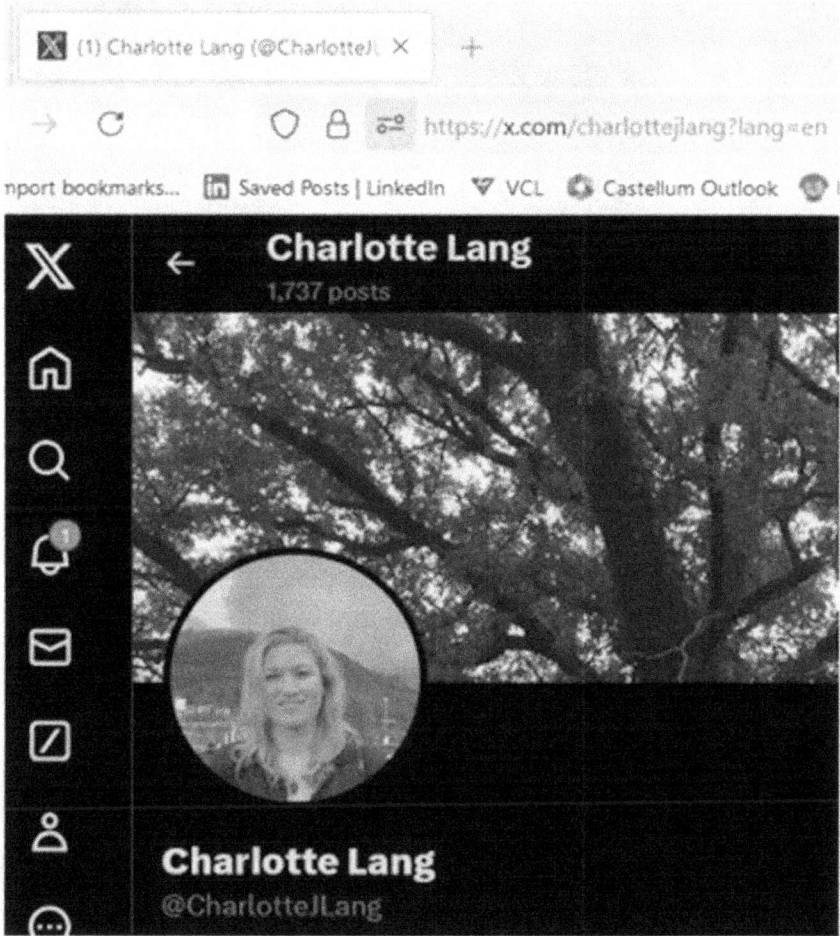

Figure 6.44   Twitter account found.

Figure 6.45   Permutate email address using just the first and last name and domain.

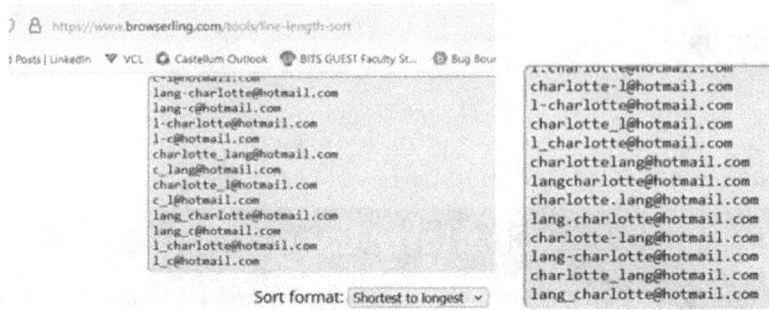

Figure 6.46   Sorting emails generated.

Charlotte Lang

```
c*********g@hotmail.com
1.charlotte@hotmail.com
charlotte-1@hotmail.com
1-charlotte@hotmail.com
charlotte_g@hotmail.com
1_charlotte@hotmail.com
```

Figure 6.47   Listing relevant email address.

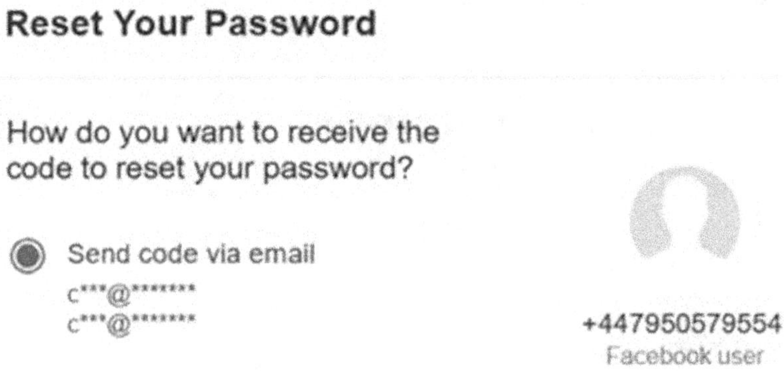

Reset Your Password

How do you want to receive the
code to reset your password?

◉ Send code via email
c***@*******
c***@*******

+447950579554
Facebook user

Figure 6.48   Use phone to verify email addresses that exist.

6.5 SEARCH BUSINESS EMAIL ADDRESS

Business emails are unique and belong to only one individual in that company, whose domain is also unique, unlike social media profile IDs on different portals, which can be the same. For example, abc@gmail.com, abc@facebook.com, or abc@x.com can belong to different persons. Business emails have a certain pattern, for example, firstname.lastname@abc.com, firstletterlastname@abc.com, or lasname@abc.com.

Use Case #1 Find the company's email pattern.

Step 1: As per LinkedIn, Charlotte Lang works with Hanbury Strategy; as shown in Figure 6.49, the first step is to find the company's email pattern.

Step 2: I recommend using the Hunter portal to search for the domain 'Hanbury Strategy.' Figure 6.50 illustrates the results as the email pattern being firstname.lastname@hanburystrategy.com.

Step 3: These emails are found by Hunter using crawlers scanning the Internet portals and sites for mentions of email addresses, as shown in Figure 6.51, for one of the people with three Internet sources.

Step 4: Using Hunter's Email Finder, we can find the email using the target's full name, as shown in Figure 6.52, which is as per the company's email pattern.

Step 5: To validate this, I tried using my name and organization email domain. Figure 6.53 reveals my correct corporate email address.

Step 6: Another tool to find the email pattern of any organization is Intelx's Phonebook [9] as displayed in Figure 6.54. This provides a list of email addresses of staff working at a certain company.

Use Case #2 Find Business Emails using Browser Extensions

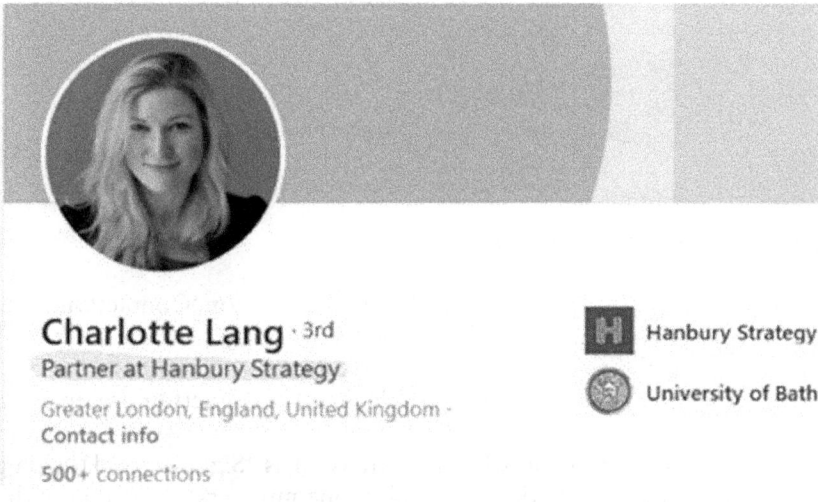

Charlotte Lang · 3rd
Partner at Hanbury Strategy
Greater London, England, United Kingdom ·
Contact info
500+ connections

H   Hanbury Strategy

    University of Bath

Figure 6.49   Target name and business organization.

Freya Thompson
freya.thompson@hanburystr...
🏢 People Manager
99%
3 sources ⌄

Niamh Fogarty
niamh.fogarty@hanburystra...
📞 +44 79 4681 3843
🏢 Partner
97%   Verify email address
13 sources ⌄

Paul Stephenson
paul.stephenson@hanburyst...
📞 +44 20 3752 6775
🏢 Partner
99%
9 sources ⌄

Jan Meinicke
jan.meinicke@hanburystrate...
📞 +44 75 0419 5699
🏢 Senior Account Manager
96%   Verify email address
7 sources ⌄

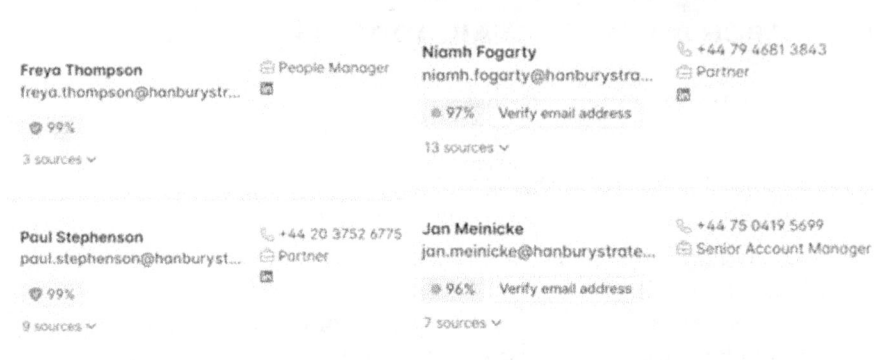

Figure 6.50   **Email domain search.**

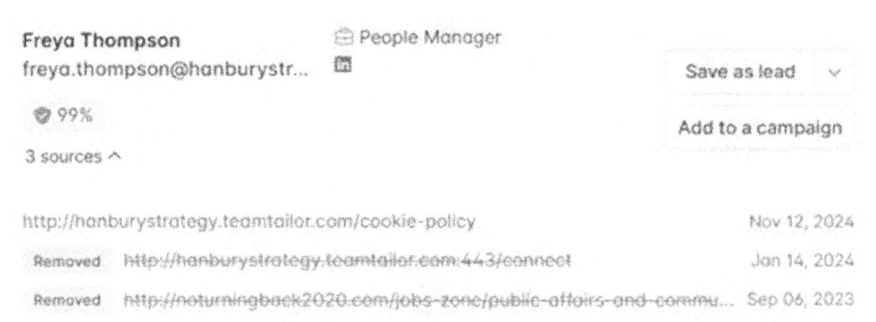

Freya Thompson
freya.thompson@hanburystr...
🏢 People Manager

99%
3 sources ⌃

Save as lead   ⌄

Add to a campaign

http://hanburystrategy.teamtailor.com/cookie-policy   Nov 12, 2024

Removed   http://hanburystrategy.teamtailor.com:443/connect   Jan 14, 2024

Removed   http://noturningback2020.com/jobs-zone/public-affairs-and-commu...   Sep 06, 2023

Figure 6.51   **Email mentions found on the Internet.**

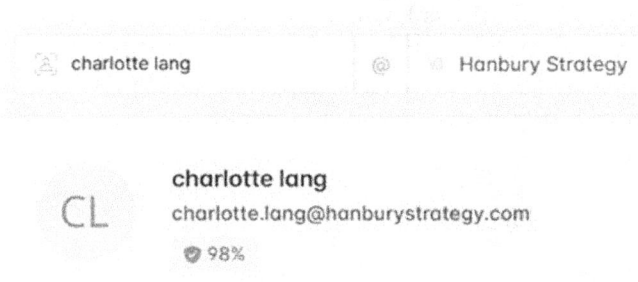

charlotte lang   @   Hanbury Strategy

CL

charlotte lang
charlotte.lang@hanburystrategy.com
98%

Figure 6.52   **Target's email address confirmed.**

Step 1: Using the Google Chrome browser extension 'ContactOut' plugin to find emails and phone numbers from public pages on the Internet and match them to the right people. Figure 6.55 illustrates a LinkedIn profile, and its associated contact details revealed using ContactOut for emails and phone numbers.

Step 2: Another Google Chrome extension is 'SignalHire' [10] plugin, which reveals the email addresses and phone numbers associated with the LinkedIn profile as shown in Figure 6.56.

Email Finder ⊙

akashdeep bhardwaj   upes.ac.in

AB   **akashdeep bhardwaj**
            abhardwaj@upes.ac.in
            ⏱ 87%

Figure 6.53 Validated another email domain pattern.

Phonebook lists all domains, email addresses, or URLs for the given input domain. You are searching 165 billion records.

2024-09-01: We are currently restricting Phonebook to paid users due to constant ₹ Phonebook license soon!

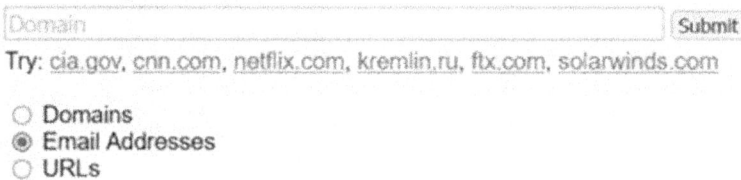

| Domain | Submit |

Try: cia.gov, cnn.com, netflix.com, kremlin.ru, ftx.com, solarwinds.com

○ Domains
◉ Email Addresses
○ URLs

Figure 6.54 Intelx Phonebook.

ContactOut 🖳   ⊙ ≡

Select all (1)

Dr. Akashdeep Bhardwaj
Experienced Cybersecurity & Digital Forensi...

🗑 Dr. Akashdeep Bhardwaj · 3rd+   ✉ ▓▓▓▓@yahoo.com ◈
Experienced Cybersecurity & Digital Forensics professional
Dehradun   ☎ +919873▓▓▓▓

Figure 6.55 ContactOut browser extension results.

Step 3: Yet another Google Chrome extension is 'GetProspect' [11] plugin, which looks up emails in seconds on Chrome browser searches and displays people like the LinkedIn profile as shown in Figure 6.57.

Step 4: Another Chrome extension is the 'Clearbit Connect' plugin [12] to get context from Gmail addresses of ideal customer profiles. This extension tags and matches every company the user wants to research as shown in Figure 6.58.

Use Case #3 Find Number Caller ID

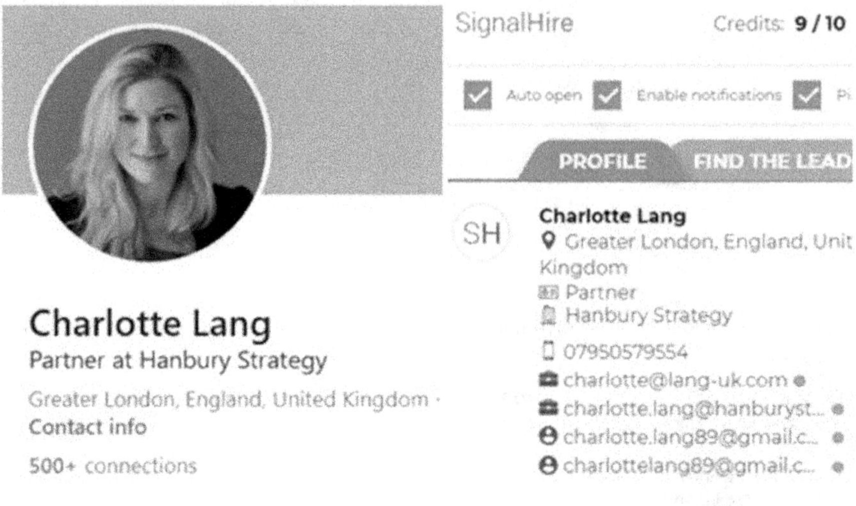

Figure 6.56   SignalHire browser extension results.

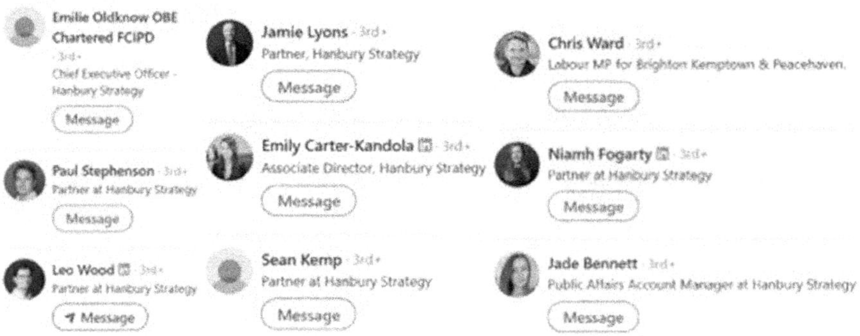

Figure 6.57   Recommendatins by browser extention 'GetProspect.'

Apart from searching for personal and corporate email addresses, this use case presents steps to find the phone number ID or the owner's name.

Step 1: The first tool I highly recommend is 'HaveIBeenPwned' portal [13], using a demo phone. Figure 6.59 presents the status of this number with one breach. This reveals that a breach happened in April 2021, leaking data related to this mobile phone, which was most likely used to create the Facebook profile. Now, by downloading or buying this Facebook database from the dark web, attackers can easily determine personal details related to this number.

Step 2: To confirm if any Facebook account was related to this number, Open Facebook and click the Forgot Password option, and check using this phone number. Figure 6.60 reveals an account associated with this phone number.

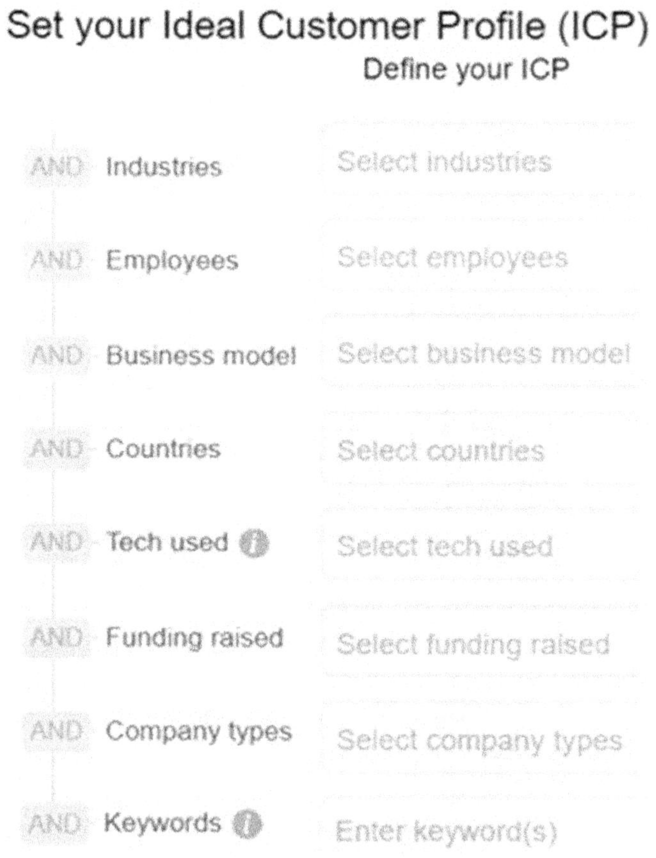

Set your Ideal Customer Profile (ICP)
Define your ICP

AND Industries   Select industries

AND Employees   Select employees

AND Business model   Select business model

AND Countries   Select countries

AND Tech used ⓘ   Select tech used

AND Funding raised   Select funding raised

AND Company types   Select company types

AND Keywords ⓘ   Enter keyword(s)

Figure 6.58 Search criteria by browser extention 'GetProspect.'

Step 3: The second option is to use 'TrueCaller' portal [14], which has a huge database of global mobile and phone numbers. Searching for this number reveals it belongs to 'Telekom Deutschland GmbgH' as shown in Figure 6.61. The initial two numbers '49' are the country code for Germany, and we even found the portal.

Step 4: To validate that the number is not a random or temporary phone, I used Amazon to sign in, which prompts for a password as displayed in Figure 6.62. This confirms that the phone number is registered on Amazon, and so this phone number is true.

Step 5: Using 'Dehashed' portal service [15] to search for compromised assets, we search for the phone number, and Figure 6.63 reveals two breaches. Since this is a paid service, investigators can buy monthly or annual accounts to gather breach details about the phone number.

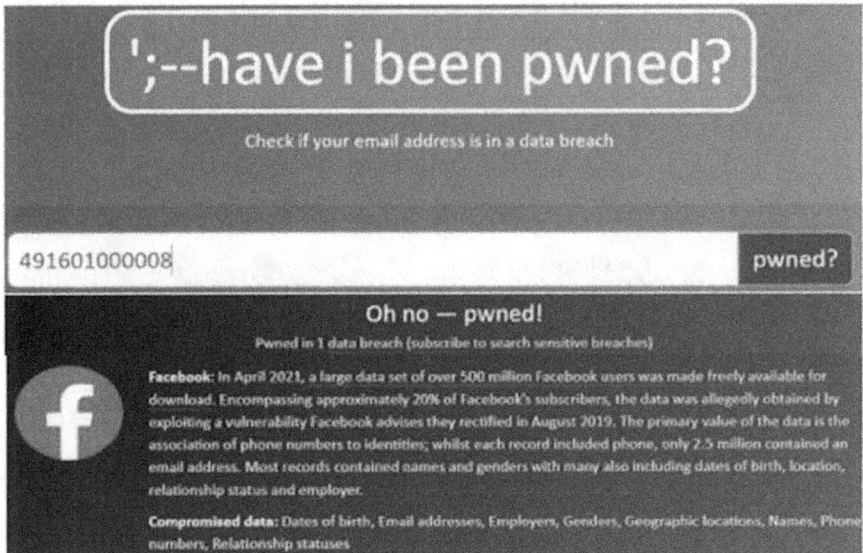

Figure 6.59 Results from 'HaveIBeenPwned.'

Figure 6.60 Found Facebook account associated with the phone number.

Figure 6.61 TrueCaller search for the phone number.

amazon

Sign in

+491601000008 Change

Password   Forgot password?

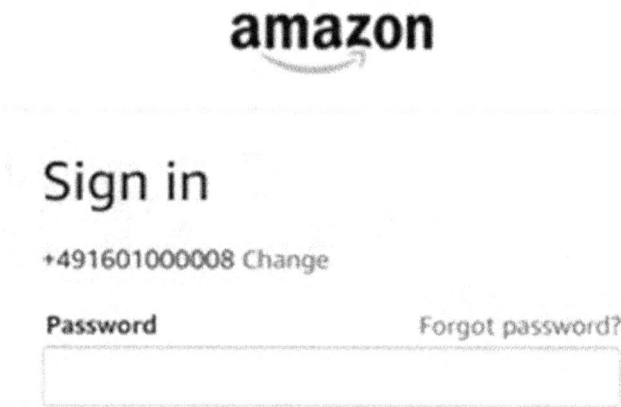

Figure 6.62   Validating the phone number using Amazon.

DEHASHED   Q 491601000008

| 2 | 326MS | 14,453,524,343 | 48,798 |
| RESULT(S) FOUND | SEARCH ELAPSED TIME | ASSETS SEARCHED | AGGREGATED DATA WELLS |

Figure 6.63   'Dehashed' breach count.

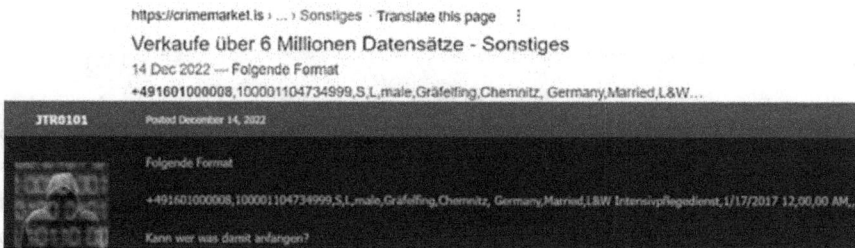

https://crimemarket.is › ... › Sonstiges · Translate this page   ⋮
Verkaufe über 6 Millionen Datensätze - Sonstiges
14 Dec 2022 — Folgende Format
+491601000008,100001104734999,S,L,male,Gräfelfing,Chemnitz, Germany,Married,L&W...

JTR0101   Posted December 14, 2022

Folgende Format

+491601000008,100001104734999,S,L,male,Gräfelfing,Chemnitz, Germany,Married,L&W Intensivpflegedienst,1/17/2017 12,00,00 AM,.

Kann wer was damit anfangen?

Figure 6.64   Dark web search for the phone database.

Step 6: By performing a dark web search as shown in Figure 6.64, we find someone trying to sell the Facebook database having this phone number on 'CrimeMarket' portal. This has the phone number along with ID, City, Country, and account creation time and date.

Step 7: Taking the profile ID from the breached database and checking on Facebook, Figure 6.65 confirms the user's name (Sven Liebscher) and profile details. Earlier Step 2 revealed two email IDs associated with the phone number, one starting with S and the other with L, which most likely would match with the name.

Use Case #4 Scan and gather information of phone numbers

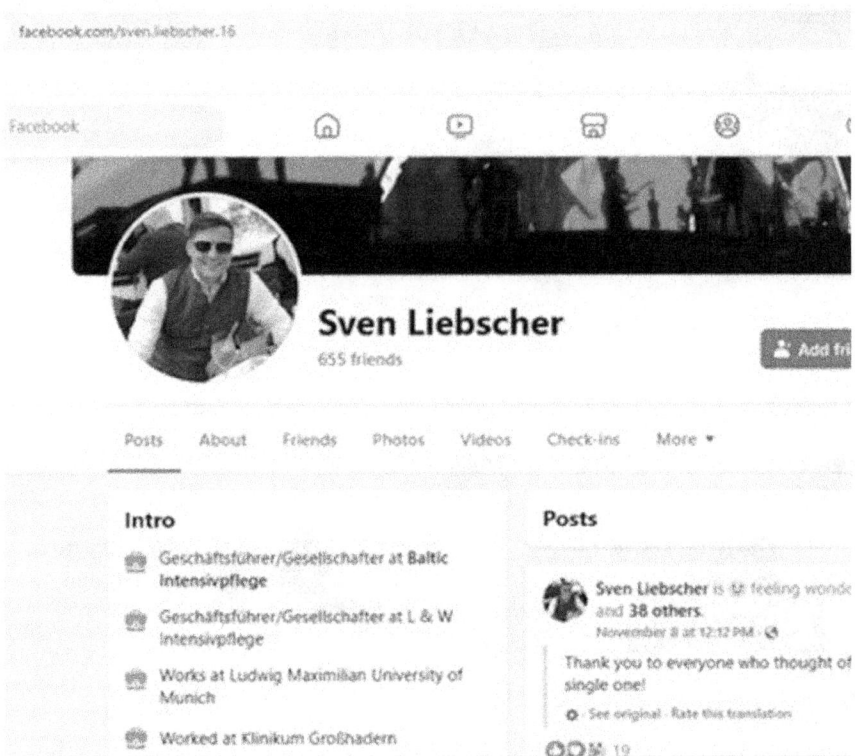

Figure 6.65   Facebook profile found.

PhoneInfoga [16] is a utility for scanning foreign phone numbers that run on Linux. You may use a variety of methods to try to locate the VoIP provider or identify the owner after first gathering basic information like nation, area, carrier, and line type. It uses a group of scanners that need to be set up for the tool to function properly. PhoneInfoga is only there to assist with phone number research; it doesn't automate anything.

Step 1: Download PhoneInfoga as Docker as shown in Figure 6.66.

Step 2: Run PhoneInfoga as a docker with Port 5000 as shown in Figure 6.67.

```
┌──(kali㉿kali)-[~/Documents/Tools/Scanners]
└─$ sudo docker pull sundowndev/phoneinfoga:latest
latest: Pulling from sundowndev/phoneinfoga
619be1103602: Pull complete
239b70fd25ff: Pull complete
Digest: sha256:b9c0eceea4048c7d8b0486d89bd9037193dc6fa38b8932794d4e9b751c28c655
Status: Downloaded newer image for sundowndev/phoneinfoga:latest
docker.io/sundowndev/phoneinfoga:latest
```

Figure 6.66   Download PhoneInfoga as the docker.

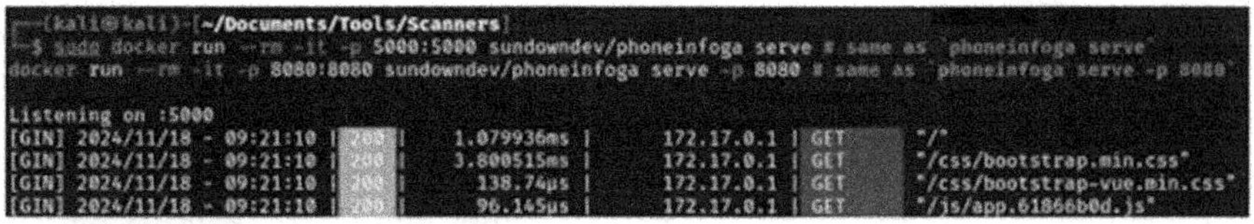

Figure 6.67   Run PhoneInfoga as the docker.

Figure 6.68   PhoneInfoga web interface.

Step 3: Open http://localhost:5000 and then enter phone numbers to scan. Figure 6.68 displays the phone number format is valid, mentioning the country (Germany or DE in our case).

6.6 CONCLUSION

The exponential growth of data has elevated its importance to a new level, making it a crucial asset in today's digital age. Email addresses, beyond their primary function of communication, serve as valuable digital identifiers that can reveal a wealth of information about individuals. Email Address Intelligence, a technique that goes beyond surface-level analysis, aims to extract deeper insights from email addresses. By connecting the dots between email interactions and other online activities, it enables businesses to gain a comprehensive understanding of their customers' preferences, behaviors, and engagement levels. This knowledge empowers businesses to deliver highly personalized experiences and strengthen their defenses against fraud and other security threats. The chapter explores various use cases that demonstrate the potential of Email Address Intelligence in uncovering and validating personal information, such as phone numbers, from social media platforms. Ultimately, the effective utilization of Email Address Intelligence can provide a significant competitive advantage and help businesses thrive in the data-driven landscape.

REFERENCES

1. "Email Address Lookup & Intelligence | Trustfull," 2024. https://trustfull.com/products/email (accessed Nov. 18, 2024).
2. "Whois.com – Free Whois Lookup," https://www.whois.com/whois
3. Laramies, "Laramies/TheHarvester," GitHub, Jun. 16, 2019. https://github.com/laramies/theHarvester
4. Palenath, "Holehe OSINT – Email to Registered Accounts," GitHub, Mar. 18, 2023. https://github.com/megadose/holehe
5. 262588213843476, "A list of all email provider domains (free, paid, blacklist etc). Some of these are probably not around anymore. I've combined a dozen lists from around the web. Current 'major providers' should all be in here as of the date this is created," Gist, Nov. 16, 2024. https://gist.github.com/ammarshah/f5c2624d767f91a7cbdc4e54db8dd0bf (accessed Nov. 18, 2024).
6. "ContactOut – Find Anyone's Email & Phone," 2024. https://contactout.com/chrome-extension (accessed Nov. 18, 2024).
7. "Sign in Hunter," https://hunter.io/search
8. "Email Permutator | Metric Sparrow Toolkit," 2024. http://metricsparrow.com/toolkit/email-permutator/ (accessed Nov. 18, 2024).
9. "Phonebook.cz – Intelligence X," https://phonebook.cz/
10. "SignalHire for Chrome, Best Email and Phone Number Finder – SignalHire," 2022. https://www.signalhire.com/extension (accessed Nov. 18, 2024).
11. "Email Finder – GetProspect," 2016. https://getprospect.com/linkedIn-email-finder-chrome-extension (accessed Nov. 18, 2024).
12. "Find Any Email Address with Clearbit Connect," https://clearbit.com/resources/tools/connect
13. T. Hunt, "Have I Been Pwned: Check If Your Email Has Been Compromised in a Data Breach," 2023. https://haveibeenpwned.com/
14. "Truecaller is the Leading Global Platform for Verifying Contacts and Blocking Unwanted Communication | Truecaller," https://www.truecaller.com/
15. "Dehashed Take Your Enterprise Security to the Next Level.| Dehashed," https://dehashed.com
16. Sundowndev, "GitHub – Sundowndev/Phoneinfoga: Information Gathering Framework for Phone Numbers," GitHub, Feb. 21, 2024. https://github.com/sundowndev/phoneinfoga (accessed Nov. 18, 2024).

Chapter 7

Imagery intelligence

7.1 INTRODUCTION

In the context of intelligence, Imagery Intelligence (IMINT) [1] is revolutionary. We obtain knowledge and insights that were previously unattainable by utilizing the power of photography. The capacity of IMINT to offer a visual depiction of the battlefield or a target region is one of its main benefits. Decision-makers need this visual information to evaluate the issue more precisely and come to well-informed conclusions. IMINT allows us to do in-depth analysis and interpretation of the photos in addition to giving visual information. We can find important features and track changes over time by looking at the imaging data. Images that have been optically or electronically replicated on film, electronic display devices, or other media are referred to as IMINT or photo intelligence. Visual photography, radar sensors, infrared sensors, lasers, and electro-optics may all produce imagery.

When gathering information, the amount of detail and analysis is crucial since it gives us a better picture of the target and its actions. To improve the overall intelligence picture, IMINT can be combined with other intelligence disciplines like Signals Intelligence [2] and Human Intelligence [3]. We can produce a more thorough and precise evaluation of the goal by integrating data from many sources. IMINT is essential to national security and really improves our intelligence capabilities. In IMINT, remote sensing is essential. It entails gathering remote imaging data using sensors mounted on platforms like satellites, airplanes, or Unmanned Aerial Vehicles (UAVs). This enables us to collect data without having to visit the target location in person.

For IMINT, satellites are especially crucial to distant sensing. They can take pictures of large areas and offer worldwide coverage. Even from far-off or inaccessible places, satellites with SAR sensors or high-resolution cameras can provide us rich imaging data. This capacity is particularly useful for gathering intelligence since it enables us to keep an eye on activity in regions of interest despite geographical obstacles. Apart from satellites, UAVs and airplanes are also important for IMINT's distant sensing. Because they may be assigned to real-time monitoring or deployed to specific regions of interest, they provide a more adaptable and dynamic approach.

DOI: 10.1201/9781003497615-7

Advanced imaging sensors on aircraft and UAVs enable the precise and detailed capturing of high-resolution imagery.

Defense and security depend heavily on aircraft detection. We can efficiently keep an eye on enemy supplies, spot possible dangers, and protect our airspace by being able to detect and track planes. The potential of aircraft detection to offer early notice of hostile aircraft or unwanted incursions is one of its main benefits. Even at great distances, we can identify and follow airplanes by using SAR satellites. This enables us to take the necessary actions to stop or eliminate any possible hazards before turning into a threat.

7.2 IMAGE INTEL USE CASES

Let's say you are trying to track down someone online, you can use reverse image search if that photo appears elsewhere or use facial recognition applications to compare the person's photo with other images to see if they match. You can also use images to uncover hidden details or use image analysis software to zoom in on a picture to reveal things not visible to the naked eye. Images can be used to narrow down a location or use satellite imagery to pinpoint a particular location and get an arial view of the area answering questions on Who, What, Where, and When.

7.2.1 Use case #1

Objective: The photo was shared on social media which looks like few houses or trees burning in the middle of the photo, a dry area with farmland having few houses, palm trees, and mountains; find the location and date.

Step 1: Refer to Figure 7.1, we could perform a Google search with those as the keywords, but these would be loosely ended search terms difficult to narrow down to get accurate results.

Step 2: We can perform a reverse image search using Google → Images link to upload this photo and find the source of this image as displayed in Figure 7.2.

Step 3: On the right, you should get several images, links, and videos as displayed in Figure 7.3.

Step 4: Browsing some of them easily leads to a new article having the exact image with the location being an ethnic village named 'Rakhine' in Western Myanmar (Burma) on May 16, 2020, as displayed in Figure 7.4. This is the power of a simple reverse image search.

7.2.2 Use case #2

Objective: The photo was shared on social media. It clearly depicts a train station. Answer the following questions:

- What is the name of the train station seen in the photo?
- What is the name and height of the tallest structure seen in the photo?

Figure 7.1 Use case #1 target image.

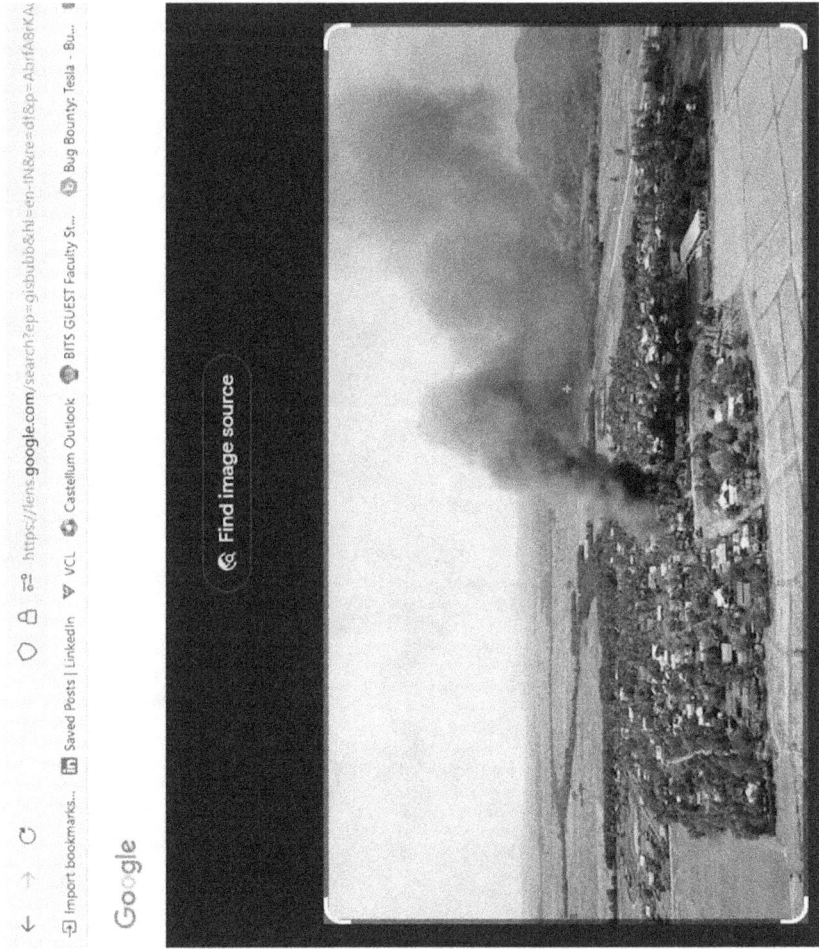

Figure 7.2   Google image search.

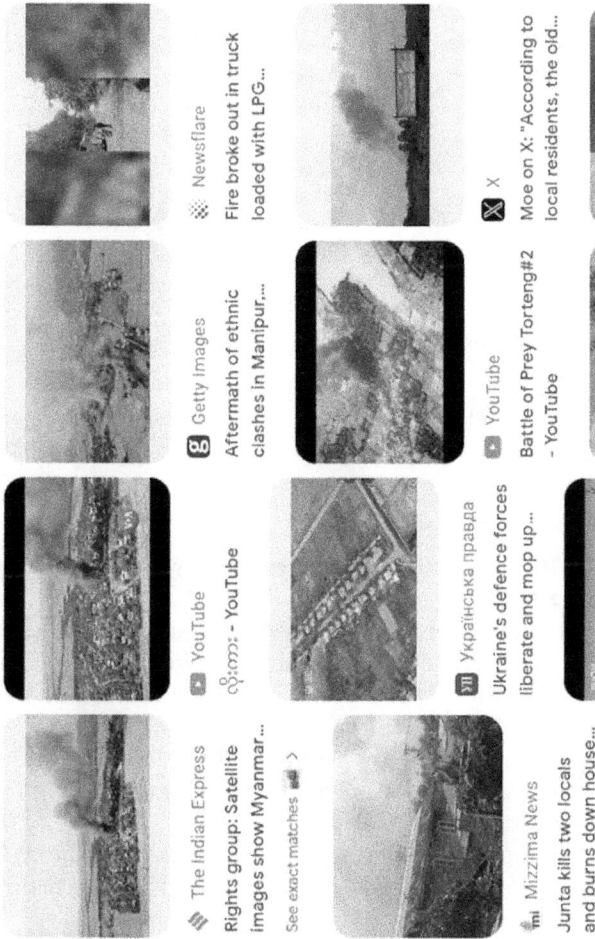

Figure 7.3 Reverse image search results.

In this photo released by the Myanmar Army, a fire burns May 16, 2020, in the predominantly ethnic Rakhine village of Let Kar in Rakhine State's Mrauk-U township, western Myanmar. (Myanmar Army via AP)

Satellite imagery that shows a village burning in a conflict zone in western Myanmar lends credence to reports that houses were set ablaze there by government soldiers, a major human rights group said Tuesday. Human Rights Watch said in a statement that an investigation is necessary to determine who was responsible for setting at least 200 buildings on fire on

Figure 7.4   Exact match found.

Step 1: Figure 7.5 displays tall buildings, blue colored train, railway station, Named 'Flinders Street.'

Step 2: Search on Google for 'Flinders Street Railway Station,' the geolocation comes to be Melbourne, Australia, as shown in Figure 7.6.

Step 3: Open Google Maps to search for 'Flinders Street' and verify photos of the railway station as displayed in Figure 7.7.

Step 4: Use Panoramic View by dropping the yellow man on a road on the map; we find a few buildings as illustrated in Figure 7.8 but no trains or railway station and tracks.

Step 5: Try the Panoramic View again; this time drop the 'yellow man' on a railway track, and here we find the track of the blue train bogies as displayed in Figure 7.9.

Step 6: Figure 7.10 seems to be the area where the photo was clicked. To find the tallest building, right click on the railway station map, copy the coordinates, and paste the coordinates to Google Earth (−37.818598324408136, 144.9665086873299); we get the exact match.

Step 7: Enable 3D, tilt, and rotate the heading till you see few tall buildings that were seen in the initial photograph as presented in Figure 7.11.

Step 8: Zoom, tilt, and face the buildings; now, we can see HWT and IBM as shown in Figure 7.12.

Figure 7.5 Use case #2 target image.

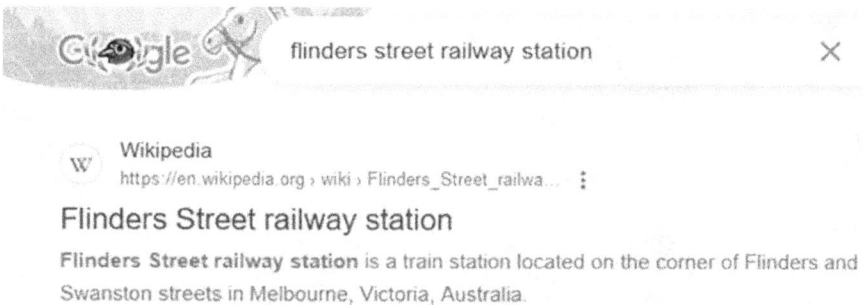

Figure 7.6 Google search for keywords.

Step 9: Move the maps toward the left and we see a white iron tower as shown in Figure 7.13.

Step 10: Drop the yellow man in front of the tower; view the panoramic photo as shown in Figure 7.14.

Step 11: Right click on the 3D image to find the name of the Tower 'Art Centre Melbourne' as shown in Figure 7.15.

Step 12: Use Google to find the height of the Art Centre Melbourne tower (162 meters) as shown in Figure 7.16.

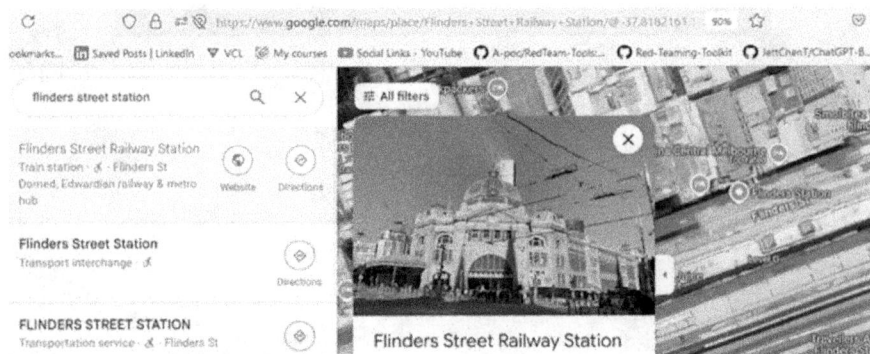

Figure 7.7   Google maps search.

Figure 7.8   Panoramic view of Google Map.

Step 13: Check the other buildings (IBM) as per the Google Maps is named The Skyscraper Centre, which is 131 meters as shown in Figure 7.17.

Step 14: However, on the right side is another tall building, called the Eureka Tower as displayed in Figure 7.18.

Step 15: Reviewing the height of the Eureka Tower Melbourne; Figure 7.19 reveals 297 meters as the highest building.

Figure 7.9 Panoramic view of tracks.

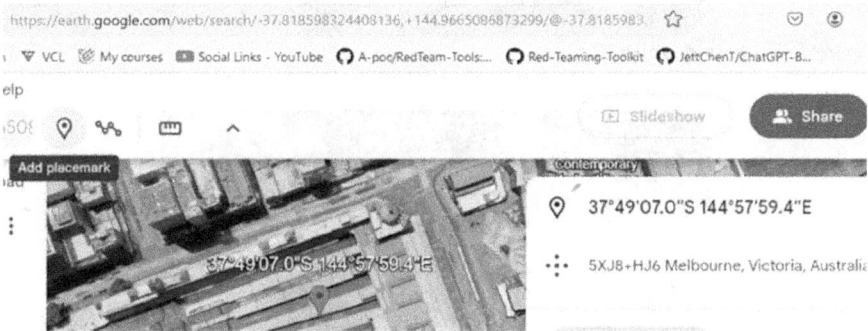

Figure 7.10 Paste Map coordinates in Google.

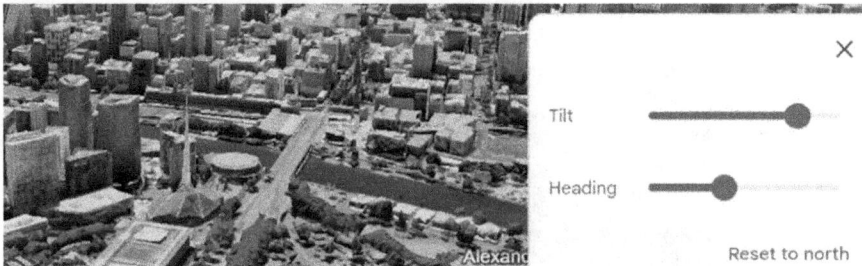

Figure 7.11 Enable 3D, tilt, and rotate map.

Figure 7.12   Zoom, tilt, and face the buildings.

Figure 7.13   Found white iron tower.

Figure 7.14   Panoramic view of the iron tower.

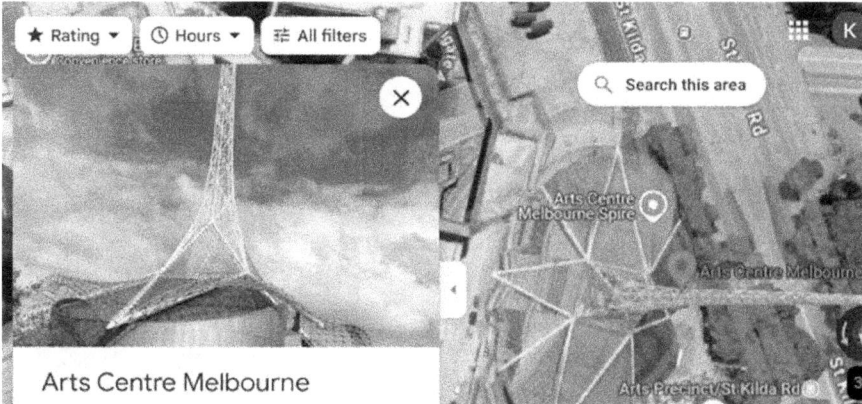

Figure 7.15   Find name of the iron tower.

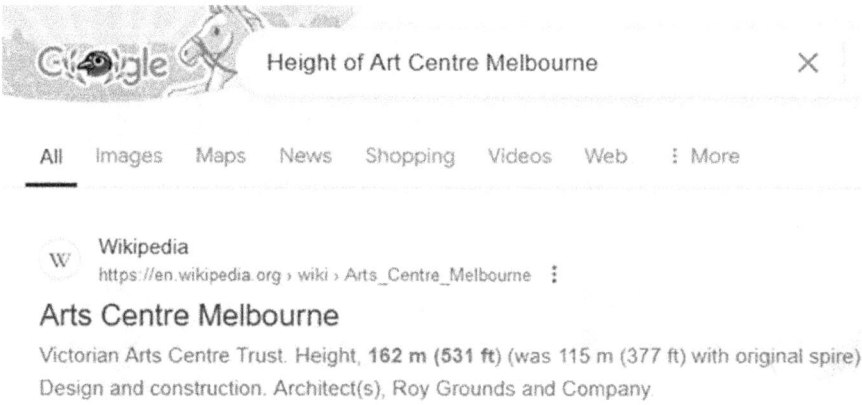

Figure 7.16   *Find height of the iron tower.*

7.2.3 Use case #3

Objective: Figure 7.20 is a photo of a resort located on an island.

a. What is the name of the resort?
b. What are the coordinates of the island?
c. In which cardinal direction was the camera facing when the photo was taken?

Step 1: Reverse Image Search using image search engines – Yandex, Bing, and Google – and install a plugin addon on Firefox Web Browser for Reverse Image Search as displayed in Figure 7.21.

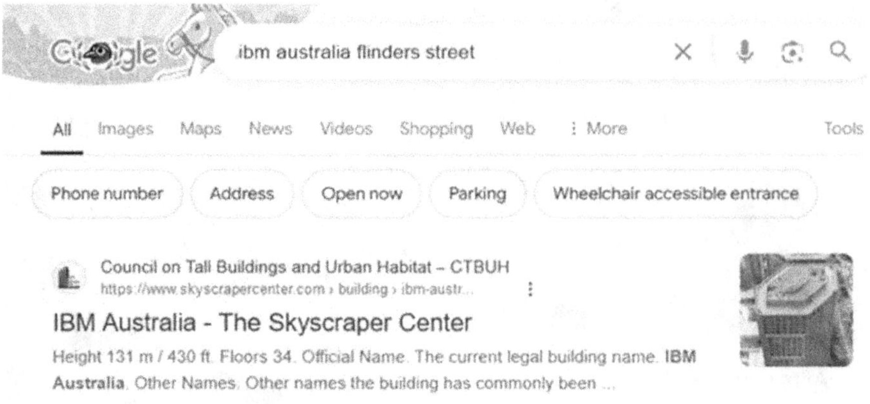

Figure 7.17   Find height of the IBM tower.

Figure 7.18   Found another tall tower.

Step 2: Google for Oan Resort as shown in Figure 7.22 for one of the search links.

Step 3: Browse the site for any Video, Email, and Phone (+691 330 5450). Verify the initial image with the link found above – this is confirmed true Positive as shown in Figure 7.23.

Step 4: Check coordinates using maps.google.com to right click on 'Oan Resort,' and find the coordinates (7.362785203417169, 151.75627903166375) as shown in Figure 7.24.

Step 5: Use Google Earth to perform 2D/3D, tilt, and rotate to find the camera direction as displayed in Figure 7.25.

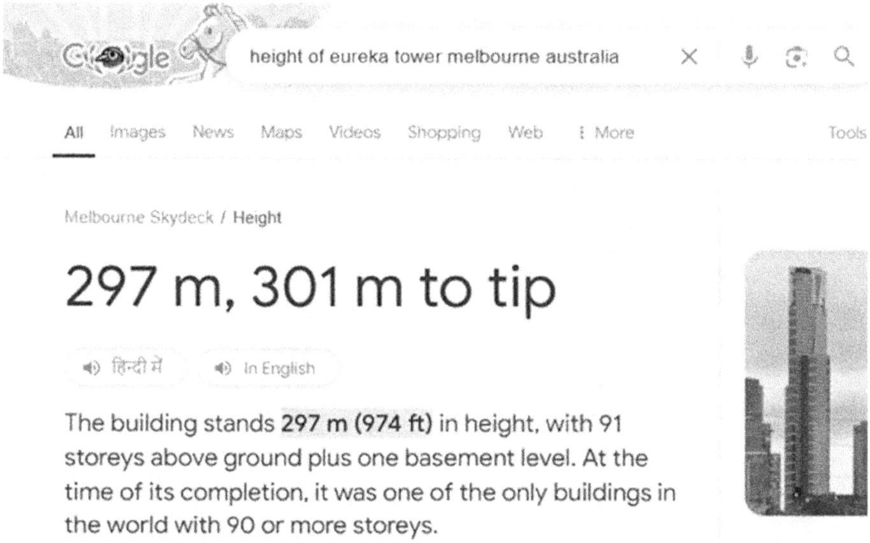
Google
height of eureka tower melbourne australia
All
Images
News
Maps
Videos
Shopping
Web
More
Tools
Melbourne Skydeck / Height
297 m, 301 m to tip
हिन्दी में
In English
The building stands 297 m (974 ft) in height, with 91 storeys above ground plus one basement level. At the time of its completion, it was one of the only buildings in the world with 90 or more storeys.

Figure 7.19 Found the tallest building.

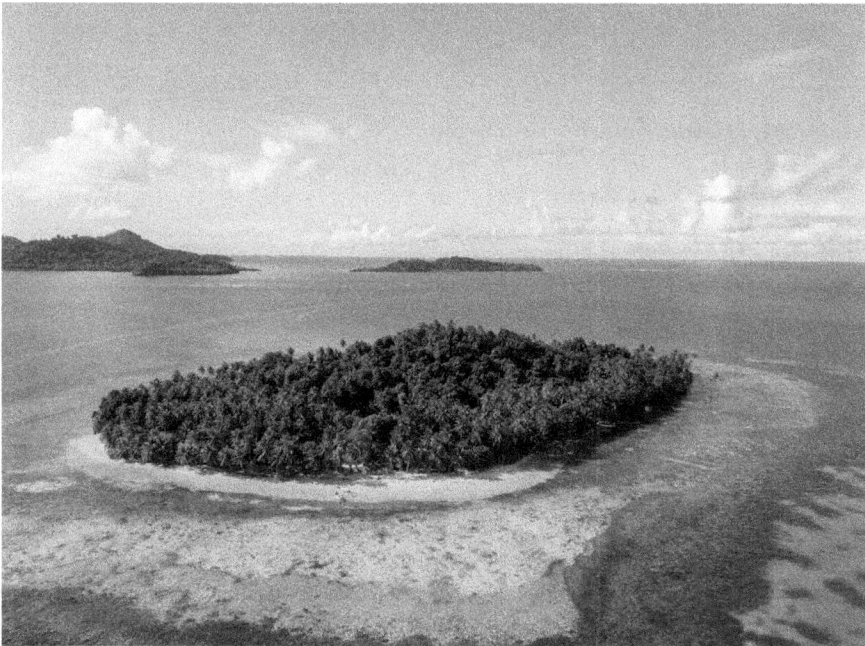

Figure 7.20 Use the case #3 target image.

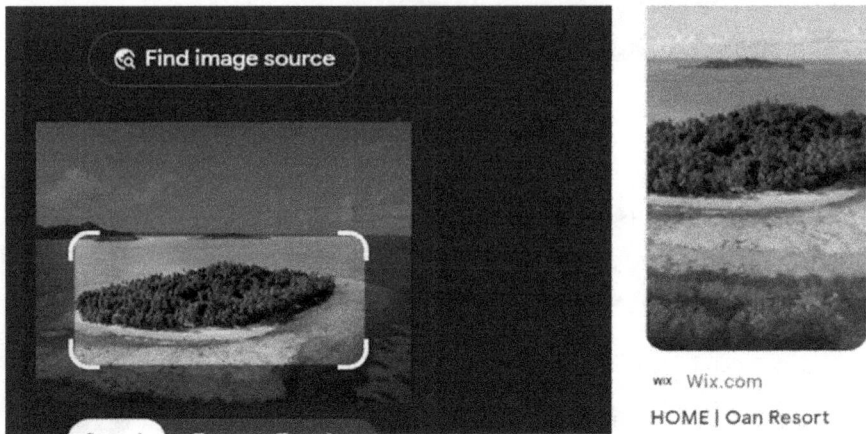

Figure 7.21   Google reverse image search.

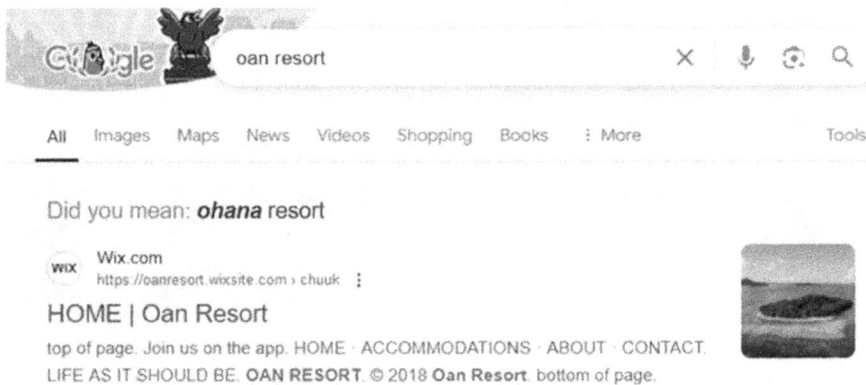

Figure 7.22   Google for Oan Resort.

7.2.4 Use case #4

Objective: The photo was taken a few years ago in a beautiful city. Your task is to find the answers to these questions:

- Where was this photograph taken?
- In which year was this photo taken?
- The big poster on the right contains a website link; what was the link?

Step 1: Looks like river or coast, tourists (people with red hair & backpacks → Americans/Europeans?) walking, wear normal (maybe it is summer) clothes even though it's cloudy, flags/poles, buildings, and rock-based pavements and road as illustrated in Figure 7.26.

Figure 7.23   Found resort site with images.

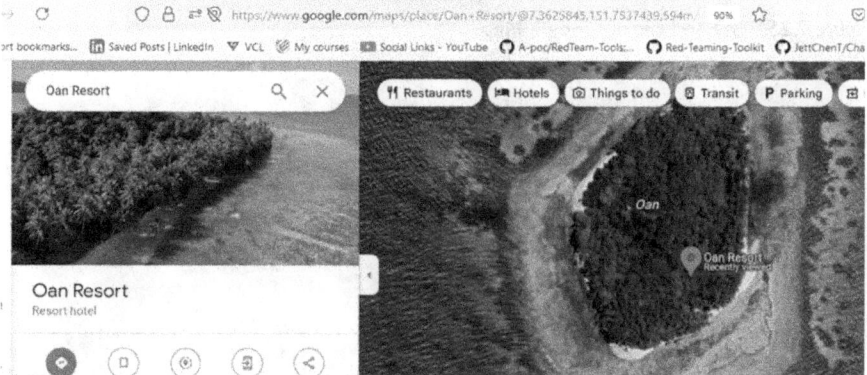

Figure 7.24   Found coordinates of the resort.

Step 2: Save and upload this image to perform reverse image search which reveals these images to be 'Centro Commercial Vasco da Gama Mall' on a sea front as shown in Figure 7.27.

Step 3: Checking other search links displays a shopping mall with the same name as shown in Figure 7.28.

Step 4: Performing a reverse image search also displays the Homem-Sol, de Jorge Vieira tower seen in the initial image, Figure 7.29.

Step 5: Performing a Google Map search for 'Homem-Sol, de Jorge Vieira' validates the image as shown in Figure 7.30.

Step 6: Utilizing the Panoramic View and dropping the yellow man in this map; Figure 7.31 displays the exact image with the tower and flags as seen in the target image.

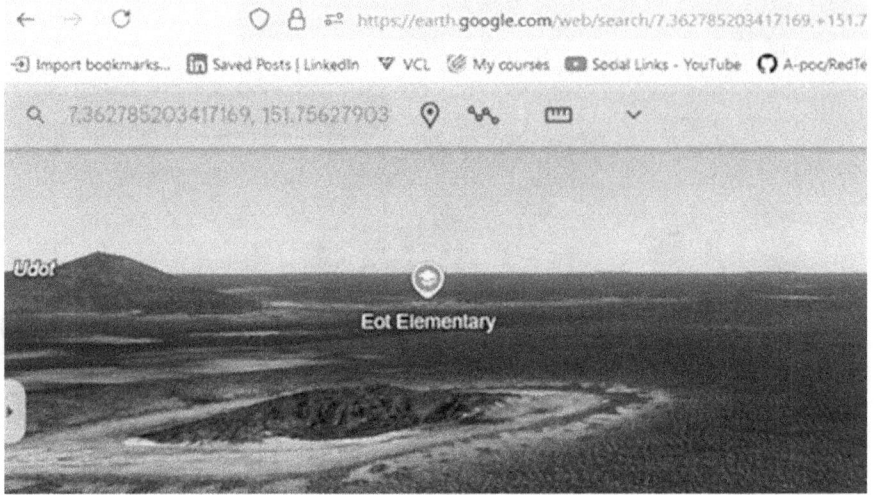

Figure 7.25   3D and tilt of Google Map.

Figure 7.26   Use the case #4 target image.

7.2.5 Use case #5

Objective: The image shows a group of people sitting in front of a large screen that reads 'Lectura en Movimiento en Lima.' A speaker can be seen standing on the left-hand side in front of three large flags.

   a. Name the speaker.
   b. Identify what he was wearing on his lapel.
   c. Find footage of his speech.

Figure 7.27   Found location name.

A huge modern shopping center Vasco da Gama:

Figure 7.28   Found the shopping mall.

Step 1: We can see a man in a dark suit, white shirt, speaking, podium with three flags, large shield at the back, screen displays 'Lectura en Movimiento en Lima' and OEI as shown in Figure 7.32.

Step 2: Performing a Google search for 'Lectura en Movimiento en Lima' displays a few images, as displayed in Figure 7.33, with the speaker being 'Juan Carlos Ruiz.'

Step 3: Performing a Google search 'Juan Carlos Ruiz' 'Lectura en Movimiento en Lima' as shown in Figure 7.34, we get a person on the stage as the speaker and 'OEI Lectura.'

Step 4: Zooming in on the person's image, we can see PIN, which displays 'OEI' as shown in Figure 7.35.

Figure 7.29   Homem-Sol, de Jorge Vieira tower found.

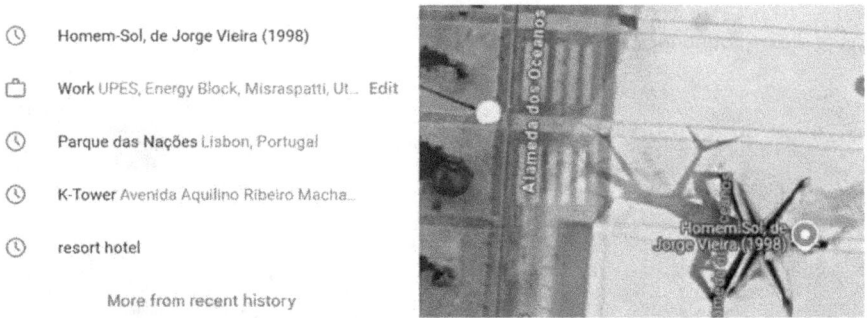

Figure 7.30   Homem-Sol, de Jorge Vieira details found.

Figure 7.31   Exact match with the tower and flags.

Step 5: Browsing the Google search, we also come across a few videos on this OEI conference as displayed in Figure 7.36.

7.2.6 Use case #6

Objective: Here, you see a screenshot from a tweet containing a photo from the city of Kiffa dated February 20, 2023, 1:45 pm. It contains all the

Figure 7.32   Use the case #5 target image.

Figure 7.33   Related images found.

Figure 7.34   Found the speaker and relevant keywords.

Figure 7.35   Found PIN label and logo.

Figure 7.36   Found related video.

relevant information necessary to help you find the exact location. Identify the coordinates of where the photo was taken.

Step 1: Image has road leading to outskirts of a city/village, few single-story buildings, desert region, gap between building & road, tree behind one of the buildings, looking like the edge of the town as shown in Figure 7.37.

Step 2: Using Google Maps displays a place called Kiffa as shown in Figure 7.38. Browsing the photographs of the map, none seem to match, although they seem similar.

Figure 7.37   Use the case #6 target image.

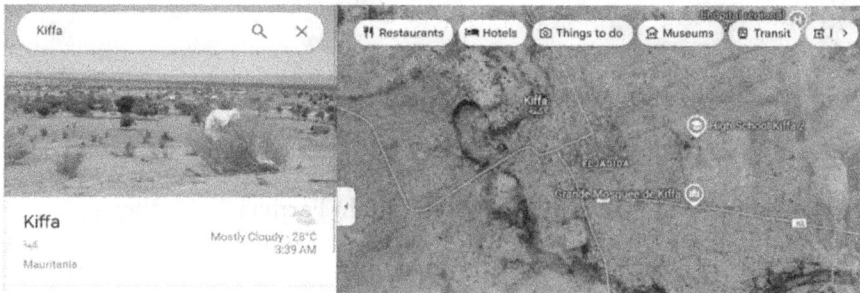

Figure 7.38   City found from Google Maps.

Step 3: If you zoom, the city is very dense, so we can enable the 'Road' view as shown in Figure 7.39.

Step 4: Notice that most roads are dirt roads, and only a few are paved roads as shown in Figure 7.40.

Step 5: Now, we can look for roads leading to outside the city with some trees, which would match with the target image in this use case.

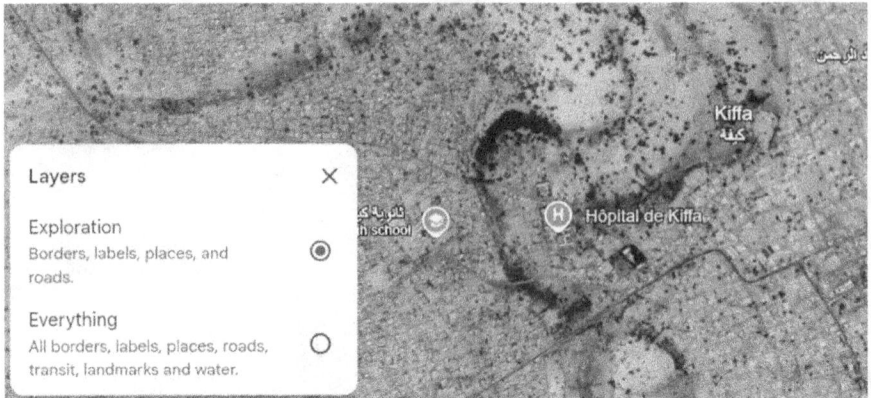

Figure 7.39   Enabling 'Road View.'

Figure 7.40   Found mostly dirt roads and a few paved roads.

7.2.7 Use case #7

Objective: In April 2017, Mohamed Abdullahi Farmaajo, the then president of Somalia, visited Turkey. Your task is to find out the name and coordinates of the location.

Step 1: Google search the above information mentions that news agencies published that photo where he was seen shaking hands with Recep Tayyip Erdoğan, the country's president. The article did not disclose where the photo was taken, as displayed in Figure 7.41.

Step 2: Reverse image search displays few matches, one on Twitter (or X) closely matching with that image, mentioning 'Presidential Complex' as shown in Figure 7.42.

7.2.8 Use case #8

This use case is about a screenshot from a zoo live cam taken on January 15, 2023, around 2 pm. Please answer the questions below:

- In which zoo are these polar bears located?
- What was the temperature at the time of the screenshot?
- What were the exact coordinates of where the bears were lying down?

Step 1: We can see Figure 7.43 displaying two polar bears resting in a rocky area, most likely a zoo.

Step 2: Reverse image search to check for any matches, but there are none, as shown in Figure 7.44.

Step 3: Since we know that the image is from a zoo with live web cameras and polar bears with the photograph date as Jan 15, 2023, perform a simple Google search for 'Polar Bears Live Cam,' which found a few links as shown in Figure 7.45.

Step 4: Checking the 'Polar Bears International' link displays a video as shown in Figure 7.46, but it does not match our target image.

Step 5: Checking the San Diego Zoom link has a web cam, which looks like the target image, so searching on Google Maps for 'Polar Bears San Diego Zoo Plunge,' we browse the photographs and videos plus we find the geolocation (32.73464212289201, −117.15458818749902) as displayed in Figure 7.47.

Figure 7.41   Use the case #7 target image.

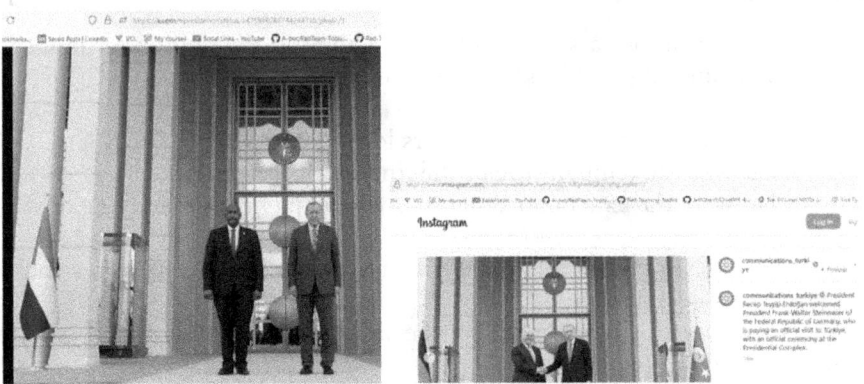

Figure 7.42   Exact location found.

Figure 7.43   Use the case #8 target image.

Step 6: Checking Google for the historical temperature [4] in San Diego reveals 62Deg F (or 15–16 Deg F) [3] on Jan 15, 2023, which matches the information of polar bears in the zoo as shown in Figure 7.48.

Step 9: The location is also verified using Google Earth for San Deago Zoo Plunge as displayed in Figure 7.49.

7.2.9 Use case #9

On January 19, 2023, a journalist with almost 140k followers on Twitter shared an image of a destroyed vehicle amidst a large cloud of smoke and fire

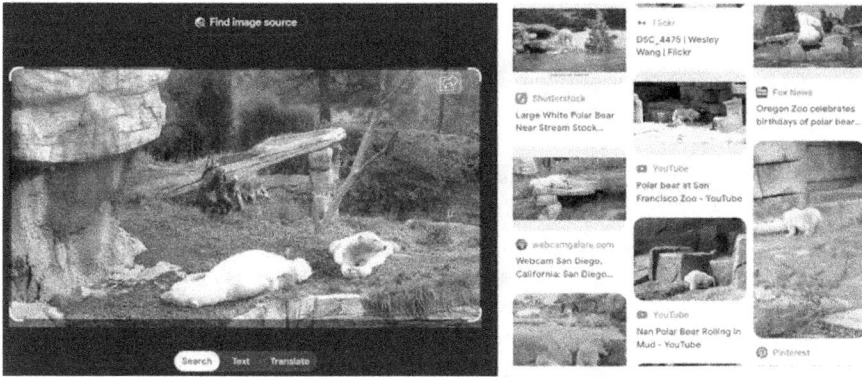

Figure 7.44 No reverse image matches found.

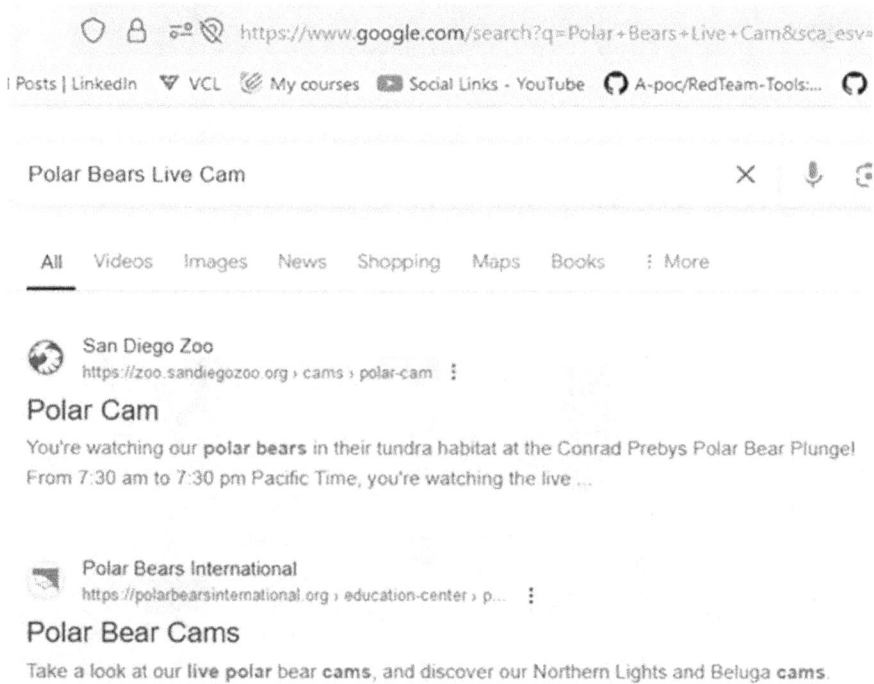

Figure 7.45 Simple Google search performed.

[5]. The tweet said: 'BREAKING: TTP carried out a suicide attack on a police post in Khyber city of Pakistan that killed three Pakistani police officers.'

Objective: Verify the photo and the statement if it is of the event described by the journalist.

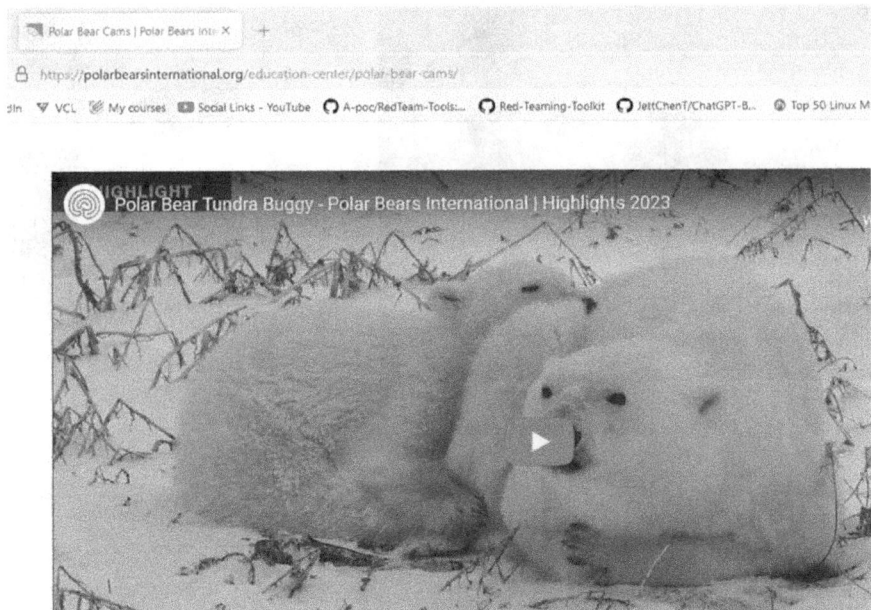

Figure 7.46   Mismatch link.

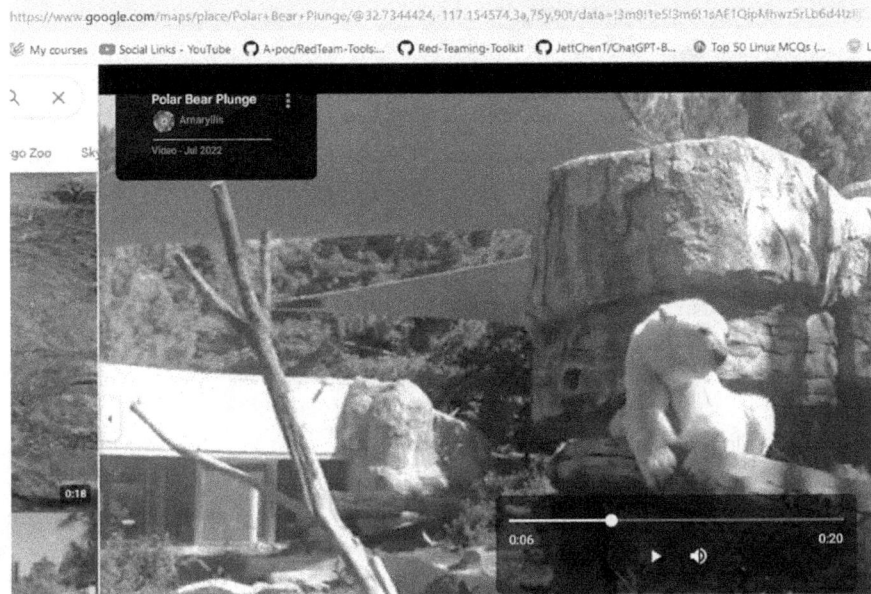

Figure 7.47   Google Map search for target zoo.

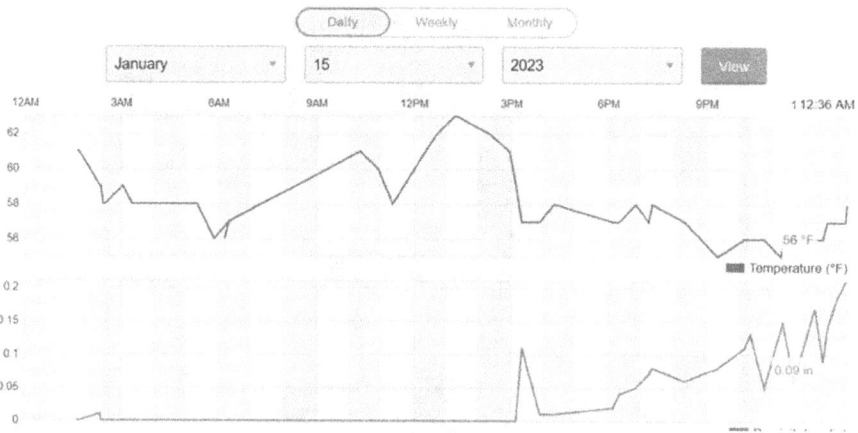

Figure 7.48 Search historical temperature in San Diego.

Figure 7.49 Google earth location match.

Step 1: The target image in Figure 7.50 looks like an improvised explosive device (homemade bomb) in a vehicle explosion.

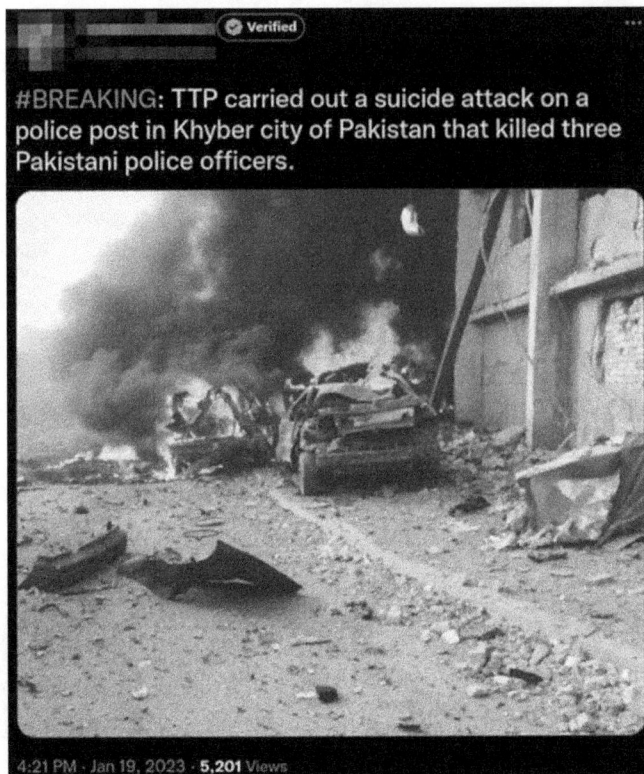

Figure 7.50   Use the case #9 target image.

Step 2: Open the image to perform a reverse image search using Google, as shown in Figure 7.51.

Step 3: Open the link to verify, which reveals the car bomb was set off by Al-Qaeda in Iraq (not Pakistan as claimed on Twitter by the journalist) as shown in Figure 7.52.

Step 4: Google to check 'MC2(SW) Eli J. Medellin' and to re-verify the image reveals a different date, time, and comment as shown in Figure 7.53.

Result: The initial photo was not taken in Pakistan; the journalist cannot be trusted, misinformation.

7.3 FIGHTING CHILD EXPLOITATION ONLINE

PhotoDNA [6] is a powerful tool developed by Microsoft and Dartmouth College to identify and track the spread of known images of child sexual abuse material (CSAM). It works by creating a unique digital fingerprint or hashes for each image. This hash is a mathematical representation of the

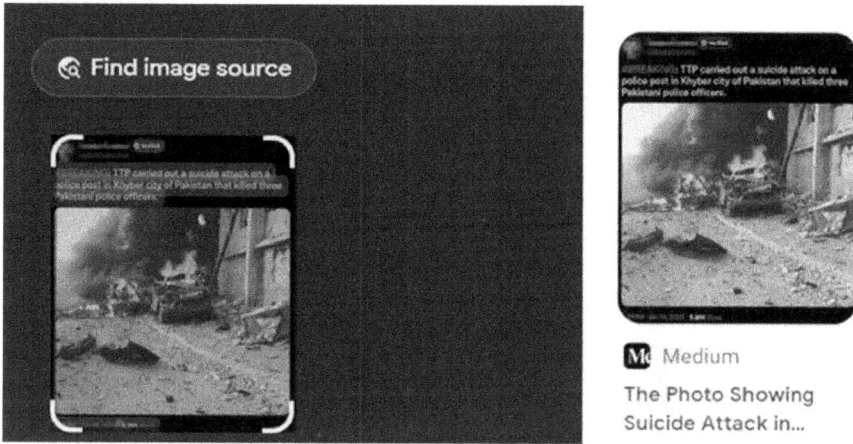

Figure 7.51 Reverse image search match found.

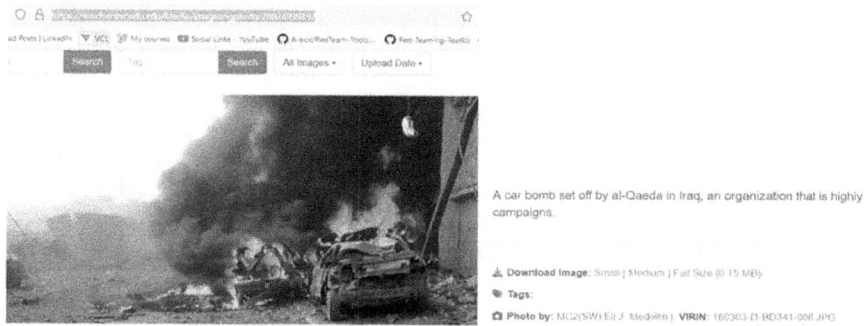

Figure 7.52 Found a different source citing the same car bomb image.

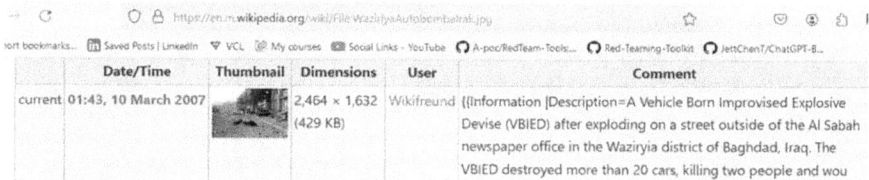

Figure 7.53 Validating the image for authenticity.

image's content, allowing for rapid identification of identical or near-identical copies. When an image is uploaded to a platform that uses PhotoDNA, its hash is compared against a database of known CSAM hashes. If a match is found, the platform can act, such as removing the image, disabling the account, or reporting the incident to law enforcement. It's important to note that PhotoDNA doesn't analyze the content of images itself. It simply compares hashes to identify duplicates. This technology has been instrumental in combating the spread of CSAM online, helping to protect children and hold perpetrators accountable.

7.4 CONCLUSION

IMINT has become a cornerstone of modern intelligence gathering, revolutionizing how we analyze visual information from photographs, aircraft, and satellites. This powerful tool provides invaluable insights for national security by enabling detailed analysis and integration with other intelligence disciplines. This chapter delves into practical applications of IMINT, highlighting its potential to extract information from often overlooked sources like images, PDFs, and videos. These non-textual formats, while frequently underestimated in open-source intelligence, can be used to pinpoint locations, identify individuals, and uncover hidden details, further solidifying IMINT's role as a critical asset in the intelligence community.

REFERENCES

1. "Image Intelligence (IMINT)," 2025. EMSOPEDIA. https://www.emsopedia.org/entries/image-intelligence-imint/
2. National Security Agency, "National Security Agency/Central Security Service > Signals Intelligence > Overview," 2024. https://www.nsa.gov/Signals-Intelligence/Overview
3. Office of the Director of National Intelligence, "What is Intelligence?" 2018. https://www.dni.gov/index.php/what-we-do/what-is-intelligence
4. "San Diego, CA Weather History | Weather Underground," https://www.wunderground.com/history/daily/us/ca/san-diego
5. "Car Bomb," 2024. https://wmdcenter.ndu.edu/Media/Images/igphoto/2002493919/ (accessed Nov. 19, 2024).
6. "PhotoDNA | Microsoft," 2015. https://www.microsoft.com/en-us/photodna?oneroute=true

Chapter 8

Tracking satellites and aircrafts

8.1 INTRODUCTION

The vast expanse of space and air has long been a realm of mystery and intrigue, a domain where secrets are hidden, and truths are obscured. In an age of rapid technological advancement and increasing global interconnectedness, the need to understand and monitor activities within these domains has become paramount. The ability to track satellites and aircrafts is a critical capability for a wide range of stakeholders, including law enforcement agencies, intelligence communities, and private sector organizations. By analyzing data associated with these entities, investigators can gain valuable insights into their movements, intentions, and potential threats. However, the sheer volume and diversity of data available in the digital age can make this task daunting and time-consuming. This chapter aims to provide hands-on use cases for conducting OSINT investigations in the realm of space and air. We will explore the fundamental principles of OSINT, highlighting its strengths and limitations in the context of tracking vehicles and vessels. We will delve into the various sources of open-source information, including social media, news articles, blogs, forums, and government websites, that can be utilized to gather relevant data.

A key aspect of OSINT investigations is the extraction and analysis of Metadata [1], which is often referred to as 'data about data' and provides valuable clues about the creation, modification, and transmission of information. By examining Metadata associated with images, videos, and other digital artifacts, investigators can determine the device used to capture the data, the time and location of capture, and any modifications made to the original content. This information can be invaluable in corroborating evidence and identifying potential inconsistencies. The second critical aspect is geolocation [2] which refers to the geographic coordinates associated with a particular piece of information. By analyzing these data, investigators can track the make, model along with the movements of vehicles, identify patterns of behavior, and pinpoint areas of interest.

Significance in tacking for Digital Forensics:

- Investigating Cybercrimes: Geolocation can help trace the origin of cyberattacks by identifying the geographic location of the devices used to launch the attacks.
- Analyzing Digital Evidence: By analyzing the geolocation data embedded in digital evidence, investigators can reconstruct the timeline of events and identify potential suspects.
- Tracking Stolen Devices: Geolocation can be used to track stolen devices, such as smartphones and laptops, by monitoring their location through cellular networks or Wi-Fi signals.

Significance in tacking for intelligence analysis:

- Monitoring Maritime Traffic: By tracking the movement of ships, intelligence analysts can identify potential threats, such as smuggling or piracy.
- Surveillant Air Traffic: Tracking the flight paths of aircraft can provide valuable information about military operations, humanitarian aid efforts, or potential threats.
- Identifying Patterns of Behavior: By analyzing the movement patterns of individuals or groups, intelligence analysts can identify potential threats or suspicious activities.

8.2 GEOINT CHALLENGES

The analysis of geolocation data is essential for drawing meaningful conclusions from OSINT investigations. By correlating different pieces of information and identifying patterns, investigators can develop hypotheses and generate leads. However, it is crucial to exercise caution and critical thinking when interpreting data, as biases and errors can lead to false conclusions. This chapter will provide practical guidance on conducting OSINT investigations, including tips on data collection, analysis techniques, and ethical considerations. Geolocation relies on a variety of technologies, including:

- Global Positioning System uses triangulation of satellite signals to determine precise geographic coordinates.
- Cellular Network Triangulation: By analyzing the signals between a device and nearby cell towers, investigators can estimate the device's location.
- IP Address Geolocation: While not always precise, IP addresses can be used to approximate the geographic location of a device connected to the internet.

- Wi-Fi Triangulation, similar to cellular triangulation, leverages the signal strength from multiple Wi-Fi access points to estimate the device location.

While geolocation is a powerful tool, it is not without its challenges. The accuracy of geolocation can vary depending on the technology used and environmental factors. The widespread use of geolocation technology raises concerns about privacy and surveillance. Geolocation can be difficult to implement in certain environments, such as indoor locations or areas with poor cellular or Wi-Fi coverage. Despite these challenges, geolocation remains a valuable tool for digital forensics and intelligence analysis. By understanding the principles of geolocation and the technologies that underpin it, investigators can leverage this powerful technique to uncover critical information and protect national security.

8.3 METADATA CHALLENGES

Beyond basic identification, Metadata empowers us to categorize and organize our digital assets, making them more manageable and efficient to work with. By assigning relevant keywords, tags, and subject headings, we can create a structured framework that facilitates seamless navigation and discovery. In the realm of digital libraries and archives, Metadata plays a pivotal role in preserving cultural heritage and ensuring long-term access to historical records. By meticulously documenting the provenance, context, and intellectual property rights associated with digital objects, libraries and archives can safeguard these valuable assets for future generations. Researchers, historians, and scholars rely on accurate and comprehensive Metadata to uncover hidden patterns, draw insightful conclusions, and advance the frontiers of knowledge.

The importance of Metadata extends far beyond the realm of libraries and archives. In the field of digital forensics, Metadata serves as a crucial tool for investigating cybercrimes and reconstructing digital events. By analyzing the Metadata embedded within digital evidence, forensic experts can uncover vital clues about the creation, modification, and transmission of files, leading to the identification and prosecution of cybercriminals. Similarly, in the realm of intelligence analysis, Metadata plays a critical role in identifying patterns, trends, and potential threats. By examining the Metadata associated with emails, phone calls, intelligence analysts can uncover hidden connections, detect suspicious behavior, and anticipate potential security risks. In the ever-evolving landscape of digital information, Metadata stands as a beacon of order and clarity. By understanding its significance and effectively utilizing its power, we can unlock the full potential of our digital assets, ensuring that they remain accessible, searchable, and meaningful for generations to come.

One common culprit is the transfer of files between devices. When we move files from one device to another, such as from a camera to a computer or from a phone to a cloud storage service, Metadata can sometimes be stripped away or altered. This is particularly true when transferring files through file-sharing services or email, as these platforms often prioritize file size and speed over preserving Metadata. Another scenario that can lead to Metadata loss or corruption is the editing and modification of files. When we edit a document, image, or video, the original Metadata may be overwritten or replaced with new information. For instance, if we edit a photo in a software like Photoshop, the original date and time of creation may be lost, replaced by the date and time of the last edit. Similarly, when converting files from one format to another, Metadata can be lost or altered in the process. For example, converting a PDF document to a Word document may result in the loss of information about the original author, creation date, and source document.

The widespread use of mobile devices further exacerbates the issue of Metadata loss. Mobile devices often automatically add location data to photos and videos, but this information can be stripped away when sharing or transferring files. Additionally, many social media platforms automatically strip Metadata from uploaded images and videos, making it difficult to trace the original source or provenance of the content. The impact of missing or incomplete Metadata can be significant. In the realm of digital forensics, incomplete Metadata can hinder the ability to reconstruct the timeline of events and identify the source of digital evidence. In the context of digital preservation, missing Metadata can make it difficult to understand the context and significance of historical documents and records. For researchers and scholars, incomplete Metadata can limit the scope of their research and make it challenging to discover relevant information.

To mitigate the risks associated with Metadata loss, it is essential to adopt best practices for handling digital files which include:

- Use Metadata-Aware Software: Employing software that preserves and enriches Metadata, such as Adobe Photoshop and Lightroom, can help maintain the integrity of digital files.
- Transfer Files in Native Formats: Whenever possible, transfer files in their original format to avoid potential Metadata loss during conversion.
- Back-Up Files Regularly: Regular backups can help preserve Metadata in case of accidental deletion or corruption.
- Use Metadata-Aware Cloud Storage Services: Consider using cloud storage services that support Metadata preservation, such as Google Drive and Dropbox.
- Educate Users About Metadata: Raising awareness about the importance of Metadata and best practices for handling digital files can help prevent accidental loss or corruption.

Incomplete Metadata can significantly hinder the analysis, search, and overall understanding of digital content. When Metadata is missing or inaccurate, it becomes difficult to accurately categorize, organize, and retrieve information. This can lead to several challenges as mentioned below.

Hindered Analysis:
- Difficulty in Identifying Relevant Information: Without accurate Metadata, it becomes challenging to identify relevant information within a large dataset. For example, if a document lacks proper keywords or subject headings, it may not appear in search results, even if it contains valuable information.
- Impaired Understanding of Context: Metadata provides context to digital content. When Metadata is missing, it becomes difficult to understand the context of the information, making it challenging to interpret and analyze. For instance, without knowing the creation date or author of a document, it's harder to assess its relevance and credibility.
- Limited Ability to Draw Conclusions: Incomplete Metadata can limit the ability to draw accurate conclusions from data analysis. For example, if a dataset lacks information about the sampling methodology or data collection process, it may be difficult to assess the reliability and validity of the results.

Hindered Search:
- Inefficient Search Results: Incomplete or inaccurate Metadata can lead to inefficient search results. Search engines rely on Metadata to identify relevant content. If Metadata is missing or incorrect, search results may be inaccurate or incomplete.
- Increased Search Time: When Metadata is missing, it can take longer to find specific information. Users may need to manually sift through large amounts of data to locate the information they need.
- Difficulty in Finding Specific Information: Without accurate Metadata, it can be difficult to find specific information, especially when dealing with large and complex datasets. For example, if a document lacks a clear title or description, it may be difficult to locate when searching for specific information.

Hindered Understanding of Digital Content:
- Reduced Discoverability: Incomplete Metadata can reduce the discoverability of digital content. If a document or image lacks proper Metadata, it may not be found by search engines or other discovery tools.
- Impaired Preservation: Metadata is crucial for the long-term preservation of digital content. Incomplete Metadata can make it difficult to understand the context and significance of digital objects over time.

- Limited Interoperability: Incomplete Metadata can hinder the interoperability of digital content. If different systems or organizations use different Metadata standards, it can be difficult to share and exchange information.

8.4 SATELLITE OSINT

Satellite [3] is any object in space that orbits around a larger object, these are two main types – Natural (like Moon and Comets) and Artificial (include International Space Stations and Starlink Constellation) [4] having about 5,500 artificial satellites in orbit. Satellite imagery has revolutionized the field of OSINT investigations, providing a unique perspective on events and activities around the globe. By analyzing satellite data, investigators can uncover hidden patterns, verify information, and gain valuable insights that might otherwise be inaccessible. One of the fundamental techniques in satellite imagery analysis is data extraction. This involves retrieving relevant information from satellite images, such as geographic coordinates, spectral signatures, and temporal data. Geolocation analysis is another critical component of satellite imagery investigations. By analyzing the geographic coordinates embedded in satellite images, investigators can pinpoint the exact location of specific features, events, or activities. This information can be used to verify claims, identify potential threats, and track the movement of objects or people.

To enhance geolocation analysis, investigators often employ techniques like georeferencing and image registration. Georeferencing involves assigning geographic coordinates to pixels in an image, allowing it to be overlaid on a map. Image registration aligns multiple images to create a more accurate and detailed representation of a specific area. By comparing satellite imagery from different time periods, change detection analysis identifies alterations in land cover infrastructure and human activity–induced modifications on earth's surface from new buildings to deforestation. By analyzing these changes, investigators can uncover patterns of behavior, identify potential threats, and monitor the impact of natural disasters or human activities. Satellite data extraction is a rapidly evolving field with numerous applications across various sectors. As technology advances, we can expect to see even more innovative techniques and tools for extracting valuable insights from this rich source of information.

There are several platform tools and software available for Satellite OSINT, data extraction and analysis. The journey into Satellite OSINT begins with accessing satellite imagery platforms which provide a wealth of visual data that offers a bird's-eye view unlocking the earth's surface.

8.4.1 Use case #1

Objective: Track any Satellite using OSINT

Step 1: Using OSINT, we can scan through public datasets to retrieve information about a satellite. Each artificial satellite in orbit is given two IDs: International Designation [5] and Catalog Number [6] (NORAD ID – nine digits assigned by US Space Command) which can be used to gather information about that satellite, including orientation with orbit, velocity, upcoming passes, etc. For example, International Space Station has the International Designation as 1998-067A, and the NORAD ID is 25544.

Step 2: Let us try to track down Starlink 31046 – this is a satellite within the Starlink constellation. For this, we will be using N2YO [7] which is an online real-time satellite tracking data for users to monitor the positions and trajectories. Visit n2io.com and enter the ID to get the general information about the satellite as shown in Figure 8.1.

Step 2: At the end this web page is a two-line element set as displayed in Figure 8.2; this is a standardized format used to describe the satellite. The first line has the satellite number, international designator, launch date, and orbit motion of the satellite, while the second line has Keplerian elements [8] which define the orientation, size, and shape of the orbit.

Step 3: Using OrbitalMechanics.info [8] Keplerian Elements help visualize the satellite orientation in space as illustrated in Figure 8.3. Enter the

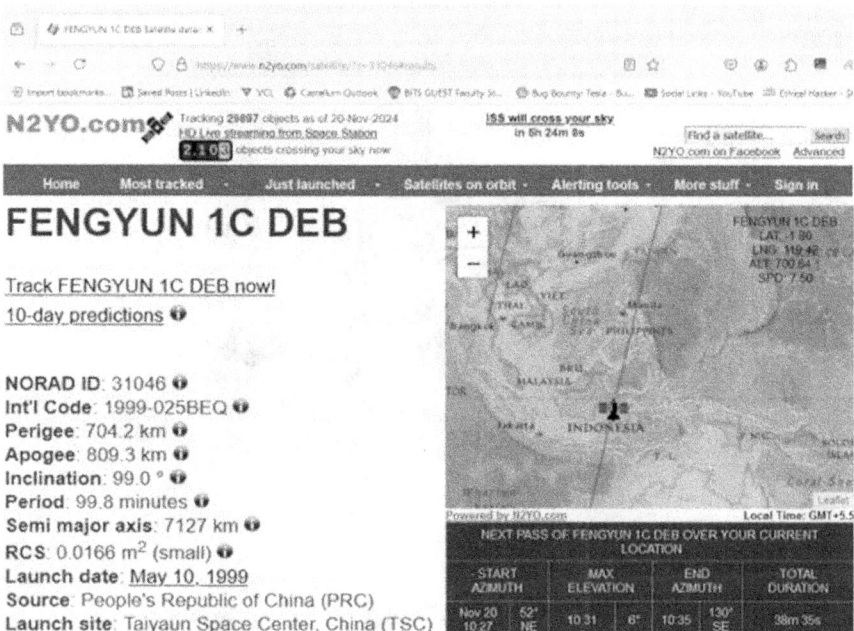

Figure 8.1   Tracking satellites using N2YO portal [7].

Two Line Element Set (TLE): ⓘ

```
1 31046U 99025BEQ 24324.21487899  .00023674  00000-0  68767-2 0  9990
2 31046  98.9748  50.8329 0073714 192.6188 197.3244 14.42695515910007
```

Source of the keplerian elements: AFSPC

Figure 8.2   Two-line descriptor about the satellite.

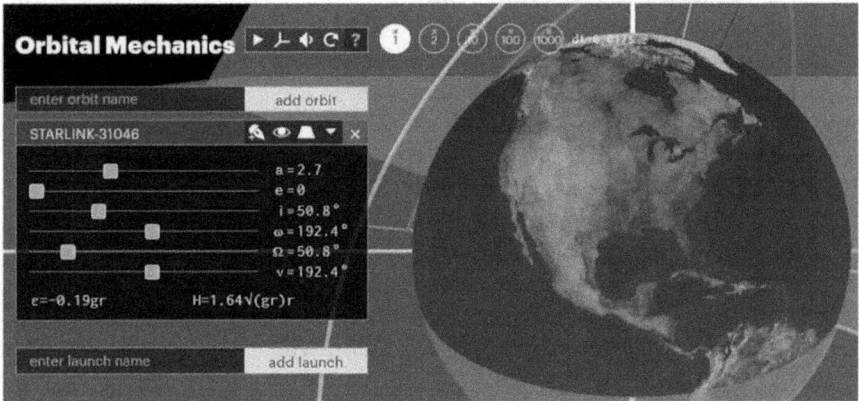

Figure 8.3   Visualizing satellite Keplerian elements.

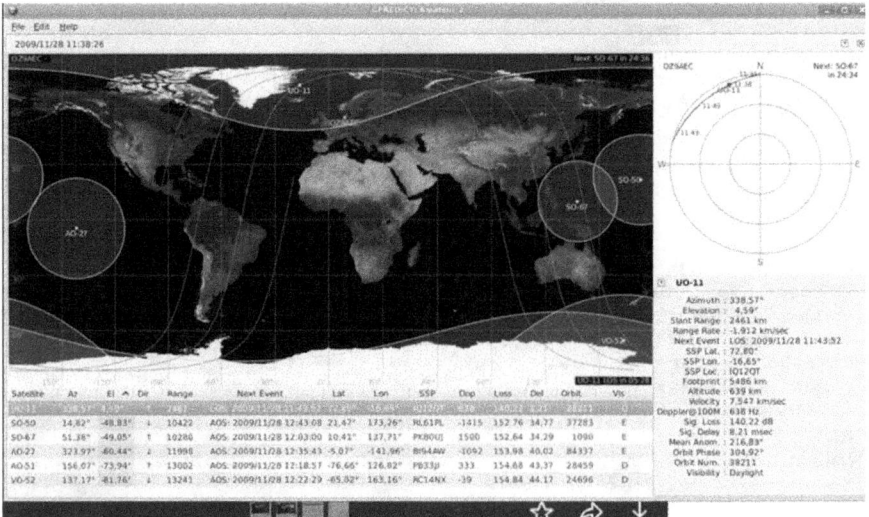

Figure 8.4   Gpredict portal.

Figure 8.5   Google Earth Pro location search.

elements as Eccentricity (e =.00073714), Orbit or Inclination (i=98.9748), Argument of perigee (192.3244), Right Ascension (50.8329), and mean anomaly (197.32).

Step 4: GPredict [9, 10] portal provides real-time orbit prediction and tracking for satellites as shown in Figure 8.4.

8.4.2 Use case #2

Objective: Use Google Earth for Satellite Imagery

Google Earth [11] provides an intuitive platform for accessing high-resolution satellite imagery, empowering users to conduct in-depth analyses of various terrains and geographic features. Its interactive capabilities, including seamless zooming, tilting, and rotating, enable users to explore the world at different scales and perspectives. This versatility makes Google Earth an invaluable tool for a wide range of applications, from urban planning and environmental monitoring to historical research and geographic education.

Figure 8.6   Changed timeline to year 2010.

Figure 8.7   Area imagery in 2024.

Step 1: Download and install Google Earth Pro on your Windows OS, type a location in the 'Search' option as displayed in Figure 8.5 and change the time to 2024. This will display the latest imagery.

Step 2: Change the timeline to an older date as shown in Figure 8.6 which displays less houses and construction.

Step 3: We can find the construction progress of a town or village in 2024 as displayed in Figure 8.7.

Step 5: Scrolling backward in time, the same area in 2013 is displayed in Figure 8.8 as per the satellite's imagery with less houses and construction.

Step 6: To verify this feature further, we checked the city 'London' city in 2023 as shown in Figure 8.9.

Step 7: Figure 8.10 displays the city 'London' in 2002, which displays blurry buildings and roads and the area changes over time.

- Sentinel Hub: Sentinel Hub is a comprehensive satellite imagery service that offers automated processing and distribution of multi-spectral and multi-temporal remote sensing data. Users can leverage its application programming interfaces to efficiently access and retrieve satellite data for their Area of Interest and desired time range from a comprehensive archive. This enables users to conduct in-depth analysis of various terrains and geographic features, empowering them to uncover hidden patterns and make informed decisions. The platform's user-friendly interface and powerful capabilities make it an invaluable tool for a wide range of applications, from urban planning and environmental monitoring to historical research and geographic education as displayed in Figure 8.11.

Figure 8.8   Area imagery in 2013.

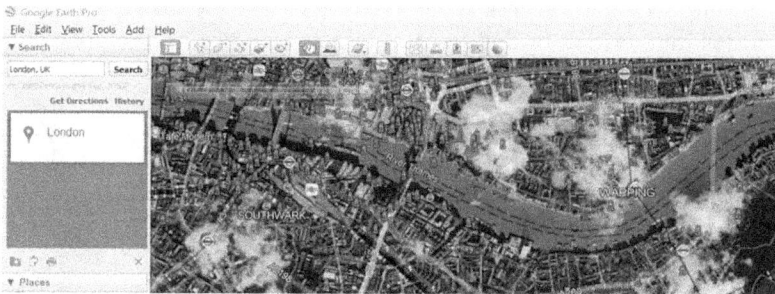

Figure 8.9   London in 2024.

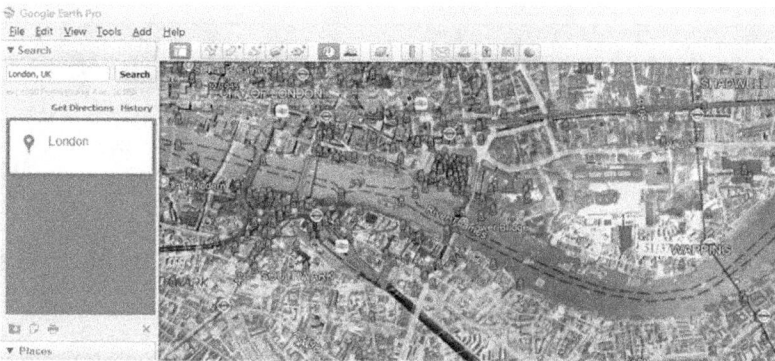

Figure 8.10   London in 2002.

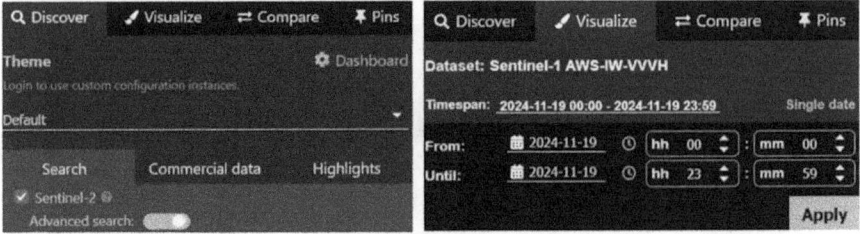

Figure 8.11   Sentinel one datasets & timeline selection.

I leveraged the SENTINEL-2 which is a European satellite system equipped with a high-resolution multi-spectral imager. This instrument provides 13 spectral bands spanning the visible, near-infrared, and shortwave-infrared regions of the electromagnetic spectrum. The versatile nature of this data enables a wide range of applications, including land use monitoring to track changes in land cover, urban expansion, deforestation, and agriculture practices. This also assess damage caused by natural disasters like floods, fires, and earthquakes to support relief efforts. The system can also be utilized to monitor water quality, air pollution, and climate change and support border surveillance and maritime security.

- Zoom Earth: Zoom Earth [12] is a powerful tool for OSINT investigations, offering a wealth of features and capabilities that can be leveraged to gather valuable information. Zoom Earth provides access to a vast library of high-resolution satellite imagery, allowing you to analyze changes in landscapes, infrastructure, and other features over time.

Figure 8.12   Zoom earth visualization on storms.

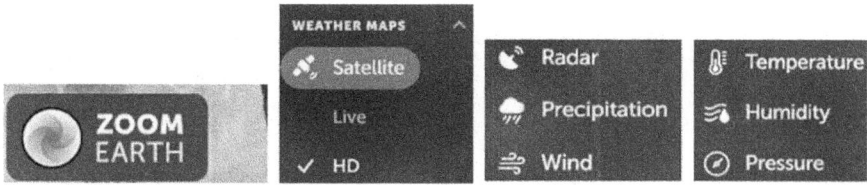

Figure 8.13   Zoom earth options.

The platform allows to create time-lapse videos to visualize changes over a period, making it easier to spot trends and patterns as displayed in Figure 8.12. This also has built-in measurement tools to calculate distances, areas, and other relevant metrics within the imagery.

We can track real-time weather conditions, including hurricanes, cyclones, and other severe weather events, to assess potential impacts on specific locations or regions and explore historical satellite images to identify changes in a particular area, such as construction projects, deforestation, or natural disasters as displayed in Figure 8.13.

- World Imagery Wayback: World Imagery Wayback [13] is a powerful tool for OSINT investigations, providing access to historical satellite imagery. It enables analysts to examine changes in landscapes over time, aiding in various investigations. The key features include access to multiple versions of World Imagery captured over the past several years, time-lapse analysis for visualizing changes, change detection to identify differences, geolocation to pinpoint locations, damage assessment to evaluate impact, and intelligence gathering for information collection as shown in Figure 8.14.

OSINT applications range from investigating natural disasters and monitoring construction projects to analyzing conflict zones, verifying news reports, and tracking environmental changes. The platform offers a range

Figure 8.14   World imagery Wayback in 2024.

Figure 8.15   Time-lapse for the same location in 2015.

of image resolutions and sources imagery from various providers. It is accessible through a web browser and provides regular updates to the satellite imagery. While it's a valuable tool, its limitations include varying image quality due to factors like cloud cover and atmospheric conditions, limited availability of high-resolution and historical imagery for certain regions, and potential privacy concerns when investigating individuals or private property as displayed in Figure 8.15.

- NASA Worldview: NASA [14] Worldview is a dynamic platform that empowers users to visualize and analyze a vast array of satellite data products in real time. This invaluable tool enables monitoring of diverse environmental phenomena, including tracking the spread and intensity of wildfires, assessing fire risk and support firefighting efforts. This also helps in monitoring volcanic activity, predicting potential eruptions and assessing ash disposal. By analyzing sea surface temperatures, marine heatwaves can be identified to study climate change impact on marine ecosystems. By observing weather patterns, this is used to track hurricanes and typhoons and predict air quality.

8.4.3 Use case #3

Objective: Find Camp Fire in California, USA

Step 1: Open WorldView Earthdata and search for overlay 'Fires and Thermal Anomalies' as shown in Figure 8.16.

Step 2: Figure 8.17 displays the image of a campfire raging in California USA; this has been captured by Landsat 8 Imager on November 8, 2018.

Step 2: The ability to visualize data from diverse sensors and sources, such as satellites, weather stations, and ocean buoys, facilitates a holistic

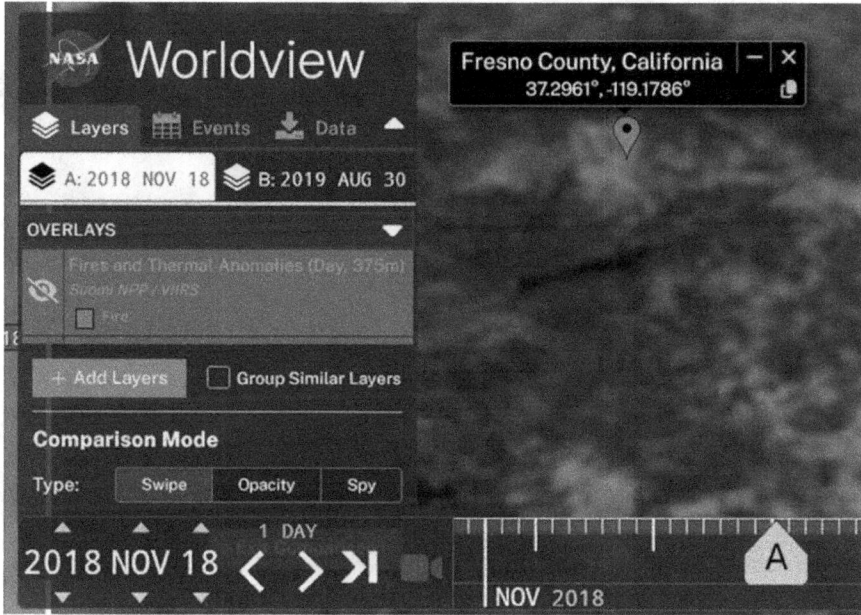

Figure 8.16   Worldview earth interface.

analysis of global phenomena. By integrating data from multiple sources, it enables a comprehensive understanding of complex interactions between different earth systems, such as the atmosphere, ocean, and land. This holistic perspective is essential for addressing global challenges, such as climate change, natural disasters, and resource management. Figure 8.18 displays lava eruptions in Reykjanes, Iceland captured on February 10, 2024, by the Landsat 9 Imager-2.

8.5 AIRCRAFT OSINT

OSINT investigations involving aircraft data offer a unique perspective on global events, enabling analysts to track movements, identify patterns, and uncover hidden connections. By leveraging a variety of tools and techniques, investigators can extract valuable insights from this rich source of information.

One of the primary sources of aircraft data is Flightradar24 [15] and Automatic Dependent Surveillance-Broadcast (ADS-B) [16] which is a surveillance technology that enables aircraft to transmit their position, altitude, speed, and other pertinent flight parameters to air traffic control and other aircraft in real time. This continuous stream of data enhances situational awareness for both air traffic controllers and pilots, leading to improved safety, efficiency, and precision in air traffic management.

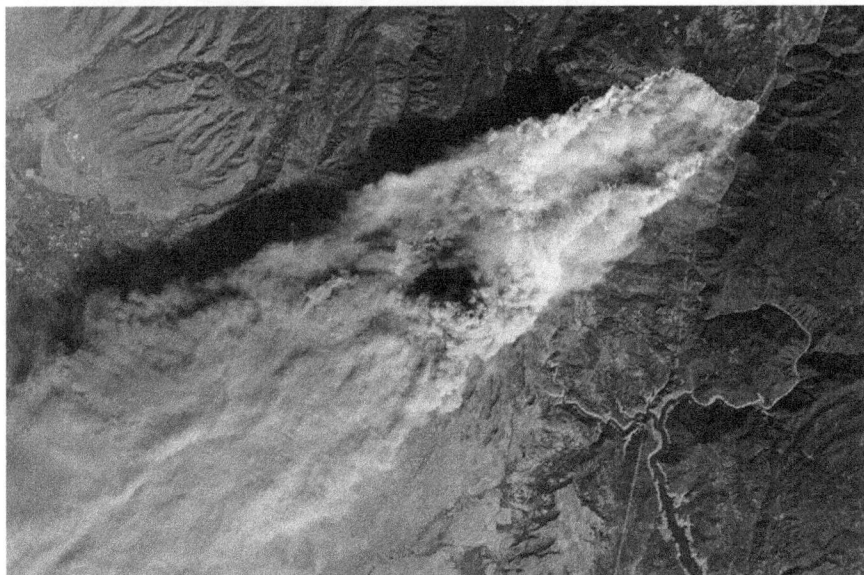

Figure 8.17   Camp fire located.

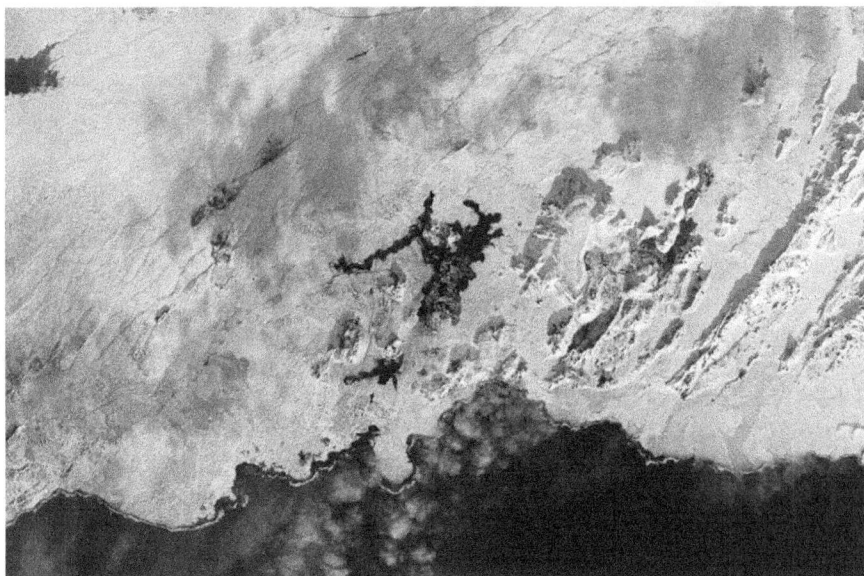

Figure 8.18   Lava eruption captured by the satellite.

By providing accurate and timely information, ADS-B [17] contributes to reduced separation standards, optimized flight paths, and enhanced coordination between aircraft and air traffic control.

Additionally, ADS-B data can be utilized for various applications, such as flight tracking, airspace monitoring, and accident investigation. This data can be accessed through various online platforms, such as FlightRadar24 and ADS-B Exchange, allowing investigators to track flights in real time. By analyzing ADS-B data, investigators can identify flight paths, departure and arrival airports, and flight durations. This information can be used to verify claims, identify potential threats, and track the movement of specific aircraft. For example, by analyzing flight patterns, investigators may be able to identify unusual activity or potential security threats. Investigators also analyze data from other sources, such as aircraft registration databases and airport databases.

By visualizing data in different ways, investigators can identify trends, anomalies, and potential insights. Flightradar24 enables real-time tracking of aircraft globally to view details such as location, altitude, aircraft type, and speed. This platform is invaluable for flight surveillance, analyzing flight paths, and monitoring weather conditions affecting flights as displayed in Figure 8.19.

8.5.1 Use case #1

Objective: Identify and Track Plane from the Satellite image

Step 1: Using Google Earth Pro search and open 'IGI Airport,' the satellite image at 9:53 am from November 2024 shows one plane landing on the tarmac in Figure 8.20. Let us try to find the airline, type, and model of this plane, where did it came from.

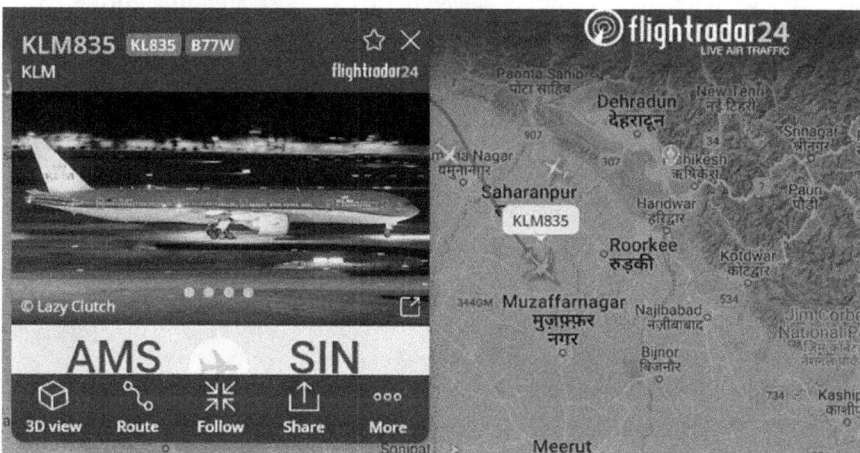

Figure 8.19 Flightradar24 interface.

Figure 8.20   Google earth IGI Airport.

Step 2: Using Flightradar24 to filter for IGI Airport, November 21, 2023 at 9:53 am UTC (Nov 20, 3:25 pm IST), notice that one plane is inbound (Callsign: IGO2192 & Flight: 6E2192) as illustrated in Figure 8.21.

Step 3: Searching the flight history for this flight (6E2192) reveals that this as an Indigo airline Code A20N Airbus A320 Serial Number 08896 is five years old. This flight started from Deoghar on November 20, 2024 at 1:20 PM IST and landed in New Delhi at 3:35 PM IST as presented in Figure 8.22 which matches with the satellite image from Google Earth.

8.5.2 Use case #2

Objective: Find airports with delays and disruptions

Step 1: Use Flightradar24 for 'Airport Disruptions [Live]' which displays 'San Francisco International Airport' with disruption index '5' indicating major problems with long delays and canceled flights as illustrated in Figure 8.23.

Step 2: Validating this on a weather portal Figure 8.24 confirms that the disruption reason is due to rains.

Figure 8.21   Found plane landing at 9:53 am.

Figure 8.22   Tracked flight details.

Figure 8.23   Live airport disruption.

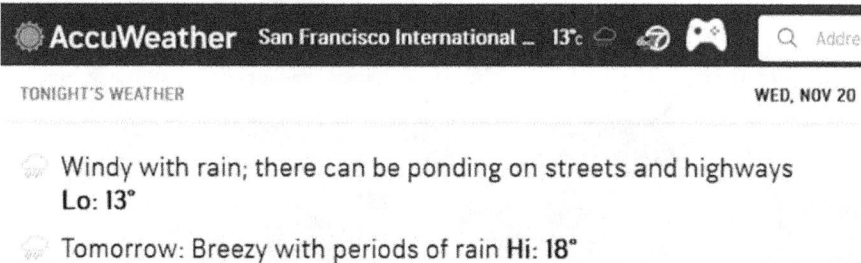

WED, NOV 20

Windy with rain; there can be ponding on streets and highways
Lo: 13°

Tomorrow: Breezy with periods of rain Hi: 18°

Figure 8.24   Validating temperature conditions.

8.5.3 Use case #3

Objective: Identify Registration and Type of Plane from Satellite image dated April 17, 2023

Step 1: Figure 8.25 illustrates an image of a destroyed plane at Khartoum International Airport, Sudan.

Figure 8.25   Satellite image of the Sudan airport.

Step 2: Figure 8.26 shows few news blogs which confirm clashes between the Sudanese army and paramilitary forces on April 17, 2023, which led to planes being destroyed.

Step 3: Checking satellite images on Google Earth for the period near the clash date reveals several large aircrafts always stationed at the same tarmac location as displayed in Figure 8.27. These seem to be of the same model and type of planes that are present at that specific location.

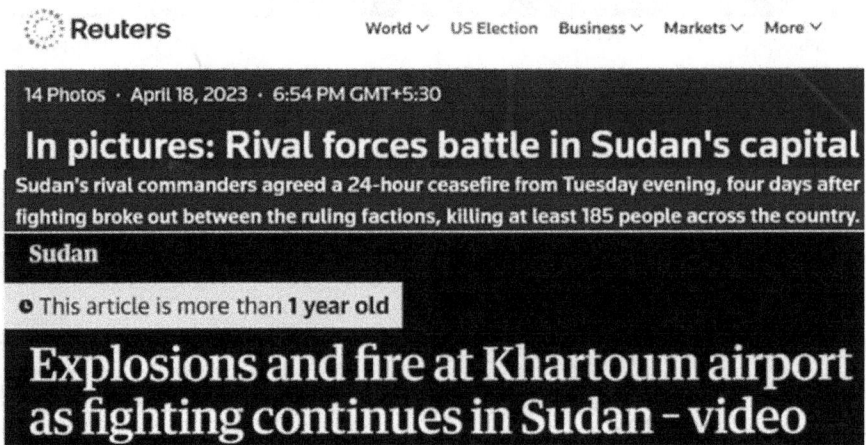

Figure 8.26   Reuter news confirms the airport attack.

Figure 8.27   Satellite image of the plane on tarmac.

Step 4: Checking the historical data in 'Arrivals' Figure 8.28 reveals that this airport always receives Alfa Airlines Aircraft 735.

Step 5: Google search for 'Alfa Airlines Aircraft 735' reveals that Alfa Airlines has one Boeing 737 which is a B735 as illustrated in Figure 8.29.

8.5.4 Use case #4

Objective: Track aircrafts and their travel history using ADSB-X

Step 1: Open Avionic Tools portal into the ICAO Calc and type the tail number of the aircraft you want to track (in our case this is 'n271dv') as shown in Figure 8.30.

Arrivals

TIME	FLIGHT	FROM	AIRLINE	AIRCRAFT
Wednesday, Nov 20				
11:30 AM	5E451	Nyala (UYL)	Alfa Airlines	735
Thursday, Nov 21				
1:00 PM	5E301	Juba (JUB)	Alfa Airlines	735
6:20 PM	5E111	Port Sudan (PZU)	Alfa Airlines	735
Friday, Nov 22				
11:40 AM	5E411	Geneina (EGN)	Alfa Airlines	735

Figure 8.28   Historical arrival data.

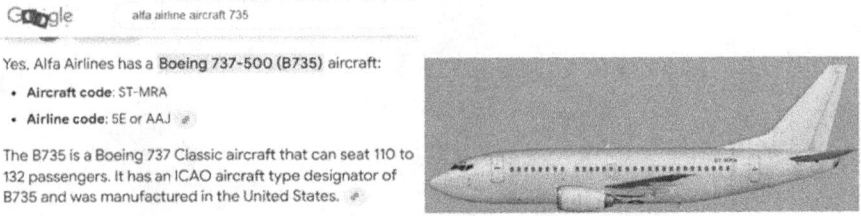

Figure 8.29   Google search for Alfa airline planes.

Step 2: This provides the HEX code of the aircraft next; we use Globe. ADBSExchange [17] to search the travel log date wise. Figure 8.31 displays flight registration number 'N271DV' having HEX code 'A2AA92' with historical travel log on February 1, 2023, confirming that this plane flew from Seattle to Los Angles.

Step 3: Searching Google as displayed in Figure 8.32 for flight registration number 'N271DV' reveals that the plane belongs to 'Jeff Bezos' who sold this private jet recently.

8.5.5 Use case#5

Objective: Using ADS-B exchange for OSINT

Step 1: Using ADS-B [17] broadcasted by airplanes for Air Traffic Controllers to correlate their radar detection to an actual aircraft.

Avionic Tools

Icao Calc

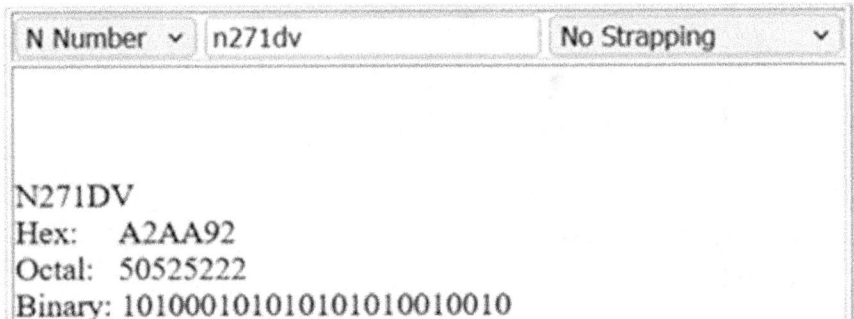

N271DV
Hex: A2AA92
Octal: 50525222
Binary: 101000101010101010010010

Figure 8.30   Avionic tools tracking planes.

EJM4
Hex: A2AA92 Copy Link
adsbexchange.com
Image © Wolfgang Kaiser
Reg.: N271DV
United States
DB flags: LADD
Type: GLF6
2015 GULFSTREAM G650
POPLAR GLEN LLC
Type Desc.: L2J
Squawk: 3555
FULL DETAILS
History
UTC day:
2023-02-01
previous next
Legs: All
previous next
Time: 23:04:10 Z
stop 1x 5x
10x 20x 40x
Click on the trace line to start playback!
SPATIAL
Groundspeed: 521 kt
Baro. Altitude: 45000 ft
WGS84 altitude: 45175 ft
Vert. Rate: 0 ft/min
Track: 167.0°
Pos.: 39.247°, -120.209°

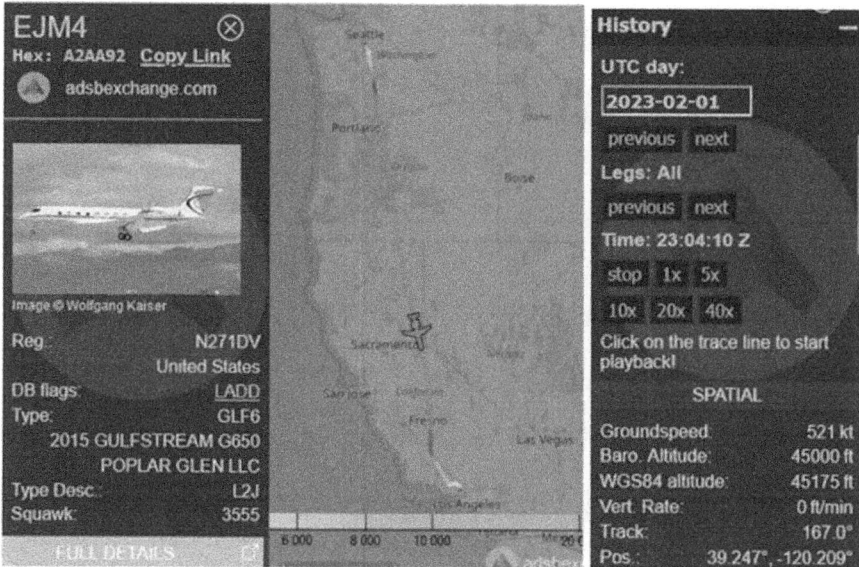

Figure 8.31 Tracking plan on a specific date.

This uses system wide information management [18] by Federal Aviation administration department providing mode details as shown in Figure 8.33 as compared to Flightradar24.

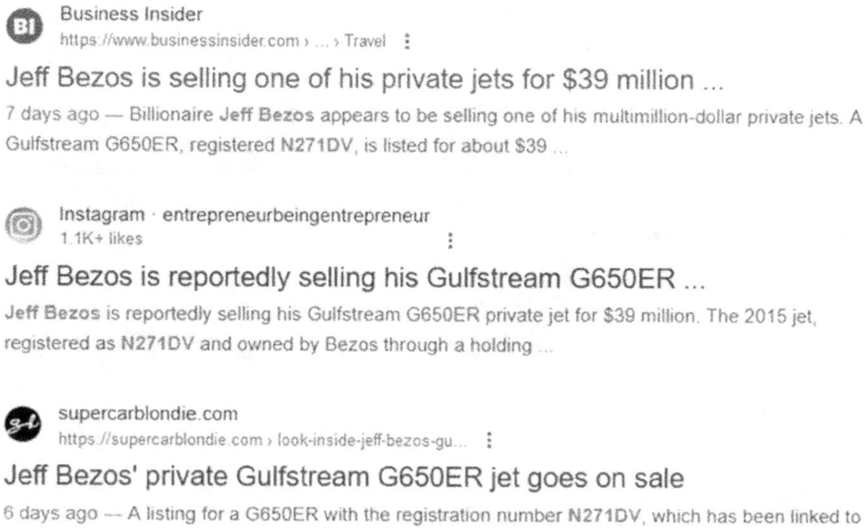

Business Insider
https://www.businessinsider.com › ... › Travel
Jeff Bezos is selling one of his private jets for $39 million ...
7 days ago — Billionaire Jeff Bezos appears to be selling one of his multimillion-dollar private jets. A Gulfstream G650ER, registered N271DV, is listed for about $39 ...
Instagram · entrepreneurbeingentrepreneur
1.1K+ likes
Jeff Bezos is reportedly selling his Gulfstream G650ER ...
Jeff Bezos is reportedly selling his Gulfstream G650ER private jet for $39 million. The 2015 jet, registered as N271DV and owned by Bezos through a holding ...
supercarblondie.com
https://supercarblondie.com › look-inside-jeff-bezos-gu...
Jeff Bezos' private Gulfstream G650ER jet goes on sale
6 days ago — A listing for a G650ER with the registration number N271DV, which has been linked to

Figure 8.32 Google search for flight registration number 'N271DV.'

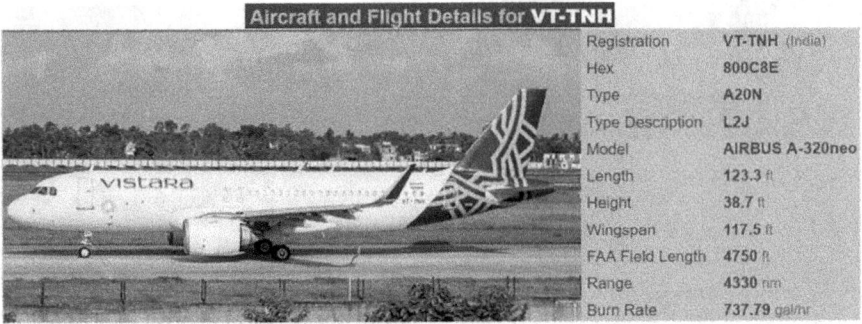

Figure 8.33   ADS-B exchange flight details.

Step 2: ADS-B Exchange Take-off and Landing historical details found as illustrated in Figure 8.34.

Step 3: We can also search for aircraft in a specific location by Call Sign as shown in Figure 8.35.

Step 4: We can even filter for aircraft by Altitude as shown in Figure 8.36 which displays only one aircraft flying at an altitude between 13,500 and 14,000 feet.

8.5.6 Use case#6

Objective: Use Python-based tool to spot aircrafts

Skytrack [19] is a Python-based command-line program for aviation OSINT spying and plane spotting. It can convert between ICAO and Tail Number designations, create a PDF report for a designated aircraft, and collect aircraft information from many data sources. Skytrack can assist you in identifying and counting aircraft for general purpose reconnaissance,

Date	Callsign	Time (UTC)	Airport	Region	Municipality	Runway
Nov 27, 2024	AIC2601	03:13	VIDP	IN-DL	New Delhi	28
Nov 26, 2024	AIC2886	14:56	VOCI	IN-KL	Kochi	9
Nov 26, 2024	AIC2885	11:15	VIDP	IN-DL	New Delhi	29R
Nov 26, 2024	AIC2822	04:21	VOMM	IN-TN	Chennai	7

Time (UTC)	Airport	Region	Municipality	Runway	Duration	Distance
17:44	VIDP	IN-DL	New Delhi	29L	2:48	1106
14:02	VOCI	IN-KL	Kochi	-	2:47	1106
09:16	VIDP	IN-DL	New Delhi	29L	4:54	951

Figure 8.34   ADS-B take-off and landing details.

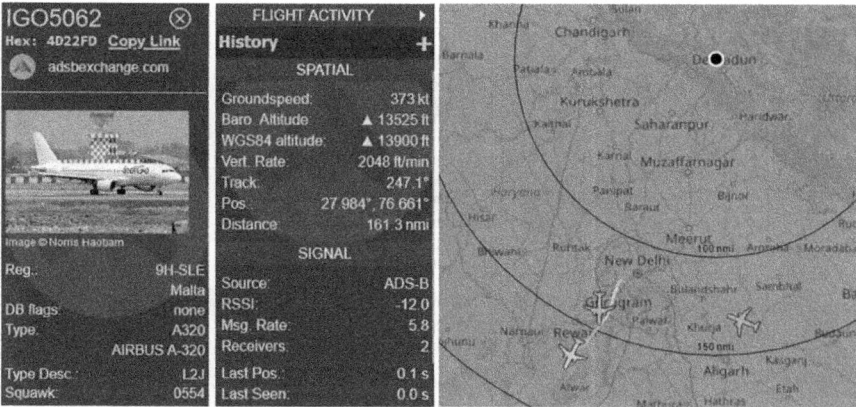

Figure 8.35   ADS-B filtering by call sign.

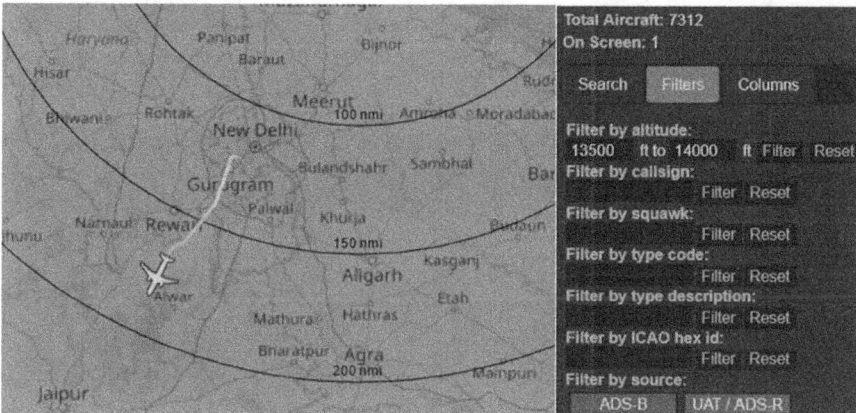

Figure 8.36   ADS-B filtering by call sign.

regardless of your level of experience as an aircraft analyst or as a hobbyist plane spotter.

Step 1: I am using Kali Linux to install Skytrack, which is Git cloned as shown in Figure 8.37.

Step 2: Install prerequisites required to run the tool as displayed in Figure 8.38.

Step 3: Run the Python script to run the Skytrack tool as illustrated in Figure 8.39.

Step 4: The tool displays four options are illustrated below in Figure 8.40.

Step 5: Choosing a Tail Number (n271dv) select option 3 and then option 1 to convert the Tail number into ICAO Designator as shown in Figure 8.41.

Step 6: We can validate this by choosing option 2 to convert ICAO Designator into the Tail Number as displayed in Figure 8.42.

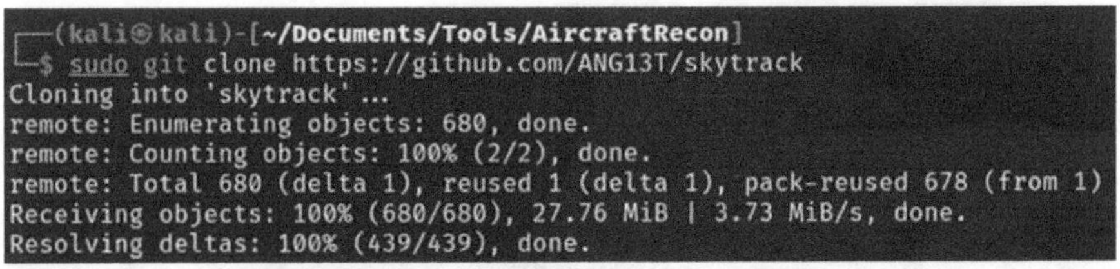

```
┌──(kali㉿kali)-[~/Documents/Tools/AircraftRecon]
└─$ sudo git clone https://github.com/ANG13T/skytrack
Cloning into 'skytrack' ...
remote: Enumerating objects: 680, done.
remote: Counting objects: 100% (2/2), done.
remote: Total 680 (delta 1), reused 1 (delta 1), pack-reused 678 (from 1)
Receiving objects: 100% (680/680), 27.76 MiB | 3.73 MiB/s, done.
Resolving deltas: 100% (439/439), done.
```

Figure 8.37   Install Skytrack on Kali Linux.

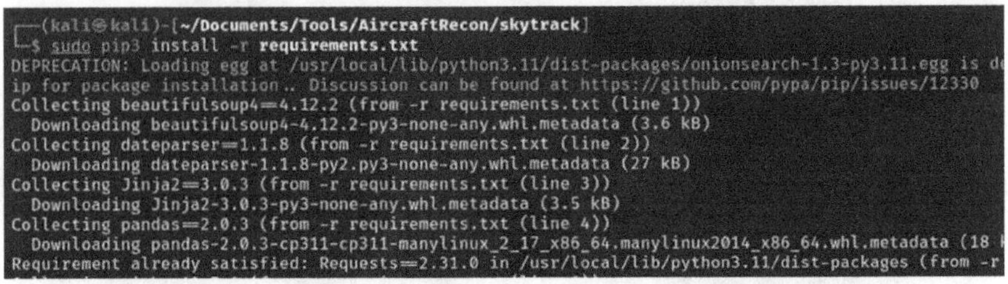

```
┌──(kali㉿kali)-[~/Documents/Tools/AircraftRecon/skytrack]
└─$ sudo pip3 install -r requirements.txt
DEPRECATION: Loading egg at /usr/local/lib/python3.11/dist-packages/onionsearch-1.3-py3.11.egg is d
ip for package installation.. Discussion can be found at https://github.com/pypa/pip/issues/12330
Collecting beautifulsoup4==4.12.2 (from -r requirements.txt (line 1))
  Downloading beautifulsoup4-4.12.2-py3-none-any.whl.metadata (3.6 kB)
Collecting dateparser==1.1.8 (from -r requirements.txt (line 2))
  Downloading dateparser-1.1.8-py2.py3-none-any.whl.metadata (27 kB)
Collecting Jinja2==3.0.3 (from -r requirements.txt (line 3))
  Downloading Jinja2-3.0.3-py3-none-any.whl.metadata (3.5 kB)
Collecting pandas==2.0.3 (from -r requirements.txt (line 4))
  Downloading pandas-2.0.3-cp311-manylinux_2_17_x86_64.manylinux2014_x86_64.whl.metadata (18 k
Requirement already satisfied: Requests==2.31.0 in /usr/local/lib/python3.11/dist-packages (from -r
```

Figure 8.38   Install prerequisites.

```
┌──(kali㉿kali)-[~/Documents/Tools/AircraftRecon/skytrack]
└─$ sudo python skytrack.py
```

Figure 8.39   Executing the Python tool.

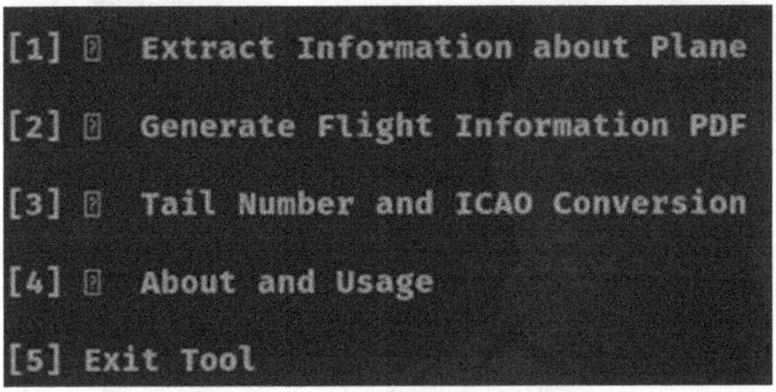

```
[1] ✈  Extract Information about Plane

[2] ✈  Generate Flight Information PDF

[3] ✈  Tail Number and ICAO Conversion

[4] ✈  About and Usage

[5] Exit Tool
```

Figure 8.40   Skytrack options.

8.6 CONCLUSION

The realm of space and air once shrouded in mystery is now increasingly accessible through OSINT. By harnessing the power of publicly available information, investigators can gain valuable insights into the activities of vehicles and vessels, unravel complex scenarios, and contribute to

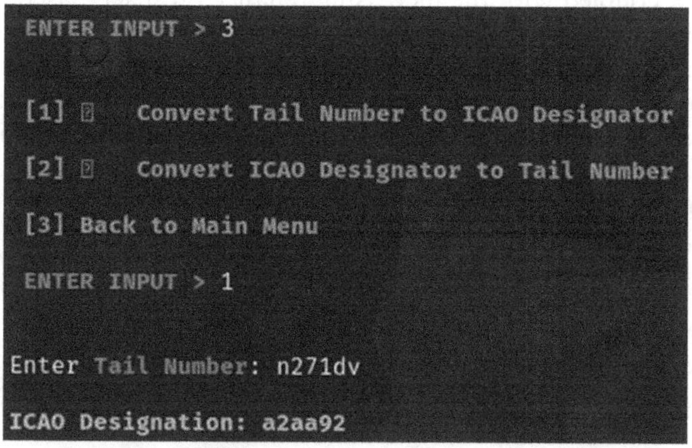

```
ENTER INPUT > 3

[1] ▯   Convert Tail Number to ICAO Designator

[2] ▯   Convert ICAO Designator to Tail Number

[3] Back to Main Menu

ENTER INPUT > 1


Enter Tail Number: n271dv

ICAO Designation: a2aa92
```

Figure 8.41   Tail number to ICAO Designator conversion.

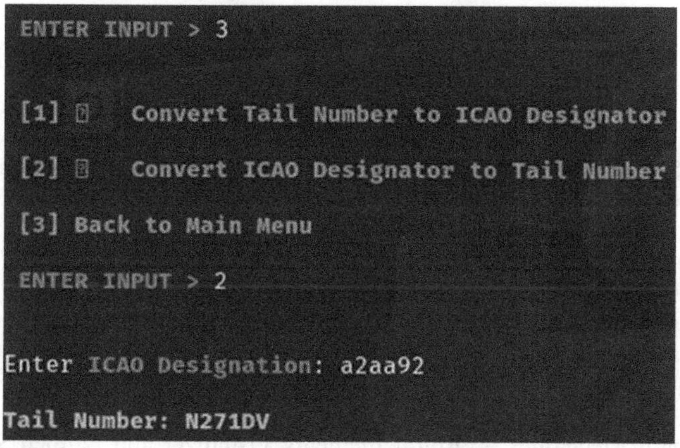

```
ENTER INPUT > 3

[1] ▯   Convert Tail Number to ICAO Designator

[2] ▯   Convert ICAO Designator to Tail Number

[3] Back to Main Menu

ENTER INPUT > 2


Enter ICAO Designation: a2aa92

Tail Number: N271DV
```

Figure 8.42   ICAO Designator to tail number conversion.

national security and international cooperation. This chapter has explored and emphasized the process of tracking satellites and aircrafts across the space and air. We have delved into the various platforms and tools, highlighting the need for careful analysis to discern credible information from misinformation. While OSINT offers immense potential, it is essential to acknowledge its limitations. The dynamic nature of online information, the constant evolution of technology, and the potential for privacy concerns pose challenges that must be addressed. By staying abreast of emerging trends and adapting to evolving methodologies, investigators can maximize the effectiveness of OSINT in the face of these challenges. As the 21st century unfolds, the strategic importance of OSINT in safeguarding our space and aviation domains will continue to escalate. The rapid advancements in technology, coupled with the increasing reliance on space-based assets and air transportation, necessitate the development and application of robust OSINT capabilities to address emerging threats and challenges. By leveraging the power of open-source information, OSINT enables us to monitor and analyze activities in the space and aviation domains, identify potential risks, and take proactive measures to ensure security and safety. By embracing the power of open-source information and honing our investigative skills, we can contribute to a safer and more secure future.

REFERENCES

1. Komprise, "What Is Metadata? Metadata Definition," May 08, 2017. https://www.komprise.com/glossary_terms/metadata/
2. M. Rashid, "Geolocation Data: Definition, Collection Methods and Uses," GeoPlugin – Resources, Jun. 06, 2024. https://www.geoplugin.com/resources/geolocation-data-definition-collection-methods-and-uses/ (accessed Nov. 27, 2024).
3. E. Howell, "What Is a Satellite?" Oct. 27, 2017. https://www.space.com/24839-satellites.html.
4. NASA, "What Is the International Space Station? (Grades 5–8) – NASA," Oct. 30, 2020. https://www.nasa.gov/learning-resources/for-kids-and-students/what-is-the-international-space-station-grades-5-8/
5. USGS, "What Are the Band Designations for the Landsat Satellites? | U.S. Geological Survey," 2023. https://www.usgs.gov/faqs/what-are-band-designations-landsat-satellites.
6. "NORAD Catalogue Number," 2024. https://www.n2yo.com/database/?name=aerocube+6 (accessed Nov. 27, 2024).
7. "Search Satellite Database," 2024. https://www.n2yo.com/database/?q=Find+a+satellite...#results (accessed Nov. 27, 2024).
8. "Glossary – k," 2025. https://www.grc.nasa.gov/www/k-12/TRC/laefs/laefs_k.html
9. "Orbital Mechanics – Orbital Elements Visualizer and Launch Simulator," 2019. https://orbitalmechanics.info/
10. "Gpredict: Free, Real-Time Satellite Tracking and Orbit Prediction Software," https://oz9aec.dk/gpredict
11. Google Earth, "Google Earth," 2024. https://earth.google.com/web/
12. Neave Interactive, "Zoom Earth – Explore Satellite and Aerial Images of the Earth," 2017. https://zoom.earth/
13. A. L. A. of the World, "World Imagery Wayback," 2025. https://livingatlas.arcgis.com/wayback/
14. NASA, "Worldview: Explore Your Dynamic Planet," 2019. https://worldview.earthdata.nasa.gov/
15. Flightradar24, "Live Flight Tracker – Real-Time Flight Tracker Map | Flightradar24," 2000. https://www.flightradar24.com/
16. Federal Aviation Administration, "Automatic Dependent Surveillance - Broadcast (ADS-B)" | Federal Aviation Administration," 2022. https://www.faa.gov/about/office_org/headquarters_offices/avs/offices/afx/afs/afs400/afs410/ads-b

17. "ADS-B Exchange – Track Aircraft Live," https://globe.adsbexchange.com/
18. Icao.int, 2019. https://www.icao.int/APAC/Pages/swim.aspx
19. "ANG13T/skytrack: Skytrack is a Planespotting and Aircraft OSINT Tool Made Using Python 🔍," GitHub, 2024. https://github.com/adsANG13T/skytrack (accessed Nov. 27, 2024).

Chapter 9

Tracking maritime and land-based transportation

9.1 MARITIME OSINT

OSINT investigations into marine vessels in the oceans and seas provide a unique perspective on tracking global trade, maritime security, and environmental issues. These include cargo ships, tankers, yachts, submarines, under-sea drones, military, and commercial ships. This includes leveraging OSINT tools and databases to gather uncover valuable information from vessel tracking and ownership to cargo analysis and potential illicit activities. By combining various techniques and data sources, analysts can investigate piracy, smuggling, illegal fishing, and environmental crimes in marine environment. This can also help gather valuable information about vessel movements, ownership, cargo, and operational history. Social media platforms are a valuable source of information for maritime OSINT. By monitoring hashtags, keywords, and user accounts related to maritime activities, investigators can identify potential incidents, news reports, and citizen-generated content. To enhance their analysis, OSINT analysts often employ a variety of techniques discussed in this chapter.

9.1.1 Geolocation analysis

By analyzing GPS coordinates embedded in satellite imagery or photographs, investigators can pinpoint the location of vessels and maritime activities. One of the fundamental applications of maritime OSINT is tracking vessel movements. By utilizing Automatic Identification Systems (AIS) data, analysts can monitor the real-time positions of ships around the globe. AIS signals provide information about a vessel's identity, position, course, speed, and destination. This data can be analyzed to identify unusual patterns, such as sudden changes in course or speed, which may indicate suspicious activity. For example, a vessel that deviates from its declared route or turns off its AIS transponder may be involved in illicit activities like smuggling or piracy. MarineTraffic enables global tracking of ships and maritime activities. Users can view the location, route, speed, and status of ships, which is particularly beneficial for those in the maritime industry and for enhancing

DOI: 10.1201/9781003497615-9

maritime security. If these safety systems are turned off or manipulated, it could be a sign that a vessel is engaged in unlawful activity, such as illegal fishing or smuggling.

9.1.2 Analyzing vessel red flags

Understanding the changes in ownership or affiliations of a vessel is crucial for maritime OSINT investigations. By delving into corporate registries, ship registries, and other public databases, analysts can uncover connections between vessels, companies, and individuals. This information can help identify potential links to criminal organizations or sanctioned entities. For instance, a vessel owned by a company with ties to a known smuggling network may be flagged for further investigation. By analyzing satellite imagery, investigators can identify specific vessels, assess their condition, and monitor their activities. Ships typically stick to the route that makes the most economic sense – to maximize their profits while delivering cargo, fishing, or transporting passengers. If the vessel deviates from their route for reasons other than weather or another reasonable event and/or makes an unscheduled stop in a port that is not typically on their historic track, this may indicate suspicious activity.

9.1.3 Monitoring maritime social media

Social media platforms have become a valuable source of information for maritime OSINT. By monitoring relevant hashtags, keywords, and user accounts, analysts can identify potential incidents, news reports, and citizen-generated content related to maritime activities. For example, fishermen may post photos or videos of suspicious vessels or illegal fishing activities on social media. Analysts can use this information to corroborate other intelligence and identify potential targets for investigation.

9.1.4 Investigating illegal fishing

By mapping the relationships between vessels, companies, and individuals, investigators can uncover complex networks and identify potential illicit activities. Illegal, unreported, and unregulated fishing poses a significant threat to marine ecosystems and global food security. Maritime OSINT can play a vital role in combating illegal, unreported, and unregulated fishing by identifying vessels involved in illegal activities. By analyzing AIS data, satellite imagery, and social media, analysts can track the movements of fishing vessels, identify patterns of behavior, and detect potential violations of fishing regulations. For instance, a vessel that frequently turns off its AIS transponder in areas known for illegal fishing may be involved in such activities. If the ship's weight (indicated by draft) drastically changes after meeting with another vessel, a researcher might want to investigate why it's happening. A sudden change in draft could indicate that cargo has been removed from the ship.

9.1.5 Detecting maritime piracy

Piracy remains a persistent threat to maritime security. Maritime OSINT can help in the detection and prevention of piracy attacks. By monitoring vessel movements, identifying vulnerable areas, and analyzing intelligence reports, analysts can provide early warnings to ships operating in high-risk regions. For example, if a vessel is reported missing in a piracy-prone area, analysts can use OSINT to track its last known position and potential routes, which may help in search and rescue efforts or investigations.

9.1.6 Monitoring environmental impacts

Maritime activities can have significant environmental impacts, such as oil spills, pollution, and damage to marine ecosystems. Maritime OSINT can be used to monitor these activities and identify potential threats. By analyzing satellite imagery and news reports, analysts can detect oil spills, track the movement of pollution plumes, and assess the impact of maritime accidents on the environment. For instance, satellite imagery can be used to identify oil slicks and assess the extent of damage to marine ecosystems.

9.2 USE CASES

9.2.1 Use case #1

Objective: Track ships and find their details

Imagine a scenario where a ship might be transmitted military or illegal weapons, when it stops at a port it weighs 5,500 tons and when it leaves it weighs 9,500 tons. Then it travels to a port to drop the cargo and again weighs 5,500 tons. Then, the ship has picked the cargo and transported it to another port.

Step 1: Portal Shipspotting [1] provides details about a ship keyword, name or number, photographs uploaded by users. Example: enter 'sig' as the search parameter in the search bar and we get ships and photos as displayed in Figure 9.1.

Step 2: Notice few keywords occur multiple times (Sigas, Sigyn, Sigma), to find ship details, select one of them clicking the photograph. Figure 9.2 reveals IMO 9 486568, photograph details, and the owner.

Step 3: This also reveals more details about the vessel including the call-sign and IMO (Registration number), cargo as shown in Figure 9.3

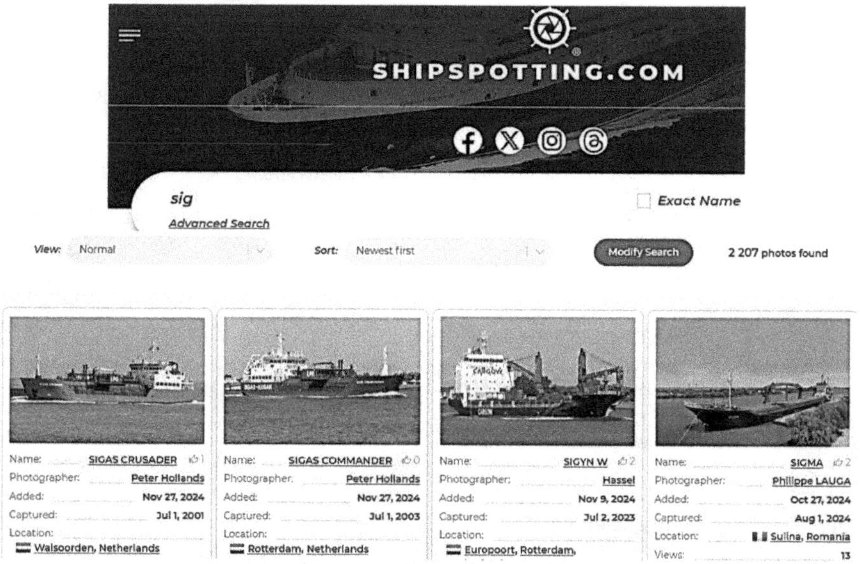
SHIPSPOTTING.COM
sig
Exact Name
Advanced Search
View: Normal
Sort: Newest first
Modify Search
2 207 photos found
Name: SIGAS CRUSADER
Photographer: Peter Hollands
Added: Nov 27, 2024
Captured: Jul 1, 2001
Location: Walsoorden, Netherlands
Name: SIGAS COMMANDER
Photographer: Peter Hollands
Added: Nov 27, 2024
Captured: Jul 1, 2003
Location: Rotterdam, Netherlands
Name: SIGYN W
Photographer: Hassel
Added: Nov 9, 2024
Captured: Jul 2, 2023
Location: Europoort, Rotterdam,
Name: SIGMA
Photographer: Philippe LAUGA
Added: Oct 27, 2024
Captured: Aug 1, 2024
Location: Sulina, Romania
Views: 13

Figure 9.1 Shipspotting search.

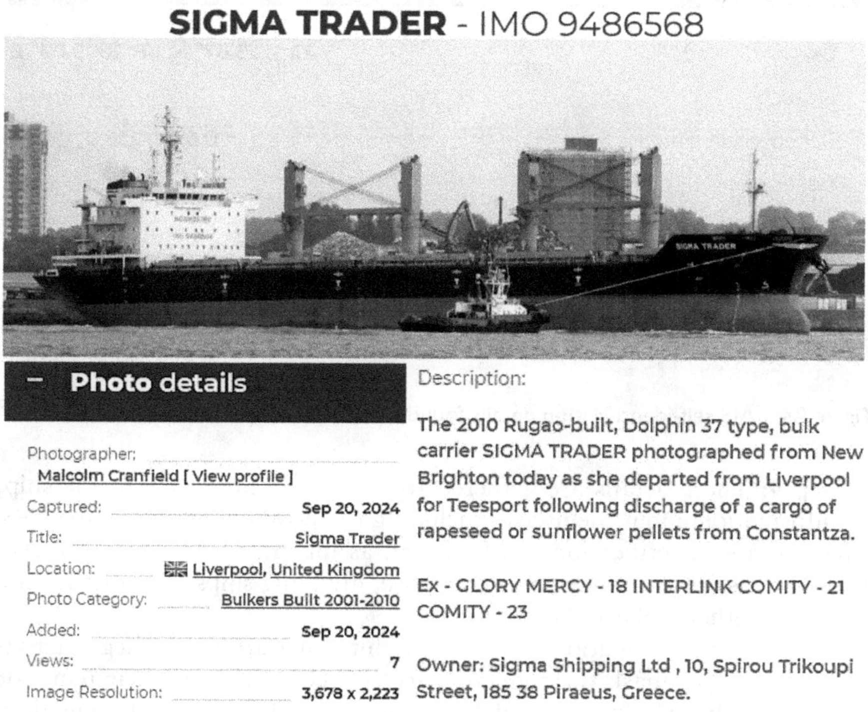
SIGMA TRADER - IMO 9486568
SIGMA TRADER
Photo details
Photographer: Malcolm Cranfield [View profile]
Captured: Sep 20, 2024
Title: Sigma Trader
Location: Liverpool, United Kingdom
Photo Category: Bulkers Built 2001-2010
Added: Sep 20, 2024
Views: 7
Image Resolution: 3,678 x 2,223
Description:
The 2010 Rugao-built, Dolphin 37 type, bulk carrier SIGMA TRADER photographed from New Brighton today as she departed from Liverpool for Teesport following discharge of a cargo of rapeseed or sunflower pellets from Constantza.
Ex - GLORY MERCY - 18 INTERLINK COMITY - 21 COMITY - 23
Owner: Sigma Shipping Ltd , 10, Spirou Trikoupi Street, 185 38 Piraeus, Greece.

Figure 9.2 Sigma trader ship IMO and photograph.

— Vessel particulars

Current name: .... **GLORY MERCY**

Callsign: **VRGF2**
IMO: **9486568**
MMSI: **538008018**
Build year: **2008**
Builder: .... **Huatai Heavy Industry - Nantong, China**
Manager: ....
  Global Marine Shipmanagement - Qingdao, China
Owner: ....
  Global Marine Shipmanagement - Qingdao, China
Class society: .... **Lloyd's Shipping Register**

Current flag: ....
  Hong Kong (China)
Home port: .... **Hong Kong**

Vessel Type: .... **Bulk Carrier**
Gross tonnage: .... **24,118 tons**
Summer DWT: .... **37,301 tons**
Length: .... **190 m**
Beam: .... **28 m**
Draught: .... **10.5 m**

Photos: ....
  63 photos by 19 photographers

Figure 9.3   Vessel details found.

— AIS Position of this ship

Last known position: .... **22°11'53.67" N, 68°28'19.09" E**

Status: ....

Speed, course (heading): .... **0.6kts, 258.6° (299°)**

Destination:

- Location: .... **Vizag**

- Arrival: .... **5th Dec 2024 / 03:00:49 UTC**

Last update: .... **5 days ago**

Source: .... **AIS (ShipXplorer)**

Figure 9.4   AIS self-identification details found.

Step 4: These details are gathered from the AIS broadcast of the ship, as information about themselves including the position, speed, course destination, and identification can be found as illustrated in Figure 9.4. AIS is used for safety and navigation purpose, allowing ships to communicate with each other and avoid collisions.

Step 5: This information is useful for ships that are doing illegal activities and tend to mask their identity, so they could change their name or callsign in the AIS system and broadcast. So 'Signal Alfa' if smuggling something could broadcast ASI name as 'Ship2' and mislead others.

However, if someone took a photograph of the ship at the same time where that ship was supposed to be, which displays 'Signal Alpha' on the side, then this can be verified that it was not 'Ship2.' Government and military track ships which might be transporting illegal cargo or oil.

9.2.2 Use case #2

Objective: Find under-sea cables and track ships

Step 1: Using Subtelforum [2], we can explore under-sea cable maps for complex global network as displayed in Figure 9.5. In case any of these user-sea cables are cut, network and internet access to that area gets disrupted.

Step 2: Searching a ship that lays under-sea cables (say Ocean Titan). Figure 9.6 reveals the AIS details.

Step 3: Marinetraffic [3] portal provides live tracking of ships as illustrated in Figure 9.7.

Step 4: Searching for a specific ship say 'Ocean Titan.' Figure 9.8 reveals its details – IMO and the departure and arrival information.

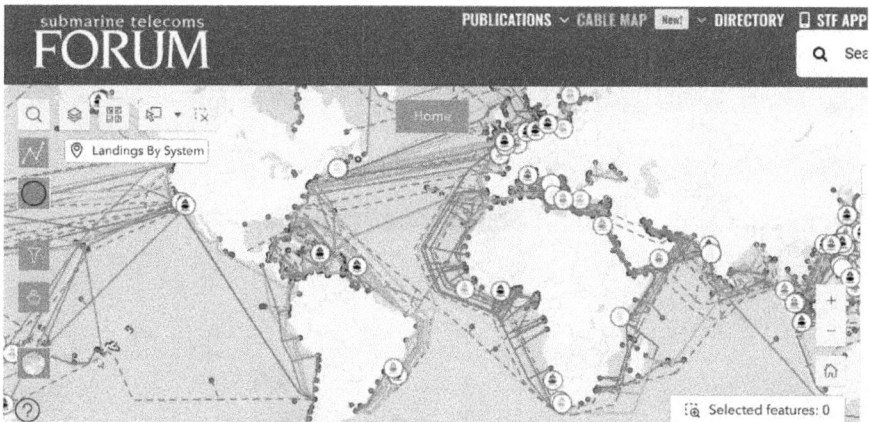

Figure 9.5 Under-sea cable routes.

Figure 9.6 Search ship by name.

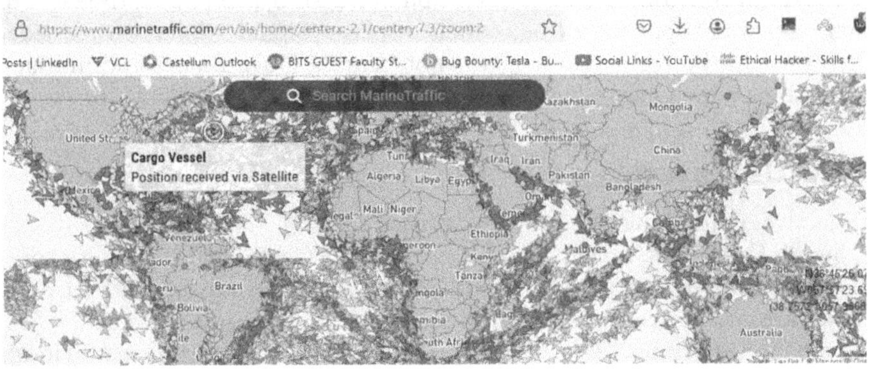

Figure 9.7   Live Marine traffic.

Research/Survey Vessel **OCEAN TITAN** is currently located in the **South Pacific** (reported **2 minutes ago**)

What kind of ship is this?

OCEAN TITAN (IMO: 8835231) is a **Research/Survey Vessel** and is sailing under the flag of **USA**. Her length overall (LOA) is 68.28 meters and her width is 13.11 meters.

Departure from Port Vila

VU VLI

Arrival at Auckland

NZ AKL

Actual time of departure:
2024-10-28 21:15 (UTC+11)

Actual time of arrival:
2024-12-02 08:33 (UTC+13)

Figure 9.8   Search for a ship.

Figure 9.9   Exact location found.

Step 5: Clicking 'Live Map' displays the live location, route, and cargo weight of the ship as displayed in Figure 9.9.

Step 6: We can even filter by types, ports, lighthouse, or companies to gather the latest details about the vessel as shown in Figure 9.10.

Latest AIS information		True heading	16 "
Navigational status	Moored	Rate of turn	0 °/min
Position received	4 mins ago	Draught	5.5 m
Vessel's local time	2024-12-03 17:03 (UTC+13)	Reported destination	AUCKLAND NEW ZEALAL
Latitude/Longitude	*Upgrade to unlock*	Matched destination	Auckland, New Zealand
Speed	0 kn	Estimated time of arrival	2024-12-02 20:00 (UTC+13)
Course	187 °	AIS source	Terrestrial - Clarks Beach

Figure 9.10   Live details found.

9.2.3 Use case #3

Objective: Track maritime ship involved in illegal cargo

Step 1: OSINT professionals track vessels and post on Twitter. As an example of a maritime vessel involved in transporting jet fuel illegally from Russia to Syria, I used the keyword 'sig' which is known to turn off its AIS, travels, and then turns on the AIS. Figure 9.11 displays the tweets about drone attack on this vessel.

Step 2: Using Shodan, we can even search for ships using 'VSAT' as shown in Figure 9.12. VSAT stands for Very Small Aperture Terminal which is a two-way satellite communication system used on ships for high-speed internet access. This uses a stabilized antenna to maintain a connection with a satellite, allowing for reliable communication even in remote areas.

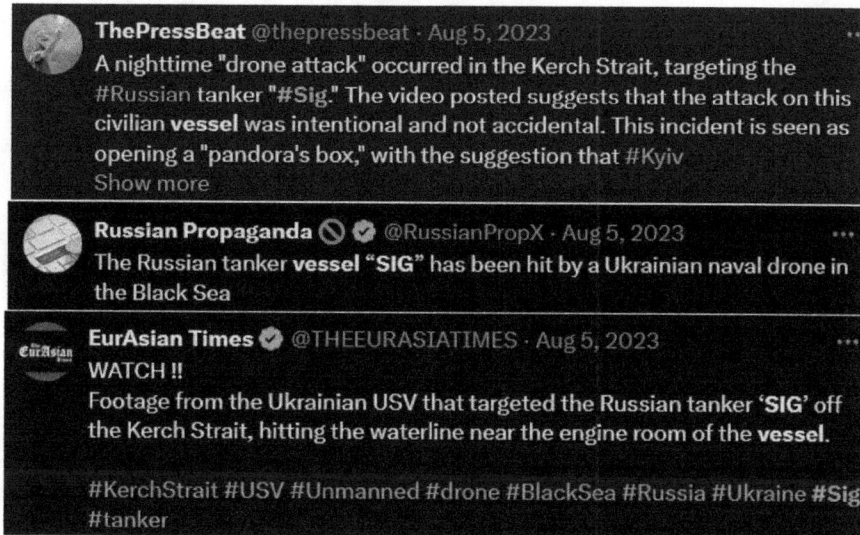

Figure 9.11   Tweets about illegal cargo ships.

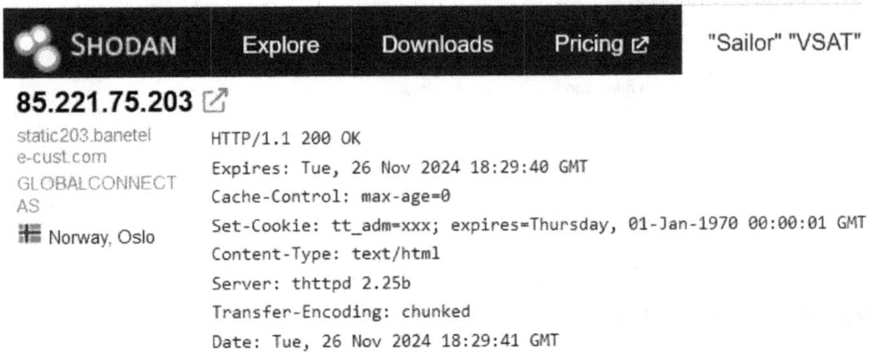

Figure 9.12   Shodan ship search.

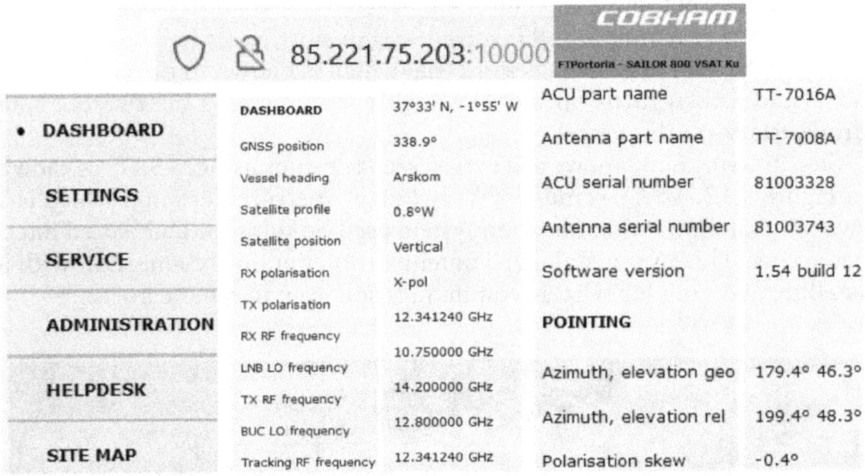

Figure 9.13   Sensitive details found.

Step 3: This specific IP (85.221.75.203) reveals the ship's dashboard, hardware and software settings, service, and admin portal as illustrated in Figure 9.13.

Step 4: Using the IP, attackers can find the geolocation of the vessel as shown in Figure 9.14. Scanning for vulnerabilities, attackers can remotely exploit the IP, access the VSAT to pivot through the ship's system and to control the ship's steering (navigation), control the weight, and change the AIS parameters (callsign and location).

9.2.4 Use case #4

Objective: Track maritime vessels using Satellite imagery tools

Permalink	https://www.ip2location.com/85.221.75.203	☐ Elevation	3m	
		☐ Usage Type	(ISP) Fixed Line ISP	
☑ IP Address	85.221.75.203	☐ Address Type	(U) Unicast	
☐ Country	🇳🇴 Norway [NO]	☐ Category	(IAB19-18) Internet Technology	
☐ Region	Oslo	☐ District	Oslo	
☐ City	Sjolyststranda	☐ ASN	AS2116 GlobalConnect AS	
☐ Coordinates of City ❶	59.921210, 10.680250 (59°55'16"N 10°40'49"E)	☐ Net Speed	(DSL) Broadband/Cable/Fiber/Mobile	
☐ ISP	GlobalConnect AS	☐ IDD & Area Code	(47) 022	
☐ Local Time	03 Dec, 2024 07:27 AM (UTC +01:00)	☐ ZIP Code	1324	
☐ Domain	globalconnect.no	☐ Weather Station	Sandvika (NOXX0033)	

Figure 9.14 Geolocation found.

Figure 9.15 Soar earth satellite imagery.

Step 1: Using 'Soar.earth' [4], we can track satellite images for various dates when it passed over a specific sea or land area as illustrated in Figure 9.15. The different dates could display cloud cover, track movement, or the progress of buildings being built.

Step 2: Also using Google Earth, we can search for a port and check ships docked on its ports, search for 'Norfolk, VA, USA' to check the ships as illustrated in Figure 9.16.

Step 3: Searching further, Figure 9.17 displays a military ship docked on the port.

Step 5: Figure 9.18 displays small boats in and around 'Norfolk' in an area called 'Little Creek.'

Step 6: Figure 9.19 displays the use of the 'Historical Imagery' feature to search for ships at prior date.

Step 7: Checking 'VesselFinder' [5], we can find details of specific ships as shown in Figure 9.20.

Figure 9.16   Google earth docks view.

Figure 9.17   Military ship found on dock.

Step 8: We can also filter for specific ships like cargo vessels, tankers, passenger or cruise, fishing, military, and high-speed yachts as illustrated for military ships in Figure 9.21.

Step 9: We can gather details about ship as illustrated in Figure 9.22 for the same military vessel.

Figure 9.18   Boats found in Norfolk, Little Creek.

Figure 9.19   Historical imagery of dock.

Step 11: Performing a Google search validates the details about this vessel as displayed in Figure 9.23.

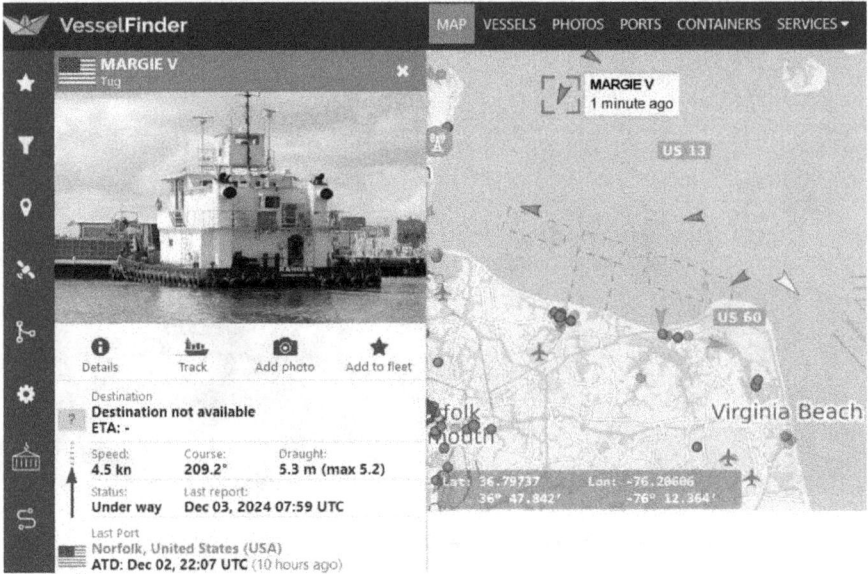

Figure 9.20   Validating vessel information.

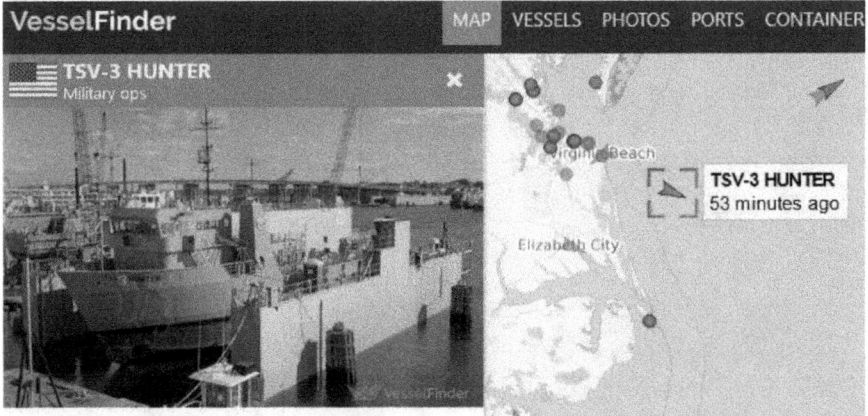

Figure 9.21   Search for military ships.

9.2.5 Use case #5

Objective: Find Piracy and armed robbery incidents

Step 1: Using 'Live Piracy Map' [6], investigators search for incident cases reported for attempted attacks, boarded, fired upon, and hijacked or suspicious vessel as illustrated in Figure 9.24.

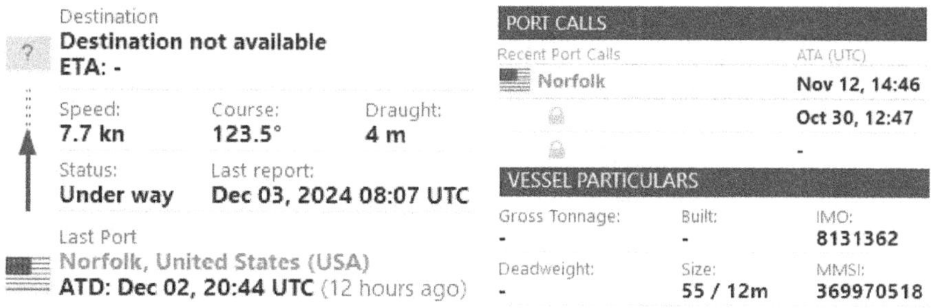

Destination
Destination not available
ETA: -

Speed: Course: Draught:
7.7 kn   **123.5°**   **4 m**

Status: Last report:
Under way   **Dec 03, 2024 08:07 UTC**

Last Port
Norfolk, United States (USA)
ATD: Dec 02, 20:44 UTC (12 hours ago)

PORT CALLS

Recent Port Calls	ATA (UTC)
Norfolk	Nov 12, 14:46
	Oct 30, 12:47
	-

VESSEL PARTICULARS

Gross Tonnage:	Built:	IMO:
-	-	8131362
Deadweight:	Size:	MMSI:
-	55 / 12m	369970518

Figure 9.22   Military ship details found.

"tsv-3 hunter"   ×   ⬤

Maritime Optima
https://marineoptima.com › pages › mmsi 369970518
TSV-3 HUNTER - Other - IMO 8131362
TSV-3 HUNTER built in 2021 is a Other vessel. IMO: 8131362, MMSI: 369970518, Callsign: NHUN. Category: Other, and is sailing under the flag of United ...

BalticShipping.com
https://www.balticshipping.com › vessel › imo
TSV 3 HUNTER, Research vessel, IMO 8131362
TSV 3 HUNTER is a Research vessel built in 1981 by QUALITY SHIPBUILDERS - MOSS POINT MS, U.S.A. Currently sailing under the flag of United States (USA).

ⓘ MarineTraffic
Ship TSV 3 HUNTER ...

▣ DVIDS
USNS Hunter (TSV 3) Undocks

Figure 9.23   Google search to validate findings.

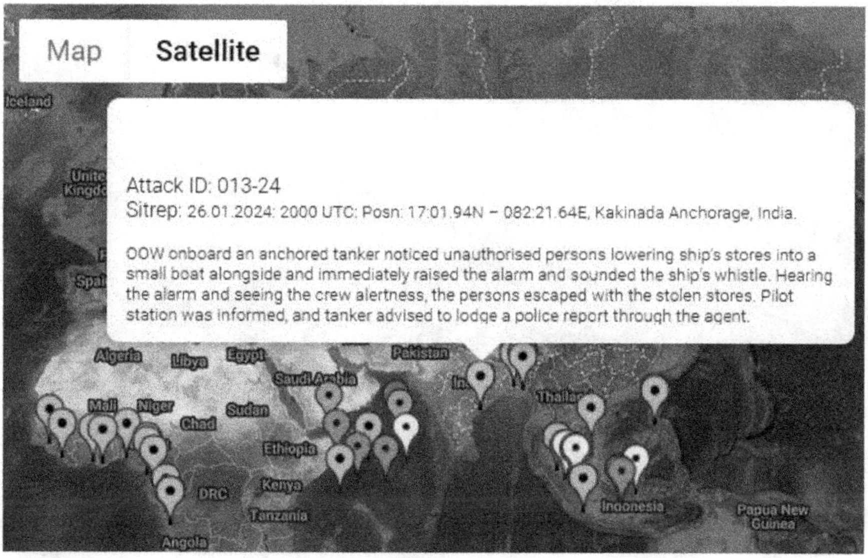

Map   Satellite

Attack ID: 013-24
Sitrep: 26.01.2024: 2000 UTC: Posn: 17:01.94N – 082:21.64E, Kakinada Anchorage, India.

OOW onboard an anchored tanker noticed unauthorised persons lowering ship's stores into a small boat alongside and immediately raised the alarm and sounded the ship's whistle. Hearing the alarm and seeing the crew alertness, the persons escaped with the stolen stores. Pilot station was informed, and tanker advised to lodge a police report through the agent.

Figure 9.24   Maritime privacy map.

9.2.6 Use case #6

Objective: Find live cams on sealines

Step 1: Skyline Webcams [7] presents list of live cams that display the sea coasts, displayed in Figure 9.25.

Step 2: Clicking a feed displays live cam feed to provide view in real time as displayed in Figure 9.26.

Step 3: Using WebcamTaxi [8] illustrates live cam feed and location as presented in Figure 9.27.

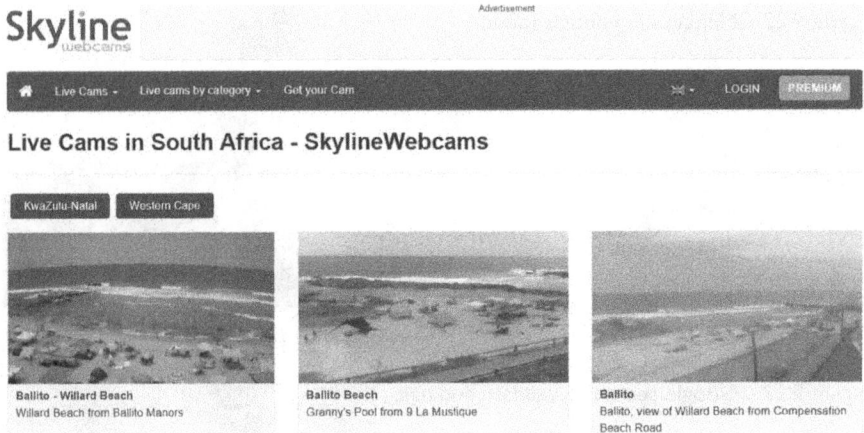

Figure 9.25 Skyline Webcams.

Figure 9.26 Live cam feed.

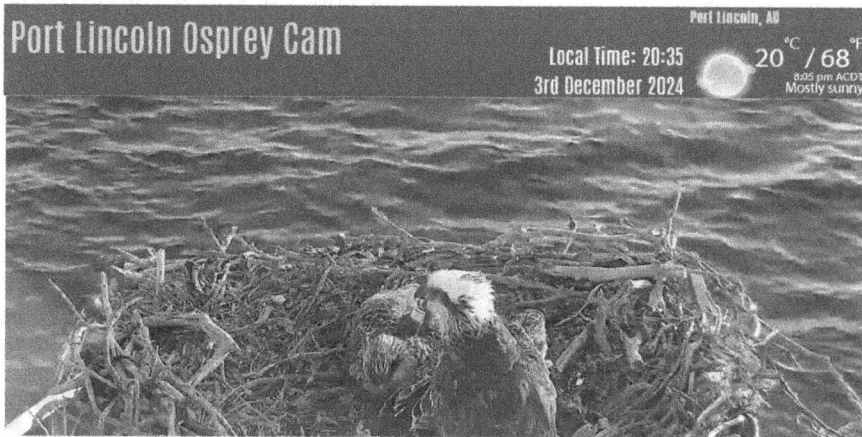

Figure 9.27   WebcamTaxi live feed.

9.3 LAND-BASED TRANSPORTATION OSINT

Road and railway OSINT helps to gain insights into land-based transportation systems. This includes everything from vehicle tracking and ownership to infrastructure analysis and potential security threats. By combining various techniques and data sources, analysts can uncover valuable information that can be used to address a wide range of challenges, such as terrorism, smuggling, and infrastructure vulnerabilities. Vehicle tracing is an important part of both cybersecurity and law enforcement for the following reasons:

- Threat Assessment: The pattern analysis of suspicious vehicles helps to prevent and mitigate future security threats, especially in areas such as government buildings and embassies.
- Vehicle Tracing in Crime Investigation: Vehicle tracing, in fact, goes very much into the fabric of criminal investigations: stolen vehicles, fraud cases, criminal networks, etc.
- Protection of Dignitaries: Public celebrities or executive leaders often face threats; therefore, vigilance regarding the suspicious vehicle and their neighbor ones plays an important role for the dignitaries.
- Counterterrorism: Vehicle tracking can be used in counterterrorism operations by monitoring suspicious patterns around sensitive locations, which could lead to early detection of potential threats.

9.3.1 Tracking vehicle movements

One of the fundamental applications of road and railway OSINT is tracking vehicle movements. By utilizing transport tracking portals (apart from Automatic Vehicle Identification systems, GPS tracking, and social media data), analysts can monitor the real-time positions of vehicles on roads and railways. This information can be used to identify unusual patterns, such as sudden changes in route or speed, which may indicate suspicious activity. For example, a vehicle that deviates from its expected route or lingers in a specific area may be involved in criminal activity; these can be tracked using the Mobility Portal [9] platform as shown in Figure 9.28.

Diving into one of the 'dots' (Train 4368) reveals the exact time and route of the train, which would follow as shown in Figure 9.29.

Geops [10] is another tracking transport application integrating applications and information systems to smartly associate factual data with geospatial data and cartographic representations. The bandwidth ranges from data analysis and visualization, information systems, and business solutions up to comprehensive server infrastructures. From the technical perspective, the company focuses on issues like environmental considerations, mobility,

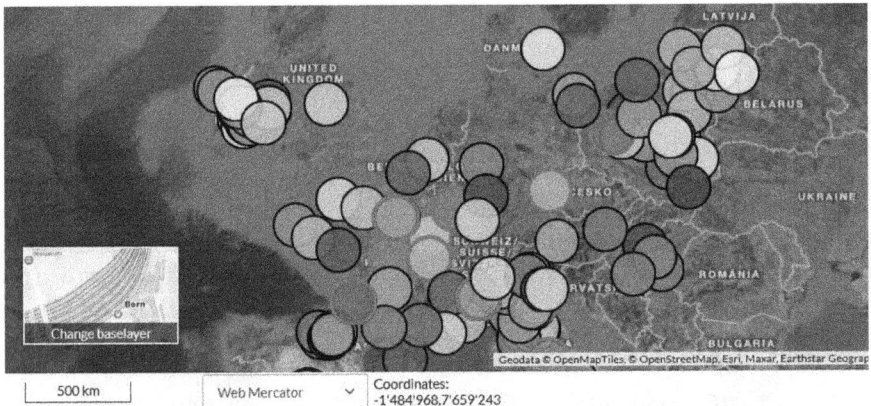

Figure 9.28   Mobility portal for trains in Europe.

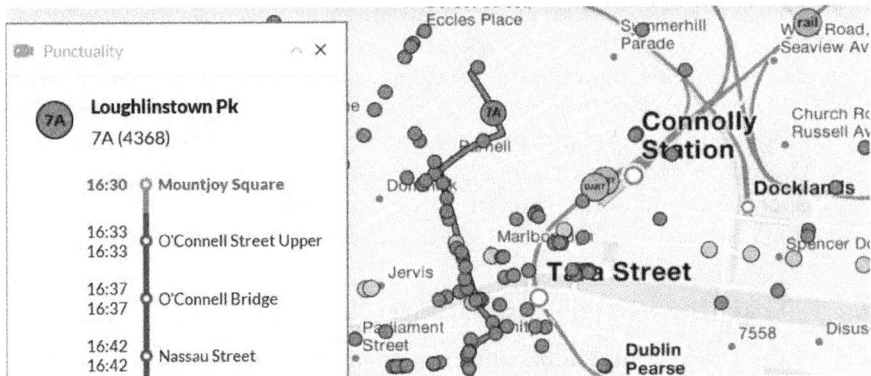

Figure 9.29   Details found for a specific train.

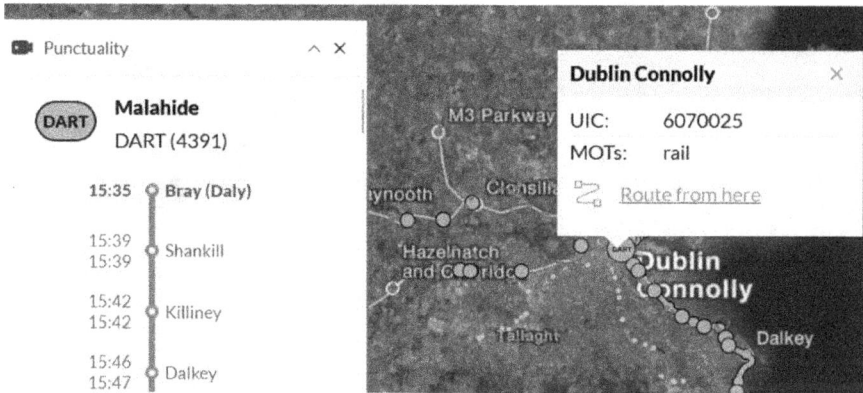

Figure 9.30   Train route details revealed.

public transportation, and logistics. Services range from IT consulting to software development, system operations, and the provision of web-based services. The platform also contains routing services for public transportation lines, as shown in Figure 9.30.

9.3.2 Analyzing vehicle ownership and affiliations

Understanding the ownership and affiliations of vehicles is crucial for road and railway OSINT investigations. By delving into vehicle registration databases, social media profiles, and corporate registries, analysts can uncover connections between vehicles, individuals, and organizations. This information can help identify potential links to criminal networks or terrorist groups. For instance, a vehicle registered to a known extremist organization may be flagged for further investigation. The first step is to identify the license plate type and understand regional patterns associated with it. Databases such as 'WorldLicensePlates' [11] have information regarding standard and diplomatic plates that aid in tracing the vehicle and its affiliations as illustrated in Figure 9.31.

9.3.3 Monitoring social media for transportation intelligence

Social media platforms have become a valuable source of information for road and railway OSINT. By monitoring relevant hashtags, keywords, and user accounts, analysts can identify potential threats, disruptions, and emerging trends in transportation. For example, social media posts about traffic jams, accidents, or protests can provide real-time updates and help authorities plan accordingly. Additionally, social media can be used to identify potential threats, such as extremist groups planning attacks on transportation infrastructure.

United States Government I

Home > North America > United States of America > United States Government I

U.S. GOVERNMENT	U.S. GOVERNMENT	U.S. GOVERNMENT
I-50855	**A2-984** DEPT. OF AGRICULTURE	**SS-1099**
1950's, Department of the Interior (1)	1960's, Department of Agriculture	1960's, Selective Service Systems

U.S. GOVERNMENT	U.S. GOVERNMENT	U.S. TREASURY INTERNAL REVENUE SERVICE OFFICIAL
NATO-16	19 **6** 64	
1960's, US Employee of NATO (1)	1964, Motorcycle (1)	1960's, U.S. Treasury Internal revenue Servce Official

Figure 9.31   Vehicle registration details.

9.3.4 Investigating infrastructure vulnerabilities

Infrastructure vulnerabilities, such as weak bridges, damaged roads, or outdated railway tracks, can pose significant risks to public safety and transportation efficiency. Road and railway OSINT can be used to identify and assess these vulnerabilities. By analyzing satellite imagery, social media posts, and news reports, analysts can detect signs of infrastructure degradation, potential hazards, and security threats. For instance, satellite imagery can be used to identify structural damage to bridges or track the construction of new infrastructure projects.

9.3.5 Detecting smuggling and trafficking

Smuggling and trafficking activities often rely on transportation networks to move goods and people across borders. Road and railway OSINT can be used to detect and disrupt these activities. By analyzing vehicle movements, cargo manifests, and social media data, analysts can identify suspicious patterns and potential smuggling routes. For example, a truck that frequently travels between known smuggling hubs may be flagged for inspection.

9.3.6 Monitoring transportation security

Ensuring the security of transportation systems is crucial for national security and public safety. Road and railway OSINT can be used to monitor security measures, identify potential threats, and assess the effectiveness of security protocols. By analyzing surveillance footage, social media posts, and news reports, analysts can detect suspicious behavior, identify potential security breaches, and assess the overall security posture of transportation systems. For instance, social media posts about security lapses or suspicious individuals at transportation hubs can be used to alert authorities.

9.4 CONCLUSION

OSINT investigations into marine vessels have proven to be invaluable in shedding light on global trade, maritime security, and environmental issues. By leveraging a combination of OSINT tools, databases, and analytical techniques, investigators can uncover hidden connections, identify potential threats, and contribute to a safer and more sustainable maritime environment. Social media platforms have emerged as a significant source of information, enabling the monitoring of maritime activities and the identification of emerging trends. Through the application of geolocation analysis, image analysis, and network analysis, OSINT analysts can delve deeper into the complexities of maritime operations. The practical use cases presented in this chapter demonstrate the real-world applications of these techniques, empowering investigators to effectively utilize OSINT for maritime investigations. As technology continues to advance, the potential of OSINT for maritime analysis will only expand, making it an essential tool for addressing the challenges of the 21st century.

REFERENCES

1. Shipspotting.com, 2021. https://www.shipspotting.com/ (accessed Dec. 19, 2024).
2. kcl@rk, "Online Map," SubTel Forum, Jan. 15, 2023. https://subtelforum.com/online-map/ (accessed Dec. 19, 2024).
3. "MarineTraffic: Global Ship Tracking Intelligence I AIS Marine Traffic," 2024. https://www.marinetraffic.com/en/ais/home/centerx:162.9/centery:-24.8/zoom:10 (accessed Dec. 19, 2024).
4. "Soar – The New Atlas," 2024. https://soar.earth/satellites?pos=28.045124007177666%2C65.81682795920716%2C4.25 (accessed Dec. 19, 2024).
5. "Vessels Database – VesselFinder," 2024. https://www.vesselfinder.com/vessels?name=norfolk&type=414 (accessed Dec. 19, 2024).
6. "Live Piracy Map," 2025. https://icc-ccs.org/piracy-map-2024
7. Live Cams, "Live Cam Kamiros Skala – Rhodes I SkylineWebcams," SkylineWebcams, 2024. https://www.skylinewebcams.com/en/webcam/ellada/naigaio/dodecanisa/rhodes-kamiros-skala.html (accessed Dec. 19, 2024).

8. "Port Lincoln Osprey Cam," 2024. https://www.webcamtaxi.com/en/australia/south-australia/port-lincoln-osprey-nest-cam.html (accessed Dec. 19, 2024).

9. "Live Train Tracker | geOps," 2024. https://mobility.portal.geops.io/world.geops.transit?z=6&s=1&x=1150450.84&y=6451274.79&l=transport&layers=paerke (accessed Dec. 19, 2024).

10. "Maps," 2024. https://geops.com/en/solution/maps (accessed Dec. 19, 2024).

11. "World License Plates," 2025. http://www.worldlicenseplates.com/ (accessed April 12, 2025).

Chapter 10

Conclusion

10.1 OPEN-SOURCE INTELLIGENCE EVOLUTION AND BASICS

Historically, intelligence gathering relied heavily on covert operations and classified sources. However, the advent of the digital age has democratized access to information, ushering in a new era of intelligence collection. In order to obtain important insights, Open-Source Intelligence (OSINT) makes use of publicly accessible sources including social media, news stories, official documents, and open-source databases. At its core, OSINT is the art and science of collecting, processing, and analyzing publicly available information to inform decision-making. From basic online searches to complex data mining and machine learning algorithms, it covers a broad spectrum of methods. By systematically sifting through vast amounts of data, OSINT practitioners can uncover patterns, identify trends, and predict future events. The ethical implications of OSINT cannot be ignored. It gives people and organizations the ability to collect data, but it also brings up issues with security, privacy, and abuse possibilities. Ethical guidelines must be established to ensure that OSINT is used responsibly and in accordance with legal and moral principles.

Key principles underpin the practice of OSINT which include:

- Relevance: Identifying information that is directly relevant to the specific intelligence requirement.
- Credibility: Assessing the reliability and accuracy of information sources.
- Completeness: Gathering a comprehensive range of information to form a complete picture.
- Timeliness: Acquiring information in a timely manner to ensure its relevance.
- Understandability: Interpreting and analyzing information to derive meaningful insights.

DOI: 10.1201/9781003497615-10

A variety of sources and methods contribute to the wealth of information available for OSINT analysis. Social media platforms, such as Twitter, Facebook, and LinkedIn, provide a treasure trove of user-generated content, offering insights into individuals' beliefs, behaviors, and affiliations. News websites and blogs offer real-time updates on current events, while government websites provide access to public records and official documents. Web scraping and data mining techniques allow for the automated collection and analysis of large volumes of data from websites and databases. Trends, patterns, and anomalies that might not be visible to the naked eye can be found using these methods. Furthermore, OSINT relies heavily on human intelligence and social media intelligence, which use social media platforms and human networks to obtain data and establish connections.

The process of OSINT analysis involves a systematic approach to collecting, processing, and interpreting information. It begins with identifying the intelligence requirement, which defines the specific information needed to address a particular question or problem. After defining the need, analysts can use a range of methods to get pertinent data from publicly available sources.

In order to get significant insights, the gathered data is further processed and examined. This might entail methods like natural language processing, data mining, and data cleansing. Finding patterns, trends, and anomalies that can guide decision-making is the aim of analysis. Critical thinking is essential in OSINT analysis. Analysts must be able to evaluate the credibility of information sources, identify biases, and draw logical conclusions. By applying critical thinking skills, analysts can avoid making hasty judgments and ensure the accuracy of their findings. As a result, OSINT is now a vital tool for people, businesses, and governments. OSINT practitioners can obtain a competitive advantage, make wise judgments, and tackle difficult problems by utilizing publicly accessible information. OSINT's position will only become more significant as technology develops. By understanding the fundamentals of OSINT and mastering its techniques, individuals can unlock the power of information and shape the future.

10.2 ONLINE PRIVACY AND SECURE BROWSING TECHNIQUES

In today's interconnected world, where digital footprints are pervasive and privacy concerns loom large, safeguarding one's online identity has become paramount, especially for those engaged in OSINT activities. This chapter delves into the essential practices and tools necessary to protect online privacy and enhance secure browsing. The digital age has bestowed upon us unprecedented access to information, but it has also exposed us to a myriad of threats. From data breaches and identity theft to surveillance and cyberattacks, the risks are real and ever-present.

To mitigate these risks, it is imperative to adopt a privacy-centric mindset and implement robust security measures.

One of the fundamental principles of online privacy is to minimize one's digital footprint. This entails adopting strong, one-of-a-kind passwords for every online account, minimizing personal information on social media sites, and exercising caution when sharing information online. By reducing the amount of personal information available to potential adversaries, individuals can significantly enhance their online privacy. Secure browsing practices are essential for protecting sensitive information and preventing unauthorized access. Using a reputable and up-to-date web browser with strong security features is a crucial first step. It is also advisable to enable privacy settings, such as blocking cookies and tracking scripts, to limit the amount of data collected by websites. A virtual private network may also be used to hide one's IP address and encrypt internet traffic, adding another degree of security against monitoring and spying. The Tor network, a global network of computers run by volunteers, provides a high level of privacy and anonymity. Tor hides a user's IP address and makes it hard to monitor their online activity by rerouting internet traffic across many servers. It's crucial to remember that Tor is not totally anonymous; thus, users should take caution while accessing private data or doing illegal acts.

A variety of privacy-focused search engines are available, such as DuckDuckGo and StartPage, which prioritize user privacy by avoiding personalized search results and tracking user behavior. These search engines provide a more private and secure browsing experience, especially for those who are concerned about surveillance and targeted advertising. Browser extensions can further enhance online privacy and security. Ad-blockers can prevent intrusive ads and reduce the risk of malicious scripts, while privacy extensions can block trackers and cookies. Password managers also lower the danger of password-related security breaches by assisting in the creation and storage of strong, one-of-a-kind passwords for every online account. People may greatly increase their online security and privacy by combining these techniques and resources. Regularly updating software and security settings is crucial as is keeping up with the most recent threats and vulnerabilities. By adopting a proactive approach to online privacy, we can protect ourselves from the ever-evolving landscape of cyber threats and ensure a safer digital future.

10.3 BUILDING OSINT SKILLS AND WORKFLOW PROCESS

One effective technique for obtaining information from publicly accessible sources is OSINT. It is a skill that is increasingly valuable in various fields, from cybersecurity to journalism to intelligence analysis. This chapter will explore the essential skills and techniques required to effectively conduct

OSINT investigations, as well as the workflow process involved. At the core of OSINT is the ability to think critically and analytically. Strong critical thinking abilities enable investigators to recognize biases, assess the reliability of information sources, and reach logical conclusions. This entails challenging the information's source, evaluating its veracity, and taking into account other interpretations.

Another crucial skill is effective search techniques. Knowing how to use search engines to their full potential is essential for efficient information gathering. Advanced search operators can be used to refine search queries and identify specific information. Search results can be greatly enhanced by, for instance, using quote marks to look for specific words or the minus sign to exclude certain terms. Social media sites have developed into a wealth of data for OSINT research. By understanding how to navigate these platforms and analyze user profiles, investigators can gather valuable insights into individuals, organizations, and events. Social media analysis tools can be used to extract data from platforms like Twitter, Facebook, and Instagram, allowing for large-scale data collection and analysis.

Data mining and analysis techniques are also essential for OSINT. By using tools like Maltego and OSINT Framework, investigators can visualize relationships between people, organizations, and events. These tools can help identify patterns, anomalies, and potential leads.

The workflow process for conducting an OSINT investigation typically involves several steps:

1. Define the Investigation: Clearly articulate the goals and objectives of the investigation. What specific information is needed? What questions need to be answered?
2. Identify Relevant Sources: Determine the most relevant sources of information, such as social media, news websites, government databases, and OSINT platforms.
3. Collect Information: Gather information from identified sources using a variety of techniques, including web scraping, data mining, and manual research.
4. Analyze Information: Analyze and process the data gathered to find trends, patterns, and irregularities. Use critical thinking to evaluate the credibility and relevance of the information.
5. Visualize Information: Use visualization tools to represent the information in a clear and concise manner. This can assist in locating connections and patterns that might not be visible in unprocessed data.
6. Draw Conclusions: Based on the analysis, draw conclusions and formulate hypotheses.
7. Document Findings: Document the entire investigation process, including the methodology, sources, and findings.

By following this workflow process and mastering the essential skills, individuals can become proficient in conducting OSINT investigations. It is important to remember that OSINT is an ongoing process, and as new tools and techniques emerge, it is essential to stay updated and adapt to the changing landscape of information.

10.4 SEARCH UNDERGROUND INTERNET

The internet, a vast digital expanse, is often likened to an iceberg. Anyone with an internet connection may access the visible part, known as the surface web. The dark web is a covert network that functions outside of censorship and conventional search engines, and it is located under this surface. A portion of the internet known as the 'dark web' is inaccessible without specialized software and is not indexed by search engines. It is built of websites and servers that are not accessible through ordinary web browsers. The dark web is well known for housing illicit operations including drug and people trafficking as well as the selling of stolen data, despite its beneficial applications, which include privacy protection and anonymous communication.

Users usually utilize specialized software like Tor (The Onion Router) to access the dark web. Through the use of a network of servers, Tor, a free and open-source program, enables users to browse the internet anonymously. By hiding the user's IP address, this technique – known as onion routing – makes it more difficult for other parties to monitor their online activity. But there are hazards associated with using the dark web. It is a lawless frontier where cybercriminals and other malicious actors operate with impunity. Users who venture into the dark web must be aware of the potential dangers, including exposure to malware, phishing attacks, and other security threats. To mitigate these risks, it is essential to adopt best practices for dark web browsing. This entails exchanging personal information with caution, avoiding downloading files from unreliable sources, and creating a strong, one-of-a-kind password for your Tor browser. To further improve security and privacy, it is also advised to use Tor in combination with a virtual private network.

It is crucial to acknowledge the potential advantages of the dark web, despite the fact that it may appear to be a strange and hazardous area. For instance, the dark web may be used by activists and journalists to safely communicate while exposing human rights violations and corruption. Additionally, researchers can use it to study the behavior of cybercriminals and develop countermeasures. However, it is imperative to enter the dark web cautiously and with a thorough awareness of the hazards. By following best practices and exercising sound judgment, individuals can safely explore this hidden corner of the internet while minimizing their exposure to potential threats. As technology continues to evolve, the dark web will likely remain a complex and enigmatic part of the digital landscape.

By understanding its nature, functionality, and associated risks, we can navigate this hidden world with informed awareness and take steps to protect ourselves from harm.

10.5 OSINT SEARCH TECHNIQUES

In the digital age, information is abundant and readily accessible. The ability to effectively search and analyze this vast sea of data has become a critical skill, particularly for those involved in OSINT investigations. This chapter delves into the intricacies of search engine techniques, exploring a range of tools and strategies that can be employed to gather, analyze, and visualize information from various online sources.

The search engine is a basic tool in the toolbox of an OSINT investigator. The most popular search engine, Google, provides a wide range of sophisticated search operators that may be used to hone search terms and find particular data. By understanding and effectively utilizing these operators, investigators can significantly enhance their search efficiency. Social media platforms have emerged as powerful sources of information for OSINT. Platforms like Twitter, Facebook, and LinkedIn provide a wealth of data, including user profiles, posts, and comments. By employing advanced search techniques and social media analysis tools, investigators can extract valuable insights from these platforms. Data mining and analysis tools play a crucial role in OSINT investigations. Tools like Maltego and OSINT Framework enable investigators to visualize relationships between people, organizations, and events. By mapping out these connections, investigators can uncover hidden patterns and identify potential leads.

Shodan, a search engine for internet-connected devices, is another powerful tool for OSINT. By scanning the internet for vulnerable devices, Shodan can help identify potential targets for cyberattacks. Additionally, it can be used to gather information about specific organizations or individuals. Google Dorks, advanced search queries that leverage Google's search syntax, can be used to find specific information, such as sensitive data leaks, hidden databases, and vulnerable systems. By mastering Google Dorks, investigators can uncover valuable insights that may not be readily apparent through traditional search methods. To effectively utilize these tools, investigators must possess a strong understanding of the underlying technologies and techniques. This includes knowledge of web scraping, data mining, and natural language processing. Investigators can optimize the potential of OSINT tools and procedures by fusing these abilities with an acute attention to detail and an innovative approach to problem-solving. It takes a blend of technical expertise, critical thinking, and inventiveness to become an OSINT master. By understanding the principles of search engine optimization, social media analysis, data mining, and visualization, investigators can effectively navigate the vast landscape of online information and uncover valuable insights. OSINT practitioners may maintain their position at the forefront of information collection and analysis by being current with the newest technologies and methodologies.

10.6 EMAIL ADDRESS INTELLIGENCE

In today's data-driven world, email addresses have evolved from simple communication tools to digital identifiers that can reveal a wealth of information about individuals. Email Address Intelligence, a powerful technique that leverages publicly available data to extract insights from email addresses, has emerged as a valuable tool for various applications, from marketing and sales to cybersecurity and intelligence analysis. At the heart of email address intelligence lies the concept of digital footprint analysis. By examining the online activities associated with an email address, investigators can uncover valuable information about an individual's preferences, behaviors, and affiliations. This includes their social media profiles, online purchases, and website interactions.

One of the primary applications of email address intelligence is in the realm of marketing and sales. By analyzing email addresses, marketers can identify potential customers, segment their target audience, and personalize marketing campaigns. For example, by correlating email addresses with social media profiles, marketers can gain insights into individuals' interests and demographics, enabling them to deliver targeted advertisements and promotions. Email address intelligence is a useful tool in cybersecurity for spotting possible dangers and reducing risks. By analyzing email addresses associated with malicious activity, security professionals can identify patterns, track cybercriminals, and develop effective security measures. Additionally, email address intelligence can be used to verify the authenticity of email accounts and detect phishing attacks. Email Address Intelligence is a potent technique for intelligence analysts to obtain data on people and organizations. Analysts can find hidden links, spot possible risks, and follow the actions of adversaries by examining email addresses linked to particular incidents or people.

Information may be extracted from email addresses using a variety of methods. One common approach is to use search engines to identify associated social media profiles, online forums, and other public websites. By analyzing the content of these websites, investigators can gain insights into the individual's interests, affiliations, and potential vulnerabilities. Another technique involves using specialized tools and databases to correlate email addresses with other pieces of information, such as phone numbers, physical addresses, and IP addresses. These tools can be used to build comprehensive profiles of individuals and organizations, providing a holistic view of their online activities. Even while email address intelligence has the potential to be a very useful tool, it must be used sensibly and morally.

There might be major ethical and legal repercussions if this information is misused. Following privacy rules and regulations is therefore essential, as is using email address intelligence for only appropriate purposes. Email Address Intelligence has become an indispensable tool in the modern world. Individuals and organizations may use publicly accessible information to obtain important insights, make wise decisions, and reduce risks by being aware of the methods and resources related to this field. Email address intelligence will become increasingly important as technology develops and the digital world grows, making it a vital ability for anybody attempting to negotiate the challenges of the digital era.

10.7 IMAGERY INTELLIGENCE

IMINT has revolutionized the way we gather and analyze information. IMINT allows us to obtain insights on a variety of topics, from environmental monitoring to military activities, by utilizing visual data, including photos, satellite imaging, and video recordings. In the realm of OSINT, IMINT plays a crucial role in uncovering hidden details and drawing meaningful conclusions. One of the most powerful tools for conducting IMINT analysis is Google Earth. With the help of this flexible platform, users may estimate distances, find possible sites of interest, and zoom in on particular regions using high-resolution satellite images. By carefully examining satellite imagery, investigators can uncover hidden structures, track changes over time, and even identify potential threats.

Another valuable tool for IMINT analysis is PhotoDNA, a technology developed by Microsoft Research. PhotoDNA can be used to identify and track the spread of images and videos online. By analyzing the unique digital signature of each image, PhotoDNA can help identify child exploitation, copyright infringement, and other illegal activities. Open-source platforms are also valuable sources of IMINT. By searching for specific keywords or locations, investigators can discover a wealth of user-generated content that can provide insights into current events, cultural trends, and social dynamics. In addition to traditional imagery analysis techniques, advanced image processing and computer vision algorithms can be used to extract information from images. These techniques can be used to identify objects, recognize faces, and detect changes over time. For example, by analyzing a series of satellite images, investigators can track the construction of new buildings, the movement of vehicles, and other activities of interest. When conducting IMINT analysis, it is important to consider the context of the image. By understanding the time, location, and circumstances in which an image was captured, investigators can draw more accurate conclusions.

Additionally, it is important to be aware of potential biases and distortions that may be present in the image. IMINT is a powerful tool that can be used to uncover hidden information and gain valuable insights.

By mastering the techniques and tools of IMINT, investigators can enhance their ability to analyze visual data and contribute to the broader field of OSINT. The potential uses of IMINT are anticipated to grow as technology develops further, making it an even more vital instrument for the future.

10.8 TRACKING SATELLITES AND AIRCRAFTS

The vast expanse of space and the intricate network of air traffic offer a wealth of data that can be harnessed for intelligence gathering and analysis. This chapter dives into the realm of tracking satellites and airplanes, examining how OSINT methods may be used to glean insightful information from publicly accessible data. Analyzing the information connected to airplanes and satellites is a basic component of tracking these entities. Data about data, or metadata, offers important hints on a file's creation date, provenance, and change history. By examining the metadata of satellite images and aircraft flight data, investigators can uncover hidden patterns, identify anomalies, and reconstruct timelines of events.

Geolocation data, which refers to the geographic coordinates of a specific location, is another critical piece of information in satellite and aircraft tracking. By analyzing the geolocation data associated with satellite imagery and flight paths, investigators can pinpoint the exact location of objects of interest and track their movements over time. A powerful tool for analyzing satellite imagery is Google Earth. With the help of this platform, users may estimate distances, identify things of interest, and zoom in on certain regions using high-resolution satellite pictures. By carefully examining satellite imagery, investigators can track changes in infrastructure, monitor environmental conditions, and identify potential security threats. For tracking aircraft, a variety of online platforms and tools can be used. Flightradar24 and ADS-B Exchange are two popular platforms that provide real-time tracking of aircraft around the world. By analyzing flight data, investigators can identify unusual flight patterns, track the movements of specific aircraft, and even predict potential security threats.

Advanced techniques like machine learning and artificial intelligence can be used to automate the examination of massive datasets in addition to the conventional ways of tracking satellites and airplanes. By training algorithms on historical data, investigators can develop models that can identify anomalies, detect patterns, and predict future events. It is crucial to remember that the moral ramifications of tracking satellites and airplanes need to be properly examined. Although there are genuine uses for these methods, such as disaster relief and national security, they may also be abused for nefarious objectives like spying. As a result, it is crucial to apply these methods sensibly and in compliance with moral and legal requirements. Tracking satellites and airplanes is an effective technique that may be used to get important information about a variety of topics. By mastering the techniques and tools of OSINT, investigators can leverage the power of publicly available information to uncover hidden truths, protect national security, and advance scientific research. The potential uses for satellite and airplane monitoring are expected to grow as technology advances, making it a crucial area of research.

10.9 CONCLUSION

In an era where information is power, OSINT has emerged as a critical tool for individuals, organizations, and governments alike. By leveraging publicly available data, OSINT enables us to uncover hidden truths, make informed decisions, and gain a competitive advantage. This book has explored the multifaceted nature of OSINT, from its historical roots to its modern-day applications. We have explored the ethical issues surrounding the use of data as well as the technological elements of data gathering, processing, and display. Through practical exercises and real-world examples, we have demonstrated how OSINT can be applied to a wide range of domains, from cybersecurity and intelligence analysis to investigative journalism and business intelligence.

The significance of OSINT will only increase as technology develops further and the digital environment grows. By mastering the techniques and tools presented in this book, readers can become proficient OSINT practitioners, capable of harnessing the power of information to achieve their goals. Remember, the future of intelligence lies in the hands of those who can effectively navigate the vast expanse of the digital world. By embracing OSINT, we can unlock the secrets hidden within the open source and gain a deeper understanding of the world around us.

For Product Safety Concerns and Information please contact our EU
representative GPSR@taylorandfrancis.com
Taylor & Francis Verlag GmbH, Kaufingerstraße 24, 80331 München, Germany

www.ingramcontent.com/pod-product-compliance
Lightning Source LLC
Chambersburg PA
CBHW060353220326
41598CB00023B/2904